MW01265156

The JFK Memorial and Power in America

Renowned architect Philip Johnson's enigmatic memorial to JFK, in Dallas, Texas, steeped in controversy, brings us face to face with the political and economic forces that shaped John Kennedy's Presidency and America.

M. D. Brosio

ISBN-10: 1492861871
ISBN-13: 9781492861874

For Denise, Cassy, Dana, and Jimmy

TABLE OF CONTENTS

FOREWORD

THIS IS NOT a book about the details of John Kennedy's assassination. It is a work about a far more important subject, the struggle for control of America's domestic, foreign, and military policies during the Cold War Years, from 1960 to 1963. The blueprint for this era was created before John Kennedy's presidency. Those plans had pre-determined the landscape of American political, economic, military, and social terrain, through the remainder of the Twentieth century. Its echoes reverberate though events today.

The Kennedy presidency represents one of the most emotionally charged eras in American history. The nation was offered a future designed by America's most elite dynasties, or a more imaginative future, eloquently expressed by America's youngest elected President. It is this author's contention, that the character of this struggle is uniquely portrayed by the rich symbolism, contained in American architect Philip Johnson's enigmatic John F. Kennedy Memorial, located in Dallas, Texas.

That discovery led to a fresh perception of John Kennedy's place in the tapestry of American and global history. It is a classic story of the men who were the most influential planners of American global supremacy in the second half of the twentieth century. Many were not elected to positions of national leadership. They believed it was their birthright and their destiny to lead the nation.

To illustrate the nature of this epic struggle, this author has chosen events, people, and conflicts, that reveal the nature of man's endless quest for power; in this case, the power to direct America's immense financial and military resources.

I invite you to journey with me, from the first moments of discovery onto the tumultuous pathways that opened before me in search of the ultimate goal - to understand the meaning and magnitude of the struggle for power in America that culminated in November 1963.

The Author

PART ONE: CREATION OF A MEMORIAL

"In architecture the pride of man, his triumph over gravitation, his will to power, assume a visible form. Architecture is a sort of oratory of power by means of forms".

— FRIEDERICH NIETZSCHE, PHILOSOPHER

1

Beginnings

"A young man from Boston set sail the new frontier,
And we watched the dream dead-end in Dallas,
They buried innocence that year."

— John Fogarty, songwriter

Field of Dreams

I could feel the twin-engine commuter jet gently leveling off at cruising altitude, ending the well-disguised tension of another successful takeoff. The simultaneous double-click of one hundred and twenty-four seat belts being released, including mine, meant settling in for the first leg of my six-hour flight. Wedged between two similarly stout fellow travelers, relief lay two hours away in Phoenix where I would regain my preferred window seating for the second leg of my trip to Dallas. Business would occupy the entire week, but I was hoping for a weekend to myself. Settling in, I opened my complimentary copy of USA Today to find the disturbing news that my S.F. Giants had been shut out by their arch-rivals to the south.

I consoled myself with the thought it was easier than being a Cubs fan, as my mid-west acquaintances reminded me. Surrendering to the plane's steady vibration, I put the paper down and thought of the first time baseball and Dallas had come together in my life. I settled in and slipped back in time, the drone of the engines gradually fading away . . . .

The hands of the round black and white clock high on the classroom wall had slowed to a crawl. Math was ending, and it was ten minutes before lunch. In a few minutes the school's lower, black-tar, parking lot would transform itself into our field of dreams for 30 minutes while our baseball fantasies came to life. The chain link fence in right-field was precisely the right distance for our best sixth grade sluggers. We used the palm side of our balled-up fists as a bat, no gloves, and a faded, half-dead tennis ball. Home runs, perfectly executed double-plays, and running catches made it all worth while. Diving catches were rare, and immediately elevated one to hall-of-fame status, or to the nurse's office for a generous application of iodine and gauze bandages.

Our school was situated at the border between San Francisco and Daly City, a hard working, racially mixed, blue-collar neighborhood, mostly known for its Friday night alcohol-fueled parties and neighborhood turf tussles, back in the day when fist-fights determined who was boss and who went home early.

Now just a minute away from baseball freedom, the school principal entered the room. A studious looking woman, middle-aged, tall, thin, dignified in round gold-rimmed glasses, she spoke quietly to our teacher for a few seconds. She turned to us with a steady controlled voice and spoke the words that are still hard to imagine, "President Kennedy has been shot in Dallas, Texas! He may have been killed! School will be closed for the remainder of the day."

There was only silence. We gathered our books, quickly glancing at each other, looking away before any inner feelings were discernible. We were young, but we felt the magnitude of the event. I can to this day, recall the feeling that day between classmates I knew well. It was a heavy, smothering sense of fear, the type you feel in your head and stomach that literally takes your breath away. None of us suspected this could happen in our time, in America, and certainly not to John Kennedy.

I was then, as now, a student of history and had read stirring accounts of Lincoln's assassination. Was this how it felt a hundred years ago? Perhaps just like those Americans a hundred years in the past had struggled to understand Friday, April 15, 1865, we could not comprehend the meaning of Friday, November 22, 1963.

Over the weekend I sat with family and close friends, listening to unanswerable questions posed by an endless stream of commentators. Riveted to our small TV sets, we watched a surreal train of incidents unfold. We listened as well-respected network anchors, reporters, authorities, and ordinary citizens were rendered helpless to explain these horrific acts, while a stream of black and white expressions of grief and shock were recorded in our memories. In an age of simplistic communication devices, the event had gone viral and had reached people far beyond our shores. We were living history, and the death of John Kennedy was a profound event that cut America to the core. We were reeling, not knowing what to expect as we watched each day, with even less to be certain of tomorrow.

Yet beneath the visible palette of shock and sorrow, there was something else, something unspoken, more troubling. It was an underlying, almost sinister current, a pervasive feeling something had gone terribly wrong, on a much higher plane, far above the daily lives working class Americans understood. Something powerful, dark, and nameless had wormed its way into our collective emotions. It had no name.

So, we listened and wondered, year after year, reflecting on the motives of the alleged assassin, the rifle's capability, the number of shots fired, the possibility of other shooters, the too-calm demeanor of Lee Oswald, and the ease which Jack Ruby gunned down the most well-known criminal suspect of the era. The events were traumatic; strong enough to leave those who cared deeply about America stunned, speechless, and searching.

"Would you like a beverage or snack sir?" The question brought me hurtling back to the present, suddenly aware of the powerful hum of the jet's twin engines and the smiling, quizzical expression on the face of my flight attendant. I smiled and made my selection, slightly embarrassed by my obvious escape to an alternate flight.

I had worked in Dallas many times prior to this trip. I had made many firm friendships, and came to admire the tough, but fair and professional approach to resolving mutual problems, shown by my colleagues in Texas. I respected their high standards and strong sense of pride in a job well done. I had never held the people of Dallas responsible for the events of November 1963, but neither could I separate Dallas from the assassination. I planned to visit Dealy Plaza again on this trip, but with a new lens, more open to thoughts beyond issues explored countless times, that had resulting in a nation torn between those accepting official conclusions and those who could not. Though many years had gone by, the historical records remained frozen in time and would speak for themselves. I felt there were essential links that had been severed between our past and our present that still existed and needed to be restored. I wanted to make another attempt at understanding what I had experienced on Friday, long ago, in front of a small black and white TV, watching America spin out of control.

*"You see, you can't see a model and say that's a beautiful building.
To make any sense at all you've got to build a building,
and have it wrap itself around you – see – that's the only test."*

— PHILIP JOHNSON, ARCHITECT

SHADOWS FROM ANOTHER AGE

Sunday, June 5, 2005, was a much-anticipated day. Business tasks had extended through Saturday, leaving a full day to revisit the place that for many generations of Americans, still invoked a sense of reverence and mystery.

Dealy Plaza is a large open airy park, a gateway into the older part of downtown Dallas. The Plaza proper has four gently sloping tracts of grass, trisected by three roads, giving the Plaza a chalice-shape when viewed from the railroad overpass at its base. The top and left sides of the chalice are a unique blend of Romanesque and mid-twentieth century buildings, strong-looking edifices of brick and stone. It is a charmingly forceful reminder of old Dallas, contrasted by stylish skyscrapers rising in the distance.

The Plaza can be a familiar experience, even for the first-time visitor. It's buildings and landscapes are among the most photographed in the world and remain burned into the collective memory of several generations. Travelers arrive from all parts of the globe and often conduct their own self-guided photo-tours of the plaza. Within the brick and mortar plaza borders visitors have a tendency to speak in subdued tones, as if inside a temple or church.

Of paramount interest is The Sixth Floor Museum and its sniper's nest, located in the former Texas School Book Depository. Other well-known locations are the raised parapet where Abraham Zapruder filmed the assassination sequence, the crude, "X" mark in the middle lane of sloping, twisting Elm Street, designating the location where Kennedy was likely struck, and the long, weathered, wooden fence atop the infamous Grassy Knoll.

Nothing of great significance in the layout of the plaza has changed since 1963. It is a time capsule, where images and sounds come to life, and replay their tragic tableau, in an endless video loop for its visitors.

After walking in and about Dealy Plaza for several hours, and confirming several of my previous discoveries, as this was not my first trip to Dealy Plaza, I shifted my area of focus to the south side of the plaza, beside the historic and renovated Old Dallas Courthouse. Affectionately named "Old Red," it has long been a Dallas landmark, designed in 1892 by Max A. Orlopp Jr. of Little Rock, Arkansas. The iconic courthouse is built primarily of red sandstone and remains an outstanding example of the Revival Romanesque architectural style, with roots dating back to the eleventh and twelfth century Romanesque architecture of Medieval Europe, featuring the beautifully designed statuary of medieval times on its outer walls and rooftop.

Towards late afternoon, I walked alongside this prolific historical embodiment of ages past, down Main Street, continuing away from Dealy Plaza. As I turned the corner to my right, looming unexpectedly in front of me, in startling contrast to all other Plaza buildings because of its stark modernistic design, was the strikingly unique John F. Kennedy Memorial. It instantly becomes an enigma, forcefully challenging its observer to find a connection to the events in Dealy Plaza and to John Kennedy.

I was vaguely familiar with the Memorial from on-line photos, but I knew nothing of its history or purpose. It is stately, but rather weighty, seemingly floating above the ground, evoking curiosity more than inspiration. On one hand, it appears too large for its cubist, roofless form, yet on the other, it is not large enough to evoke a sense of grandeur. The absence of ornamental or inspiring features leaves the viewer searching for some indication of its direct statements about John Kennedy. I took only slight notice of the round medallions placed in single vertical rows at the corners and portals, as they seemed more functional than decorative, like oversized rivets holding the structure in place.

The John F. Kennedy Memorial in Dallas, Texas

The inscription on the raised pedestal in front and to the right of the Memorial reads:

President John Fitzgerald Kennedy (1917-1963) was assassinated in Dallas, Texas on November 22, 1963. This event changed the city – and the world – forever. As a tribute to this extraordinary man, John F. Kennedy Memorial Plaza was dedicated on June 24, 1970. In the years since, it has become an integral part of the city's urban landscape and cultural heritage.

"a place of quiet refuge, an enclosed place of thought and contemplation separated from the city around, but near the sky and earth."

— PHILIP JOHNSON, ARCHITECT

An engraved marker embedded in the ground near the Memorial entrance reads:

The joy and excitement of
John Fitzgerald Kennedy's life belonged to all men
So did the pain and sorrow of his death

When he died on November 22, 1963, shock and
agony touched human conscience throughout the world
In Dallas, Texas, there was a special sorrow.

The young President died in Dallas. The death
bullets were fired 200 yards west of this site.

This memorial, designed by Philip Johnson,
was erected by the people of Dallas. Thousands of
citizens contributed support, money and effort.

It is not a memorial to the pain and sorrow
of death, but stands as a permanent tribute to the joy
and excitement of one man's life.

John Fitzgerald Kennedy's life.

The Monument's curator, the Sixth Floor Museum, located in the Texas School Book Depository offers the following description of the JFK Memorial:

Philip Johnson's design is a "cenotaph," or open tomb, that symbolizes the freedom of Kennedy's spirit. The memorial is a square, roofless room, 30 feet high and 50 by 50 feet wide with two narrow openings facing north and south. The walls consist of 72 white precast concrete columns, most of which seem to float with no visible support two feet above the ground. Eight columns extend to the ground, acting as legs that seem to hold up the monument. Each column ends in a light fixture. At night, the lights create the illusion that the structure is supported by the light itself. The corners and doors of this roofless room are decorated with rows of concrete circles, or medallions, each identical and perfectly aligned. These decorations introduce the circular shape into the square architecture of the Kennedy Memorial.

Over the years, as my knowledge and understanding of the structure grew, I often returned to this enlightened description of the monument's features. Little did I suspect how well these descriptive words would validate the singular inspirations of its creator's extraordinary Memorial.

When one first walks inside the open, roofless Memorial, there is a profound sense of vacuity, unusual for a memorial with so much potential for heartfelt emotional and historic significance. There are simply no features or decorations, save the flat cold block of black granite in the center at the base of the Memorial, arising a few feet from the floor, that bears John Kennedy's name. The Memorial is without doubt a "room," where one is fully conscious of the closeness of the surrounding walls; a room without statement, devoid of color, decor, and quite efficient in creating a still, quiet chamber, encouraging contemplation and allowing one to fall captive to the silence within.

The opposing walls are not connected, nor enclosed. The walls are detached from the ground except for minimally required supports at widely spaced intervals. The walls were obviously not intended to be grounded, but rather to float, as if detached from the heaviness of the black symbolic crypt. Underneath the concrete pillars there are lights placed at precise intervals to illuminate the concrete walls at night.

For the seeker, the admirer, the conspiracy-minded, or the visitor simply wishing to pay their respects, the challenging task lies in replacing the initial feeling of emptiness, by looking inward to find personal affinity with the life and death of John Kennedy. The Memorial is ingeniously

Cenotaph for John F. Kennedy within the JFK Memorial.

effective in erasing preconception and bias. With the mind and the senses cleared, the visitor is free to spontaneously experience emotion and memories. Perhaps the emptiness of the "sede vacante" - the empty throne of a fallen leader, allows one to recall the charm and energy John Kennedy possessed, or the fading recollections of a time when America embraced challenge, hope, and either the possibility of nuclear Armageddon, or a world at peace.

At this moment in time my mind was cleared, the pathway to the imagination opened, and previous questions of assassin's lairs, bullet trajectories, and escape routes ceased to exist. I found myself locked inside of a riddle of a different nature, and I was intrigued by the possibility of drawing new understanding from the design of the Memorial.

As the moments passed in silence, I keenly felt the oppressing emptiness of the "room" in which I stood. The architect had offered nothing to "uplift" the weary traveller arriving with the greatest of expectations, save the open sky above, which seemed to emphasize the abysmally low-lying symbolic crypt bearing John Kennedy's name. His symbolic sepulcher seemed almost purposely diminished, or in the worst of all scenarios, trivialized in utter defeat, its honoree vanquished, entrapped at the lowest position within his own cenotaph.

I thought of John Kennedy as an American legend, larger than life, and a powerful force during his time. It was difficult to accept this as a fitting statement to the memory of a man who inspired people throughout America and across the waters. To many struggling to elevate themselves above their repressive or impoverished societies, he represented a reenergized world, offering hope for freedom, human rights, and perhaps a time of peace.

As I stood silent and alone with my struggling emotions, something to my left caught my attention – an element of light, or perhaps a shape, or a shadow. Something within the Memorial had subtly and silently moved. The level of light in the interior had changed. It had grown darker, colder, and more oppressing. As I looked at the wall to my left, a vague, shadowy pattern was forming and moving upwards on the memorial wall, in opposition to the setting sun.

As I stood entranced, three blurred shapes began their slow but steady ascent, carried upwards upon a sloping surface toward the top of the memorial. As they approached the top of the wall, the shapes gained focus. I rushed outside of the memorial and looked upwards towards the setting sun to understand the source of these shadows. There, far above me, in the overpowering glare of the setting sun, loomed the Renaissance-inspired rooftop architecture of "Old Red". From their towering positions atop this venerable structure, the medieval symbols of power - the castle turret capped by a monarch's scepter, the dragon, and the obelisk had been projected directly onto the interior walls of the Kennedy Memorial. Majestically and inexorably rising, as day turned to night, they were escaping from their prison of oblivion, imposed by their solar master, fleeing unopposed to rule the darkness of night.

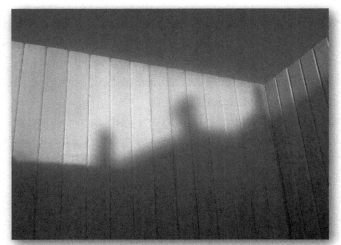

Shadows on the interior wall of the JFK Memorial.

Rooftop architecture "Old Red," Dallas Courthouse.

I returned inside the memorial and watched as the medieval tableau completed its unstoppable ascent, sensing the vague outline of a darker intention in the powerful metaphorical display I was witnessing. The historic representations of man's power were "soaring" from within this open cenotaph, in a naturally occurring daily ritual, yet the spirit of John Kennedy lay hopelessly confined in granite, at the base of his symbolic tomb.

It was an enthralling and yet a sad moment, leaving me struggling with the seemingly contrary messages within the memorial, for it was certainly not John Kennedy's spirit soaring from the structure dedicated to his memory. No longer a sterile and tranquil place of refuge and remembrance, the memorial was operating as a living theater, using the interplay of sunlight, shadow, stone, and the natural motion of the earth, to suggest a deeper meaning and interpretation.

There, alone with the creeping shadows of darkness, my first sense of the Memorial's intent began to take shape. From Medieval history and before, the castle fortress has been the foremost symbol of man's endless quest for power, the rule of the few over the many, the residence of the king, nobility and the elite, a clear distinction between the home of powerful men and the common man; between those who rule and those subject to rule. Cruel or benevolent, or in any combination thereof, the power to decide the fate of man historically resided within castle towers.

There were no others present inside the Memorial that day - no one to interrupt, or share my thoughts, as I concentrated on the unique, natural show taking place before me. Borne upwards, alongside the castle turret, was an obelisk, the ancient symbol of mankind's power through renewal and regeneration. The obelisk appears in man's earliest civilizations, and represents his attempt to elevate his species, aspirations, character, or alternately to claim affinity with the powers he conceives are above him.

Carried upwards alongside the obelisk, was the form of a dragon, in this case, a wyvern. The wyvern has a distinctive two-legged stance with bat-like wings, eagle-like talons, a beak-like jaw, and a deadly barbed stinger at the tip of its tail. In medieval lore, wyverns were depicted as aggressive entities, associated with war, power, and conquest, capable of spreading plague, a heinous charge in medieval Europe reeling from the horrors of the Black Death, making them fearsome carriers of death and suffering. They have been used as an allegory for Satan, associated with suffering, pestilence and sin. Wyverns have served as heraldic emblem, symbols of ruthless power to those who bore their images on pennants, shields, and coat-of-arms. In England, they are referred to as 'dragonets' and are prominently displayed on the coat of arms of the City of London. Since 1849, wyvern statues have been the ceremonial guardians to the seven gateways into the City of London, the financial heart of the British Empire.

Wyvern atop Dallas "Old Red" Courthouse.

Wyvern, City of London.

Wyvern, City of London.

I felt excitement and fear - when a hidden door bearing unknown secrets has been opened. The initial feelings I had experienced in November 1963, watching and listening as America wrestled with the unexplainable, were still pushing me forward. For the first time, I felt there might exist some visible purpose and meaning behind those events, but its nature and consequences would require examination through a different lens, the wider lens of history and man's quest for power. I understood this was a profound change in direction and would need a much closer examination of the era in which JFK lived and died, his vision for America, and his adversaries.

On that serene April afternoon, standing within the quiet "room" Philip Johnson had built, alone with no movement save the relative motion between earth and sun, the memorial had given up one of its secrets. My perceptions had been transformed by the resulting interplay of light and shadow. It was an experience Philip Johnson was well qualified to understand, and re-create, as I would soon discover.

I knew if I chose to step forward and follow this pathway, I would be leaving the comfort of known signposts and trail markers behind. For the first time, I sensed that the shots fired only a few blocks away, had never held the keys to unlocking the true meaning of November 22, 1963. There was a larger story, one of timeless historical importance, directed not by random or chance events, but by the steady hand of man.

In 1963, America and the world were moving simultaneously toward the abyss and the promised land, and the choices were expressed as survival or destruction. For those in the highest positions of power, it was all or nothing.

2

THE JFK CITIZENS MEMORIAL COMMITTEE

1963 - DALLAS IS THE KEY

ON SEPTEMBER 12, 1963 John Kennedy issued these remarks in a speech at the Cortez Hotel in El Paso, TX:

> "There is a story about a Texan who went to New York and told the New Yorker that he could jump off the Empire State Building and live. The easterner said, "Well, that would be an accident." He said, "Suppose I did it twice?" The easterner said, "That would be an accident, too." "Suppose I did it three times?" And the easterner said, "That would be a habit." (Laughter)
>
> "Texas twice, in 1952 and 1956, jumped off the Democratic band wagon. We are down here to see it is not going to be a habit (applause)."[1]

With these statements, John Kennedy formally kicked off Democratic Party strategy to capture Texas in the presidential race just 14 months away. It was an opportunity to demonstrate Kennedy-Johnson solidarity, heal some widening rifts, and take advantage of lucrative fund-raising opportunities, in a state with an extraordinarily high number of millionaires.

Texas was a mixed bag of changing political loyalties. These were turbulent and highly emotional days, not only in Texas but across America. There were many issues uniting and dividing Americans of all backgrounds. Segregation, cold war tensions, changing standards of morality, as well as political extremism, were swirling in the consciousness of Texans and the nation, as Americans began their march into the Sixties, an era of tremendous reexamination of the nation's direction, mindset, and character.

The Texas political landscape had been shifting since the mid-1950's. As the affluence and influence of Southwestern oil and banking industries increased, so did the perception of an increasingly intrusive federal government. The state's historic vein of self-governance and political independence, coupled with the Kennedy administration's liberal positions, were fueling right-wing agendas in Texas and across the nation.

Houston and Dallas were the new centers of wealth and political power in the American Southwest. Three years prior, in the1960 presidential election, the metropolitan areas of Houston, Dallas, Tarrant, and Harris counties, had given Republican candidate Richard Nixon 390,352 votes to Kennedy's 296,536 votes, nearly a 100,000 vote difference. The Kennedy White House knew that Dallas support was essential to placing Texas in the Democratic win column. Victory in 1964 was the cornerstone upon which Kennedy's emerging vision for America would be realized or rejected. Whatever risks a Texas visit posed, they would have to be accepted if John Kennedy was to become Chief Executive of the government of the United States in fact, and not just in name.

Texas and Dallas' state and local leaders were not blind to the dangers and challenges of a Kennedy visit. Relatively small but disturbing acts of violence had already occurred in Dallas before Kennedy's visit. Texas Governor John Connally, Dallas Mayor Earle Cabell, Dallas law enforcement, and city leadership publicly denounced these odious attacks in the strongest possible terms and called for a more civilized and tolerant political behavior in preparation for Kennedy's upcoming visit.

The Dallas Police Department's Intelligence Division had been actively engaged in identifying extremist groups and their potential plans for unrest during Kennedy's upcoming visit. A November 18, 1963 report forwarded by Captain W.P. Gannaway of the Special Forces Bureau of the Criminal Intelligence Section of the Dallas Police Department, identified subversive political groups in Dallas, both right and left, several of which had been infiltrated by Gannaway's department.[2] The groups listed were:

The Ku Klux Klan
Indignant White Citizens Council
National States Rights Party
John Birch Society
Dallas White Citizen's Council
Oak Cliff White Citizen's Council
The General Edwin A. Walker Group
American Opinion Forum
Dallas Committee For Full Citizenship
Young Peoples Socialist League
Dallas Civil Liberties Union
Texas White Citizens Council
Black Muslims

Hannaway's report noted that several of the groups under surveillance planned to stage active demonstrations during Kennedy's visit to Texas:

The Indignant White Citizens Council had prepared signs to embarrass Mr. Kennedy and planned to picket the Dallas Trade Mart during Kennedy's speech.

The General Edwin A. Walker group planned to embarrass the President by picketing along the parade route, and at the Dallas Trade Mart.

Prior to the President's visit, information was obtained that members of the Young Peoples Republican Club were meeting with the General Walker group and making plans. According to a reliable source, the group indicated they intended to "rub the President's [genitals] in the dirt."

The report stated that only a few individuals demonstrated at the Dallas Trade Mart, and six individuals were taken into protective custody.

In contrast to the Gannaway Report, it is clear from the abundant newsreels and movie footage of the President's visit, that enthusiastic crowds turned out in force at many locations to offer John and Jacqueline Kennedy admiration and Texas hospitality, and none more so than the citizens of Dallas. It was in this spirit that Governor Connally's wife, Nelly, turned and commented to John Kennedy while riding in the Dallas motorcade,

> "You certainly can't say that the people of Dallas haven't given you a nice welcome, Mr. President." The President replied, "No, you certainly can't!"

John Fitzgerald Kennedy, husband and father of two, Congressman, United States Senator, and 35th President of the United States, who inspired the world with his charm and grace, was pronounced dead at 1:00 PM Central Standard Time, November 22, 1963, at Parkland Memorial Hospital, in Trauma Room Number One.

Forty-eight hours and seven minutes later at 1:07 PM Central Standard Time, his alleged assassin, Lee Harvey Oswald, husband and father of two, former United States Marine with "Confidential" level security clearance, son-in law by marriage to Colonel Ilya Prusakova of Russia's Interior Security Service, repatriated American defector, leftist New Orleans political provocateur with right-wing Dallas connections, was pronounced dead at Parkland Hospital in Trauma Room Number Two.

The brazen murders of John Kennedy and Lee Oswald, while under protective custody of local police, was the ultimate expression of a city unable to control its most virulent elements, and portrayed city leadership's attempts at restoring justice and order woefully inadequate. Dallas was also coming under attack nationally and internationally for statements made by local officials, seeming to indicate the case was closed, by virtue of evidence in the hands of Dallas law enforcement.

These events, occurring 48 hours apart, sent the world, the nation, and in particular, the citizens of Dallas, spiraling though a state of physical, mental, and spiritual turmoil. Condemnation, caustic criticism bordering on the obscene, self-consolation, suspicion, soul-searching, and open mistrust were expressed in repetitive cycles during the months following the assassination. The civic and collective soul of Dallas writhed in anguish. There was also a strong emerging conviction that Dallas must join the nation in honoring a fallen leader. So began the painful process of self-examination and healing, under the weight of overwhelming traumatic events, and beneath the caustically critical eyes of the nation and the world.

"Should this Committee concern itself only with a local memorial, only with a national memorial, or both."

— FROM THE MINUTES OF THE FIRST MEETING OF THE
JFK CITIZENS MEMORIAL COMMITTEE
DECEMBER 3, 1963

WHAT SHOULD DALLAS DO

On November 24, 1963, two days after the assassination, Dallas County Judge Lew Sterrett proposed that a memorial should be erected in memory of the late President. On the very next day, Mayor Pro Tem, Carrie Welch, recommended that the Dallas City Council approve the creation of a memorial plaza near the assassination site. The recommendation was approved. Welch stated the plaza should be "an effort to express the sympathy and dedication of the people of Dallas." Mayor Earle Cabell then proposed that the memorial should not be constructed in Dallas, but elsewhere, perhaps in Washington D.C., as a national monument. As JFK Memorial Committee member Stanley Marcus recalled, "There was a great difference of opinion on what we should do, but we had a feeling Dallas had the obligation to do something to recognize that the President was killed here." The struggle to define the city's response to one of the most significant events in American history was underway.

Mayor Earle Cabell had raised the first and perhaps most important of the controversies regarding memorial construction: should a Kennedy Memorial be located in Dallas, Texas? The question bore serious ramifications for Dallas leadership in terms of effort, obligation, and political will.

Two days later, the *Dallas Times Herald* reported that the Dallas Parks Board wished to construct a local monument. Again, Mayor Cabell spoke in favor of a national monument, while Welch again advocated for a local monument. To create momentum for a memorial outside of Texas, Cabell requested "through appropriate channels" a committee be named in Washington, D.C. to oversee funding for a John F. Kennedy national memorial. He stated that Dallas, although it may play an active and even leading part could not provide a monument of sufficient magnitude. Given the city's well-known wealth and social connections, both in finance and the arts, this was an entirely mis-leading and deceptive statement, but from a state, county, and local government perspective this proved to be true. But Cabell had underestimated the magnitude of the heartfelt outpouring of contributions from the citizens of Dallas, as well as their instinctive desire to shoulder their share of the nation's and the world's sorrow, rather than risk the paths of denial and further isolation. Underestimation could not have persisted, as the Cabell's office began to receive a steady flow of mail from individuals and businesses offering assistance and suggestions for a Kennedy memorial. The Earle Cabell Collection of Private Papers at Southern Methodist University contains many emotional letters sent by individual citizens of Dallas, and from citizens throughout the nation. Their archived correspondence remains a silent but strong testimony to the wishes of the citizens of Dallas and American people, irrespective of race, faith, and social status, to remember John Kennedy in a fitting and dignified manner.

Emphasizing Dallas's need to move towards positive local action, was the news reported by the *Dallas Morning News* on November 27. Joe Ratcliff, a business consultant and former state representative from Dallas, was gathering local civic leaders to raise funds for scholarships, educational grants, and a memorial.

Persistently pursuing his efforts at establishing the future JFK memorial at a national location, Mayor Cabell on November 29, 1963 sent a letter to President Lyndon Johnson, advocating initiation of a national Memorial Commission to determine the best location and funding for a Kennedy memorial. However, citizen response was moving faster than official channels, as monetary donations were being received at Dallas City Hall from all over the world, accompanied by letters expressing citizen's desires to begin creation of a memorial in Dallas. A little more than a week after the assassination, the citizens of Dallas, America, and the world were already taking the lead in stating their wish for a memorial of some type in Dallas Texas.

On December 2, 1963, Mayor Cabell and County Judge Lew Sterrett issued a joint statement requesting a group of prominent Dallas citizens to form a Citizens Memorial Committee to work in conjunction with any memorial commission that might be appointed by President Lyndon Johnson. Their initial charter was to:

> "collaborate with any such President's commission in determining form, location or locations, method of financing, and/or any other area of study or recommendation requested."

It was a request made under tumultuous conditions. Jack Ruby, Oswald's killer, was being held in a Dallas jail. Revelations of his connections with Dallas Law Enforcement and his unsavory past as Jacob Rubenstein of Chicago Illinois, with connections to the Chicago-based Capone crime family were rumored in the press. Rumors of Lee Harvey Oswald's extraordinary past were emerging, with possible links to U.S. intelligence agencies as a paid informant.

On December 2, Dallas democrat Mike McKool, and Dallas Republican Maurice Carlson, both requested the powerful Dallas City Council to authorize the development of a monument to the memory of President John Kennedy in Dallas. McKool and Carlson advised the Council this was an appropriate direction in view of the mounting wishes of Dallas citizens. McKool and Carlson stated the site should be within Dallas City limits for Dallas to claim true ownership of the memorial.

The Memorial Committee's first executive meeting was held on Tuesday, December 3, 1963, with Mayor Cabell and Judge Sterrett in attendance. The twenty appointed Memorial Committee members were:

J.D. Francis	Mercantile National Bank
Joe Dealey	Dallas Morning News
Jim Chambers	Dallas Times Herald

Louis Nichols   Dallas County Bar Association
Dr. Ben Merrick   Dallas County Medical Society
John Stemmons   Greater Dallas Council of Churches
Ray Hubbard   Dallas Park Board
Dr. Willis Tate   President, Southern Methodist University
Dawson Sterling   Dallas Assembly
Robert Callum   President, Dallas Chamber of Commerce
Charles Meyer   United Fund
C.A. Tatum   Dallas Citizens Council
Clay Roming   President, Junior Chamber of Commerce
Stanley Marcus   President, Neiman-Marcus Retailers
Durwood Sutton   Grand Prairie State Bank
James Smith   President, Negro Chamber of Commerce
Rev. Caesar Clark   Pastor Good Street Baptist Church
Rabbi Levi Olan   Temple Emanu-El
Allan L. Maley   Dallas AFL-CIO Council
Ed Maher   Chairman, Parkland Memorial Hospital

Mayor Cabell and Judge Sterrett each spoke briefly concerning the objectives and responsibilities of the Committee outlined in their December 2, 1963 joint statement.

Most of the five agenda items were routine Committee business. The Committee acknowledged citizen's desires to contribute to the memorial process in Agenda Item Number 3 by inviting the populace of the entire county to submit written suggestions for Committee consideration. Two additional points were presented for consideration and they clearly represented the difficulties facing Dallas leadership and the Committee:

1. Should other memorial committees in the city be combined with this Committee.
2. Should this Committee concern itself only with a local memorial, only with a national memorial, or both.

Stanley Marcus, President of Neiman-Marcus Retailers commented that he felt the Committee should keep an open mind, as to both a national and a local monument. He stated he was aware of a movement to establish a Kennedy memorial library at Harvard University. During the meeting, the Committee was informed that many citizens had already forwarded contributions and suggestions to memorialize John F. Kennedy. These citizen recommendations consisted of:

- an Arts Center, containing existing works of art,
- educational funds to train students to repair deteriorating homes,
- a Kennedy Nobel Prize,
- scholarships,
- prayer cards,
- a trust fund to support Parkland Hospitals Emergency Care facilities,
- a psychiatric research center,
- a series of funded special lectures and seminars on mental retardation,
- a plaque with proper landscaping at an appropriate location,
- donations to the Foundation for Retarded Children
- a hospital and research center in Dallas devoted to Mental Retardation
- a seven-foot hand carved white marble Celtic Cross
- a marble bust of the late President
- an eternal flame on a grassy slope (location to be determined)
- an inscription "Friend to All Races, Creed, Colors. Crusader for Peace.
- a cairn erected at Elm and Houston Streets
- a tower, bell, or carillon
- a lighthouse type of memorial with chapel for all denominations.

In a second letter to President Lyndon Johnson on December 3, 1963, Mayor Cabell formally extended the services of the JFK Citizens Memorial

Committee. This action on Earle Cabell's part was consistent with his initial letter to LBJ, suggesting the merger of a national memorial committee with the Dallas Memorial Committee. When Dallas citizen Pat M. Greenwood, warned Mayor Cabell that a permanent memorial in Dallas "would only serve to inflame public opinion still further", Cabell agreed.[4]

On the very next day in support of Mayor Cabell's views, former Dallas Mayor, Robert Thornton, stated he was opposed to the establishment of a monument in Dallas. Thornton said in a newspaper article on December 4, 1963, "For my part, I don't want anything to remind me that a President was killed on the streets of Dallas. I want to forget."

The second meeting of the JFK Citizens Memorial Committee convened on December 10, 1963. Stanley Marcus stated he was aware of a movement to rename the National Cultural Center in Washington, D.C., the Kennedy Cultural Center.

Temporary Committee Secretary, Dr. Luther Holcomb, reported that as of the time of this meeting, the Committee had received 260 letters of suggestions, and the substance of each suggestion received would be provided to each Committee member for review.

Committee member, Rabbi Levi Olan, presented a new perspective by stating there was another pathway to view the dilemma, that of a living memorial which would have ongoing intrinsic value.

Committee member Joe Dealey brought another perspective to the discussion, one that assumed a memorial would be erected in Dallas. Dealy suggested the memorial location should not be in the exact spot as the assassination, but should be in another location, perhaps on an existing monolith located at Young Street, south of Elm Street. This existing structure could be modified with a legend carrying the name of John F. Kennedy along with his date of birth and death. Mr. Dealey felt by removing the marker some distance from the actual site, and allowing for the forgetfulness that comes with time, the spot will not be used as an assembly point for demonstrators of one kind or another. He went on to say the city might change the name of a street or avenue or rename a park, preferably one that does not at present bear a name. He also suggested the

Committee combine its efforts, financial abilities, and leadership with an over-all national committee which most assuredly will be formed, if not now, sometime in the near future.

Committee member Allan Maley commented the general feeling is there should be a marker of some kind beside the spot where the shooting took place, even if it were a simple historical marker. It was pointed out such markers are scattered throughout the state, marking sites of historical importance, and certainly this will become one of those sites in years to come.

The second Committee meeting was adjourned in a quandary, not only over the decision to place a memorial within Dallas or in a national location, but if the Memorial was located in Dallas, what would be a suitable place, or should the memorial itself be a real structure, or a living memorial with on-going social benefits. At this point it must have seemed to Committee members that reaching final consensus would be a far more difficult task than anticipated.

The Third Meeting of the of the JFK Citizens Memorial Committee was called to order on December 16, 1963. The committee named officers for the future term of the organization, confirming W. Dawson Sterling as permanent Chairman and the Reverend Luther Holcomb, who headed the Dallas Council of Churches as permanent secretary. Suggestions for the memorial were still being received, and Committee members continued to receive these suggestions for evaluation.

The Fourth Meeting of the of the JFK Citizens Memorial Committee was called to order at 3:30 p.m., CST, on Thursday, January 16, 1964.

The following statement was read by Committee Chairman W. Dawson Sterling:

1. The Committee today endorsed a proposal by the Texas State Historical Survey Committee for placement of an official historical marker near the spot where President Kennedy was assassinated.
2. The proposal will be recommended to the City of Dallas which owns the property on which the marker would be placed.

Mr. Sterling went on to state the marker was in line with many suggestions received by the Committee. Of 570 suggestions submitted so far, he stated that 234 favored some kind of identification at the assassination site. Mr. Sterling emphasized however, that the Dallas Committee does not contemplate its endorsement of the state committee's proposal would be in lieu of other possible action by the committee, and that study of other proposals received by the Committee will continue. The marker, as proposed by the Texas State historical Committee, would be of cast aluminum with a Swedish steel effect, and bear a Medallion of the State of Texas at the top, along with a suitable inscription. Rabbi Olan moved that this statement be approved and the Chairman be authorized to release it to the press. The motion was unanimously passed. In previous meetings the Committee had indicated it did not want to act in haste. The general consensus at this meeting was that time was now an important consideration.

Two moving letters on January 19, 1964 were emblematic of the self-examination the city of Dallas was undergoing. One was written by Rabbi Levi Olan, spiritual leader of Temple Emanu-El in Dallas Texas, and Memorial Committee member. Sensing the deep inner conflicts dividing city leadership, and fearing Dallas was straying from its meaningful self-evaluation following the assassination, he took a strong and resolute stand. Rabbi Olan acknowledged the apprehension that existed before Kennedy's visit. He recalled Dallas law enforcement pleading with Dallas citizenry in the newspapers, television, and radio to behave decently during the President's visit. "We were all afraid of an incident," wrote Rabbi Olan, undoubtedly with remembrances of the Adlai Stevenson and Lady Bird Johnson attacks. He courageously asked the question why Dallas had become a haven for the most extreme expressions of the mood of anxiety which was felt throughout cities across America. He cuttingly questioned why the Dallas political structure, taking a high platform of political idealism, tolerated a sub-par public education system, with a shameful dropout rate, and refused federal lunch programs for impoverished students because its high principles included distrust for national government. In closing Rabbi Olan offered this challenge,

"What should Dallas do now? For its psychological well being it ought to accept blame and responsibility for its behavior and act upon that now.

Perhaps to paraphrase the late President, our value system in Dallas ought to be, "Ask not what Dallas can do for me, but what can I do for Dallas?"

He asked Dallas to focus on social and political renewal, and initiate a pragmatic approach to government, rather than the uncompromising politics of high idealism and exclusion that existed before November 22, 1963.

The second letter released on January 19th, 1964 was authored by Professor Frederick S. Carney, a highly respected professor at the Perkins School of Theology at Southern Methodist University in Dallas. It was titled "Crisis in Conscience in Dallas". Professor Carney stated that ultimately how Dallas responded to this crisis in conscience, was predominantly in the hands of two groups: the clergy which would provide spiritual and moral guidance for the community, but in a more visible sense, it would be the group wielding the most power within the City of Dallas. He was referring to the Dallas Citizens Committee, or DCC, a group of businessmen that formed the real power structure in Dallas. Professor Carney, as well as Rabbi Olan, both pointed out the City had properly engaged in an honest attempt at self-examination in the days immediately following November 22, but since then there seemed to be a mood change in which city leadership was retreating into defensive patterns amid concern for the public image of Dallas. Professor Carney reminded the DCC it had in the past, "succeeded in calling forth from its members a spirit of personal sacrifice and hard work that has undoubtedly contributed to the rapid economic and population growth of Dallas."

Throughout this period of civic tumult in Dallas, powerfully moving burial ceremonies for John Kennedy in Washington, D. C. and countless scenes of remembrance had taken place throughout Europe, Asia, Pacific-rim nations, and South America. Accompanied by the somber brassy precision of Washington military bands, the gently fluctuating oscillation of tone bowls in Shinto and Buddhist temples, the dulcet tones of Bolivian flutes, and the ancient drone of Celtic bagpipes in Eire, people the world over were sharing their common sense of grief. There was a global sense of loss of hope with the shocking death of this young, charismatic, American President, who for a brief moment, spoke so eloquently of the possibilities of peace, and the ascent of the rights of man. Without the benefit of instantaneous telecommunications through cell phones, pods, pads, and tablets, televised images of worldwide solidarity and remembrance honoring the life of John Kennedy, were globally shared and symbiotically understood. Yet within the councils of Dallas leadership, there remained an element of obstinancy and conservative obstruction.

Unfortunately, in Dallas, it was still a time of grasping for politically acceptable answers, where an improper response might appear be detrimental to the future of the city. These concerns were on the minds of conservative Dallas political and business leaders. Some were guarding against over-memorializing John Kennedy with a Dallas monument that would create a permanent mecca for Kennedy admirers, and possibly perpetuate Dallas's new reputation as the "City of Hate".

The Dallas Citizens Committee recognized an official response could not be long in forthcoming while the city was, like it or not, forced to work under the glaring light of the national and world media. After the shooting, Dallas residents were harassed. In isolated incidents, phone operators disconnected long-distance calls from Dallas, and some out-of-state restaurants refused service. In Pennsylvania, a gas station attendant threw a fistful of coins in a Texas driver's face. In Detroit, a Dallas man was ejected from a cab, and in Europe, foreigners exclaimed when introduced to a Dallas history professor, "Oh, you're from Dallas? That's where they kill presidents."[3]

The DCC also understood the ramifications of allowing the label of "The City of Hate" to stand unchallenged. But their own camp remained divided. Some would, as Professor Carney stated, prefer to take no action other than emphasizing the strengths and virtues of the City of Dallas. This however, would have been a morally vacant pathway, sidestepping conscience and compassion, with the risk of further isolating the city. Perhaps there could be a response that would satisfy both camps, highlighting their humanitarian efforts, while also endeavoring to minimize the memory of violent assassination on the streets of Dallas.

Throughout this period of indecision, a powerful independent force was quietly at work - freed from the inner workings of conservative Dallas politics, moving faster and with more certainty, but relentlessly driving Dallas leadership - was the unheralded force of Dallas citizens. They took it upon themselves to acknowledge the assassination and legacy of John Kennedy's Presidency, and the responsibility of forcing city leadership into action. They instinctively understood what needed to be done. A steady

Citizens memorial to JFK in Dealy Plaza, Dallas Texas.

outpouring of impassioned letters were received in the office of Dallas Mayor Earle Cabell. Many expressed outrage and criticism, but many more were asking and suggesting how ordinary citizens could honor the memory of John Kennedy. It was impossible for city leadership to ignore the rising strength of public sentiment in Dallas to respond in a compassionate manner. Nor could the city leaders ignore the immediate need for damage control to prevent a political and economic disaster.

Memorial Committee members were eager to move forward, and many courageously did their best to do so. But in the conflicted world of Dallas politics, it would be seven long years of effort, controversy, and frustration before a lasting memorial to President John F. Kennedy would arise for dedication.

Following another meeting on Feb 5th, the JFK Citizens Memorial Committee Chairman prepared a statement to be released.

FOR RELEASE AT 3 p.m., SATURDAY, FEBRUARY 22, 1964.

The following statement was issued today by W. Dawson Sterling, Chairman of the Dallas John F. Kennedy Citizens Memorial Committee:

After receiving and studying more than 700 suggestions for appropriate memorials to the late President John F. Kennedy and after many additional hours of conference, the Dallas John F. Kennedy Memorial Committee has reached unanimous agreement.

The decision was reached in conference with representatives of the Kennedy family, and not only has the endorsement and approval of Mrs. Jacqueline Kennedy, but represents as well, her feelings that it would please the late President.

Our decision involves two separate actions. First, we have endorsed and pledged our efforts to seek contribution in as substantial numbers as possible to be designated for a particular memorial sector of the proposed John Fitzgerald Kennedy Library to be established close to the scene of the President's youth in Boston. Second, we have approved the creation of a dignified and modest memorial near the assassination site.

As a spiritual expression of our community, your committee hopes that all will join wholeheartedly in supporting these efforts.

The committee met for several hours yesterday with Mr. Stephen E. Smith, a brother-in-law of the late President Kennedy, who presented the family's viewpoint.

Arrangements for the Kennedy Library are already underway but architectural plans are not yet available. When these are ready it is the Dallas committee's feeling that some specific part of the Library can be selected for our particular memorial undertaking.

Mr. Smith said that Mrs. Jacqueline Kennedy, whose almost sole preoccupation is now concerned with the accomplishment of the Library project, and others involved in the project will work with the Dallas committee toward that end.

While the Library will be a memorial to President Kennedy, it will be more than a monument. Not only is it to contain a fitting memorial room but it is also to include several working components—a Museum, an Archive, and an Institute – which would introduce new concepts for preserving and displaying historical records and for teaching history and political science.

It is estimated that the Library with its components will cost $10 million, of which more than $4 million has already been received nationally in cash or in pledges.

Final detailed drawings of the memorial at the Dallas site are not yet finished. As soon as the are complete they will be made available to the public.

So, the decision was made to participate both in the effort to create a national monument near Boston at Harvard University, and the creation of a Dallas memorial to John Kennedy. This then would be the compromise between those that had championed a memorial outside of Dallas, supported by more resources and ultimately providing a more fitting and grander memorial, but also recognized the wishes of the citizens of Dallas to commemorate John Kennedy. As Chairman Sterling reported in the minutes of the Fourth Meeting of the Dallas Committee, 234 of the 570 suggestions received favored a local memorial close to the assassination site. Public opinion had truly played a significant role in allowing those in the committee favoring a local monument to gain a decision in their favor. Without this level of public support, it is possible those favoring only a national monument outside of Dallas would have carried the day.

"It is good to have an end to journey toward; but it is the journey that matters, in the end."

— ERNEST HEMINGWAY, AUTHOR

THE LONG MARCH

First contact between the Memorial Committee and a Kennedy family member regarding the type of memorial that would be constructed in Dallas had taken place on February 21, 1964 with Stephen Smith, husband of Jean Kennedy. Smith communicated Jacqueline Kennedy's wishes for a memorial that was simple, modest, and dignified, a request that would reverberate through the creative process of the memorial's design. Memorial Committee Chairman Sterling subsequently announced plans for a modest memorial near the assassination site. Initial plans envisioned a semicircular wall of marble, at a yet unnamed site.

After failing to secure funding from Dallas city, state, or county leadership, committee members appealed to the public sector. In the end, neither the City of Dallas, Dallas County, nor the State of Texas would provide any funding for the Dallas memorial structure itself. At this time, the Dallas School Board suspended a restriction on soliciting funds within Dallas school districts. This seemingly small act would have significant impact on the creation of the JFK Memorial. The major source of funding would come from over 50,000 individual donations totaling over $200,000. Many donations consisted of a few pennies each, donated by the school children of Dallas, as a result of the School Board's action. Four months later, in March of 1964, it was reported that families of Dallas school children had already contributed over $10,000 toward the creation of a memorial park.

Various suggestions had been forthcoming concerning the location and form of the Dallas memorial and each had been rejected. Fort Worth city leaders considered building a memorial and had requested the City Parks Board to consider this. The Board had already rejected a previous proposal for a memorial across from the Hotel Texas as being too costly and did not view the new proposal favorably. The Dallas JFK Memorial Committee had originally suggested an official marker near the assassination site, with a semicircular memorial wall. This idea was placed in abeyance and eventually dropped. In late March, the Committee proposed a memorial location at North Elm and West Houston Streets. Four days later the Dallas City Department of Traffic Control denied this proposal due to traffic control issues, in anticipation of the large number of visitors expected to visit the memorial. By the early part of 1964, the various city departments, boards, and committees could would reject one proposal after another, as if they were working in concert with Dallas city, county, and state officials.

The project regained momentum on March 18, 1964 when Dallas County Commissioners and Judge Lew Sterrett offered two blocks of land to be designated as the JFK Plaza. This location would eventually become the site of the present-day memorial. However, work on the park plaza could not begin until the new courthouse was completed in April of 1965. This offer from Dallas County officials enabled the project to move forward, however, a major impediment to swift completion of the Memorial lay ahead as County and City planners as well as the JFK Committee, would become entangled in competing and conflicting priorities.

In the midst of the drive to create the JFK Memorial, there was a change in the office of mayor. Earle Cabell, whose grandfather, William L. Cabell, and father, Ben E. Cabell both served as mayors of Dallas, resigned his office to run for Congress.

Cabell's chief opponent was the fiercely conservative Republican incumbent, Congressman Bruce Alger. In 1960 Alger was the principal organizer of a protest in Dallas against then Senate Majority Leader, Lyndon Johnson. The rally had disintegrated into a personal attack, and Lady Bird Johnson was spat upon by a protestor. But Alger's ultraconservative credentials and the strength of his support would be a significant hurdle for any challenger. His tenure ran concurrently from 1954 to 1963, as the only Republican in the Texas delegation. He had successfully defended his congressional seat against two formidable Democratic challengers. In 1956, Alger defeated Dallas County attorney Henry Wade, who would later emerge as a principal spokesman during the chaotic days of November 1963. Wade would later become the defendant in the Roe v. Wade abortion case in 1973. In 1958, Alger defeated Democrat Barefoot Sanders, a popular figure in Dallas political and legal communities, United States District Judge, and later counsel to President Lyndon Johnson.

Alger had become expendable. His association with Dallas political extremism had made him a liability by 1964. Defeating Alger was an important step for the Dallas Citizens Council to showcase a more tolerant political climate. Earle Cabell was the only candidate with sufficient prestige, Democratic tradition, and fully supported by the powerful DCC to unseat Algers. With Earle Cabell's direct line to the Democratic political power structure in Washington D.C. that included President Lyndon Johnson and Cabell's brother, Air Force General Charles P. Cabell, former Deputy Director of the Central Intelligence Agency, Earle Cabell won with 57.5% of the votes to Alger's 42.5%.

As Mayor of Dallas, Earle Cabell had performed well under extreme circumstances. He had led Dallas through the most trying times an American city would face, before the tragedies of 9/11 and Katrina. His attempts to divert the memorial's location away from Dallas are understandable, given his focus on the political and economic health of Dallas, and he was not alone in wishing to minimize reminders of the November tragedy. He would be criticized for the violence that had occurred in 1963, and no doubt felt a heavy responsibility as mayor. What once were his strongest political assets of ties to LBJ, and his brother Charles Cabell in the nation's intelligence apparatus would later be viewed as suspicious, placing him amidst a mix of conspiratorial intrigues. No one could have expected Earle Cabell to provide all the right answers, and the correct political responses, to quell the controversy and anger over one of the most horrific events in American history.

Succeeding Cabell as mayor of Dallas was Erik Jonnson, former president and chairman of the board of Texas Instruments, who was instrumental in the development of the University of Texas at Dallas, and a key member of the Dallas Citizens Council.

Planning for the JFK Memorial continued during 1964. A new facet of the memorial site's development began taking shape, one which would delay the construction of the Memorial for six years. Dallas County leadership had earlier envisioned an underground parking garage beneath the memorial site, to spur urban renewal in this area of Dallas. Years later, speaking at the dedication of the JFK Memorial, Judge Sterrett would trumpet the fact that the creation of the Kennedy Memorial Plaza had helped transform the surrounding area by the removal of seamy urban blight, which consisted of thirty-seven flophouses, numerous beer joints, and liquor stores.[6]

With Mayor Erik Jonsson now at the helm, a proclamation was issued designating the period from June 13 through June 30 as a time for the community to focus on the development of the Kennedy Memorial. The underground garage would be funded by the County of Dallas, and the JFK Memorial project would be funded by private citizens through the guidance of the John F. Kennedy Memorial Citizens Committee. The County's timetable and requirements would always trump the Committee's timetable, as the engineering and construction requirements for completion of the underground facility would necessarily come first.

Mayor Jonsson's proclamation was a reminder to those dedicated to memorial development that urgent efforts were needed to regain and sustain momentum. With renewed efforts, it was announced near the end of June that contributions for the memorial had exceeded $100,000. By early August, contributions and pledges had passed the $200,000 mark. The fundraising campaign was successfully concluded on August 6, 1964, less than nine months from the date of the assassination. Contributions had ranged from a few pennies from school children to $2000 from local Dallas businesses.

Dallas had every reason to be proud of the response from its citizens and local businesses. The Memorial to John Kennedy would forever remain a spontaneous and heartfelt gift from the citizens of Dallas to a fallen leader. Even after the conclusion of the fund-raising campaign, it was reported that individuals continued to deliver contributions and signed scrolls at fire stations around the city of Dallas.

Throughout the long march to completion of the memorial, the citizens of Dallas proved much to impatient to wait for a formal memorial. They had their own timeline for demonstrating remembrance and created many ad-hoc memorials in Dealy Plaza, with commemorative floral wreaths, cards, messages, and flags. These spontaneous outpourings suggested an adamant resolve to directly confront the reality of the assassination and take the first step in returning life to normal. It was reported Dallasites had been parking their cars along the curving descent of Elm Street and stepping out into traffic lanes, risking becoming additional fatalities, to photograph the commemorative wreaths lying beneath the Grassy Knoll - taking with them fleeting but proud, photographic remembrances of the days when Dallas came together as a city.

Jacqueline Kennedy was kept abreast of Dallas plans for contributing to the Kennedy Library, originally planned to be built at Harvard University, and for Dallas plans for a local memorial. She was also keenly aware of the primary source of the funds. In August of 1964, she sent a letter to the City of Dallas which read:

"I am most deeply grateful for the contribution sent to the Kennedy Library Fund, especially because you worked so hard to earn the money. Of all the many tributes to the memory of President Kennedy, I am sure that none would have pleased him more than the touching response of young people that have worked to help the fund. When the library is finished your name will always be on file there. You and your children and all the generations to come who visit the library will be proud to see it there and to know that you had a part in making the President Kennedy Library possible. I know that you will retain the wonderful spirit embodied in your gift to the library that would have meant so much to President Kennedy. With deep appreciation, Jacqueline Kennedy"

The *Dallas Times Herald* reported that by September, approximately $225,000 had been collected, and there was still more expected from corporate donors.

Working in the background but remaining a steady forceful voice for a Dallas-located memorial was Committee member, Harold Stanley Marcus, who would prove to be a significant mover in accomplishing that goal. Marcus received his Bachelor of Arts Degree from Harvard in 1925, the same school attended by Memorial architect Philip Johnson. In 1950, upon the death of his father, Stanley moved to the top of the fashion world, as president and CEO of the haute-couture' Neiman-Marcus retail chain. But there was far more than high fashion to this well-spoken, genteel, sophisticated man. He was also a highly visible organizer and contributor to the advancement of the arts in Dallas. He is remembered for taking politically unpopular stands in the conservative world of Dallas politics, doing his utmost to encourage freedom of expression, unencumbered by the fear of ostracism or censorship. He was one of the hosts for John Kennedy's scheduled luncheon at the Dallas Trade Mart after the motorcade through Dallas. Being well-connected in the worlds of art and finance, Marcus had solicited donations from the collections of David Rockefeller and his brothers, and from other noted national business leaders, for a 1952 exhibition of abstract art.

Marcus also involved himself in issues of civil rights and social justice. One unusual case involved three male students at a Dallas high School who, in 1966 were stopped at the school's front door and ordered to cut their hair to be admitted to the school. The young men filed a lawsuit against the Dallas Independent School District, claiming the restriction interfered with their constitutional freedom of expression. Despite not knowing the boys involved, Marcus took out a newspaper ad defending their choice and offered legal support if needed, noting "I don't like long hair any more than the principal does, but I will fight for the rights of those students to wear hair any way they choose."[7] The case was lost and then appealed all the way to the U.S. Supreme Court without success. Such was the noble nature and humanitarian characteristics of the man who served as the critical link between the Memorial Committee and the extraordinary individual who would design the JFK Memorial.

Stanley Marcus remembered Philip Johnson from his days at Harvard, and was aware Johnson was practicing architecture successfully in Texas. Marcus had seen many of Johnson's works in Texas such as the exquisitely designed Amon Carter Museum, and had visited Philip's most notable structure, the Glass House, Johnson's home in the forested beauty of Connecticut. Marcus knew Johnson's social connections extended into the highest reaches of American society, and that Johnson enjoyed the patronage and support of the Rockefeller and Kennedy families during his tenure as Director of Architecture at the New York Museum of Modern Art.[8]

To many influential persons in Dallas, Johnson's work was gaining acclaim, as well as notoriety, although Johnson himself was still considered an outsider. For Marcus, Philip Johnson was the only choice for the job. Marcus remembered Johnson's pioneering work in introducing America to the European International Style of Architecture. In Marcus's artistically appreciative mind, this style would be an appropriate architectural form for the memorial, with its predisposition for straightforward, powerful statement, and its lack of emotional or excessive adornment. Johnson enthusiastically accepted the assignment, and waived his architectural fee, very likely made aware of the severe budget constraints surrounding the Memorial project. It was likely that Philip was also desirous of donating his efforts to a fallen President, a man he admired.

Two years and two days after the assassination, the memorial funding, the site, and the architect were in place. On the day before Christmas 1965, *Time Magazine* carried an artist's rendering of the proposed design for the John F. Kennedy Memorial in Dallas, Texas.

Action began in early 1966 at the Memorial site. To coordinate activities between the Memorial Committee and Dallas County, Judge Lew Sterrett appointed four county commissioners to work in conjunction with the Memorial Committee to develop and beautify the memorial site.

Sterrett also thought it prudent to have County Auditor, George Smith, attend all meetings between the two groups.

At a tumultuous meeting held on June 15, 1966, the Memorial Committee stated they were under severe pressure to complete the Memorial without delay. Contributions had accumulated for nearly two years, and the Committee had been expected to move forward without delay. Monuments to John Kennedy were being completed around the world, yet in the city where he was slain, no visible action had yet been taken.

W.W. Overton, a prominent Dallas executive, who had suggested the underground parking garage to County Commissioners, now proposed the memorial be constructed, stored at a temporary site, and moved to the final site after completion of the underground garage. Committee members stated this was not structurally feasible, therefore County Commissioners ruled the garage must be completed first, despite the Memorial Committee's strenuous insistence that it was inappropriate, from a variety of significant viewpoints, to delay the Memorial any longer. County officials estimated the construction of the garage would delay the memorial for at least a year and a half. Concerned Dallas citizens expressed a desire to have the memorial completed in time for the five-year anniversary of the assassination. And so ended 1966.

In mid-February 1967, the Texas State Legislature approved a revenue bonds bill to finance the underground garage. In a meeting between the County Commissioners and the Memorial Committee, Judge Sterrett formally announced the eighteen month delay in Memorial construction. Memorial Committee Chairman W. Dawson Sterling restated, with admirable restraint, that the Memorial Committee was under considerable pressure to accomplish their mandate, and did not have a choice, as the site was located on county ground. In retrospect, delays might have been inevitable when the Memorial Committee accepted land under jurisdiction of County officials in the early days following the assassination. The Memorial Commission had no city or county authority. It was not provided with funding, and originally chartered by Cabell and Sterret only as an advisory body. Mayor Cabell's original statement that Dallas would not be able to provide a memorial of sufficient magnitude might have been fact, if not for the intense and persistent drive of Dallas citizens, and its Memorial Committee, to patiently overcome each successive hurdle for a greater good.

By the end of June 1967, The *Dallas Times Herald* reported Kennedy Plaza had become a visual disgrace suffering from blight and neglect. Judge Sterrett had previously appointed four County Commissioners to coordinate beautification of Kennedy Plaza, but this clearly had not been done. Responsibility for maintenance of the plaza seemed to be no one's responsibility to the consternation of Dallas citizens and concerned civic leaders. The project was floundering in a miasma of unresolved details, unexpected turns, and unforeseen delays.

Pressure from Dallas citizenry and Memorial Commissioners remained unrelenting. By October of 1967, County Commissioners had responded. The sale of revenue bonds had begun, traffic detours had been agreed upon for the construction phase, final demolition plans were resolved, relocation of the historic John Neely Bryan log cabin was determined, and the final geological survey was nearing completion.

A new glitch was reported by the *Dallas Morning News* when it was discovered there were underground cracks below the garage site due to earth faults. It was thought this might cause additional delays in construction of the garage facility.

In April 1968, the *Dallas Times Herald* reported that Memorial Committee Chairman, W. Dawson Sterling, again stated the Committee was ready to proceed after waiting for approval from the County Commissioners, as they had been doing for three years. Sterling hoped to dedicate the Memorial before the six-year assassination anniversary on November 22, 1969. The next month, the Memorial Commission, formerly known as the JFK Citizens Memorial Committee, announced the construction site would be ready in August.

John Schoellkopf, *Dallas Times Herald* Washington correspondent and president of the Citizens Charter Association, was named the new President of the Memorial Commission. Schoellkopf took an active role in the development of the Memorial and often accompanied architect Philip Johnson during Johnson's trips to Dallas to oversee construction of the Memorial's concrete components. Johnson visited Dallas several times before the assembly of the Memorial, locating the correct materials, along with builders and craftsmen fitting the assignment and the cost. Frank Welch, in his excellent work, *Philip Johnson & Texas,* recounts Schoellkopf's comments about one of Johnson's visits to Dallas:

"He would run his hand over the brush-hammered surfaces saying "This is good" and, "This is not good and won't do" until the finishes were acceptable. He was very polite about it, but his standards were very high. I knew zip about architecture and was sort of the "errand boy" for the commission.

It was now several years after the assassination, and while the original commitment was intact, the intense emotion of the early days after Kennedy's death was waning. Johnson was very kind to me, a junior executive with an afternoon newspaper, while he was probably wondering where the CEO's were."[10]

Other newly selected officers of the Memorial Commission were Robert Callum named as Vice President, and Robert H. Stewart as Secretary-Treasurer. One month later, in June 1969, the *Dallas Times Herald* reported Committee member and Dallas building contractor, Robert McKee of Robert McKee Inc, who's company built the underground garage, had agreed to build the JFK Memorial, with an estimated completion date of January 1, 1970.

In November of 1969, Commission Chairman Schoellkopf, announced further delays and now projected a probable completion date of March 1970, or later. Concrete elements of the Memorial, scheduled to arrive in August, did not arrive until late December of 1969. Work on the JFK Memorial began that month and the first wall of the Memorial was completed on December 22. The Memorial was being erected on "neutral ground," not at the assassination site, yet not distant, and would be a peripheral element in the family of structures forming the Dealy Plaza complex.

All told, the Memorial costs were $175,000 including donated labor and materials.

The John F. Kennedy Memorial was completed and dedicated in a public ceremony on June 6, 1970, with several hundred people in attendance. No Kennedy family members attended the ceremony. Memorial Commission Vice President, Robert Cullum addressed the assemblage with these remarks:

"The traumatic event, crashing down upon us near the culmination of the keenly anticipated, warmly exuberant, almost triumphant visit with the President of the United States, is etched poignantly and permanently and personally upon our memories."

Present on the speaker's podium were Memorial Commission Chairman Schoellkopf, Vice President McCullum, Judge Lew Sterret, Memorial architect Philip Johnson, and Bishop Thomas A. Tschoepe. All spoke of the city's ultimate triumph which began amid the sorrow and chaos of the assassination when Judge Sterret and Mayor Cabell had first proposed a monument to honor John Kennedy.

The story of the JFK Memorial does not end with the hopeful anticipation of a long and revered life as a well-preserved national memorial. By the late 1990s, nearly 20 years after its initial dedication, the Memorial had fallen into a pitiable state of neglect. The walls of the monument had become chipped and stained from exposure. The structure was attacked by a man who vandalized the Memorial with a spray can, leaving the monument grossly defaced. Following this vicious attack on the historic edifice, the City and County of Dallas took notice of the neglect.

In 1999, the Sixth Floor Museum at Dealey Plaza undertook management of the Memorial, and with the support of the city of Dallas, and Dallas County, became a driving force behind restoration of this most uniquely expressive architectural work. Today the Sixth Floor Museum retains its proud position as custodian of the John F. Kennedy Memorial.

The Museum's goal was the full restoration of the structure, including enhancements to explain the Memorial's history and interpretation. Philip Johnson helped guide the restoration process, which eventually cost $80,000. The work was performed pro bono by Phoenix 1 Restoration and Construction Ltd. and numerous local suppliers who donated their time, labor, and materials to restore the Memorial to its original pristine beauty. Dale Sellers, of Phoenix 1 Restoration found subcontractors willing to donate their time and materials during the restoration project. According to Sellers, "It was as simple as picking up the phone! The memorial represents the living Kennedy. When I look at it, I think of all the things he tried to do."

The restoration was a three-month project and included the installation of interpretive plaques at the front and rear of the Memorial to answer questions that visitors had posed over the years. Senator Edward Kennedy released a statement saying, "I am pleased to know that my brother's memory still continues to inspire such public service."

The story of the struggle to bring the John F. Kennedy Memorial into existence remains a fascinating tale of a city overcoming many soul-wrenching issues. There are many unrecognized heroes, many who have since passed, who advocated for a memorial to restore civic pride, and a more compassionate climate of tolerance. Courageous men and women in Dallas, not only advanced the cause of the JFK Memorial, but also spoke out forcefully in Dallas sermons, public forums, and newspapers, urging the city to examine its civic soul, face the reality of the past and present, and restore the city's shattered esteem and its moral compass, in a way the entire world would recognize and understand. Memorial Commission members, city and county officials, and Dallas citizens and school children and their families, everyday Americans of every nationality, faith, and occupation, had a voice in resurrecting Dallas from the horrific events of 22 November 1963. It may not be the form and shape many wished would capture the essence of John Kennedy, but in its ingenious and yet sublime form, it portrays the nature of man's historic struggle for power. Its existence is firm and dignified testimony to the moral resolve and compassionate power of the citizens of Dallas that could not be denied.

3

Philip Cortelyou Johnson

*"In architectural works, man's pride, man's triumph over
gravitation, man's will to power assume visible form.
Architecture is a veritable oratory of power made by form."*

— Friedrich Nietzsche, philosopher

The Ascent of Man

In 2005, when I first visited the JFK Memorial, my initial reaction was
one of overwhelming curiosity. The Washington Monument speaks of
towering leadership; the Jefferson Memorial evokes classical wisdom; the
Lincoln Monument depicts the larger-than-life courage of the visionary;
the Grant Memorial presents the adamant resolve of the warrior. The
Kennedy Memorial, 1300 miles from the center of American government,
does not, at first glance, invoke these characteristics.

Because of the plain, unadorned, although striking presentation of the
monument, I originally suspected its designer to be of modest talent and
fame - perhaps an obscure local or regionally famous architect. Perhaps he

or she was one of the many talented artists often working in relative obscurity, creating artistic works to revitalize inner city neighborhoods beyond the sameness of urban architecture.

My expectations were proven woefully wrong and suggested a glaring weakness in my understanding of modern architecture, and most-especially, American architects of renown. Phillip Johnson played a major role in shaping American architecture of the Twentieth Century and beyond. Within this ancient art form, he was a superstar of the highest magnitude, an acknowledged genius and an internationally famous trendsetting virtuoso. He was the guiding force in introducing the International Style of Architecture to America in the 1930s. This structural building form has been the primary catalyst for shaping America's modern skyscraper city skylines and avant-garde dwellings coast to coast since its introduction. He was also the first Director of Architecture at New York's famous Museum of Modern Art, or MOMA, as it is popularly known.

Philip passed away in his sleep in 2005, at the age of 95, at his fabled home, the Glass House, in New Canaan, Connecticut. He was acclaimed by many as the foremost of American architects in company with his friend, enemy, critic, and colleague, Frank Lloyd Wright. Although this narrative is not meant to be a biographical study of Philip Johnson, it is essential to understand the man and the influences that shaped his approach to the creation of the Dallas JFK Memorial. Biographies and collective studies of Philip Johnson's accomplishments offer minimal commentary on his Dallas Memorial. For this author it added to the mystique of the structure, as I learned of its designer's potential for creating works that stretched the limits of accepted form. The memorial also suggested the subtle power of the architect's force, for despite the limitations he encountered within the JFK memorial project, he was able to create an inspiring living theater that encourages imagination and awareness.

Philip Johnson was born in 1906, into a moderately wealthy family in Cleveland, Ohio, and with his sisters, was raised in an environment that sparked their interest in the fine arts. They were attended by a German-born governess who taught them to speak German. Philip also learned to speak French fluently, and the two languages later provided the communication skills needed to gain a first-hand understanding of the architectural and political environments of Europe. Fluency afforded Philip the ability to serve as an effective translator for the International Style of Architecture that significantly influenced the future of American architecture.

The family vacationed frequently in Germany, which at that time was a vibrant center of European cultural. Teutonic-based music, art, and literature were favored in the Johnson home, reinforcing Philip's attraction to Germanic culture which remained throughout his personal and professional life.

Through his inheritance from his father, he was a millionaire at the age of 20, and able to sustain the costs of youthful adventurism, allowing him to travel when and where he pleased. He enjoyed a world of exploration unavailable to most young men of his time. He experienced the overwhelming sensations of historical connection within the Parthenon, then again beneath the soaring interiors of Europe's great Medieval cathedrals. He ventured forth in Arabian garb, as a young Lawrence of Arabia in the exotic surroundings of Cairo and its fabled Museum. He traveled through Europe in his powerful American-built convertible, a young Indiana Jones, in search of exciting discoveries and architectural treasure.

In the summer of 1928, his visit to the Parthenon in Athens affected him so deeply he was moved to tears by its classic, timeless architecture. In later years he remembered his experience on the Acropolis as a life-changing moment, leading him towards his conversion to architecture as a high art form. Its powerful, yet simple and straightforward design, even in a state of ruin, transmitted the force of Hellenistic intellectualism and culture across the millennia. Through the beautifully symmetrical interplay of the *rectangle and the cylinder* [italics are the Author's] it made a lasting impression on Philip.

In America, his wealth and social connections gained him entry into New York's elite company of artists and patrons. His patrons included members of the Rockefeller, Morgan, Vanderbildt, de Menil, and Kennedy families. In 1930 he was introduced to Alfred H. Barr, Jr. at his sister's graduation from Wellesley College. Barr had recently been chosen to lead the new Museum of Modern Art. Barr's vision was of a unique institution, a symbiosis of all the modern arts behind one intellectual banner of avant-garde artistic activity. It would be located in the middle of Manhattan, dedicated, in Barr's words, to "The art of now." No establishment with such a mission existed.

Sometime during their first meeting, Barr asked Philip, "Do you want to help start a modern art museum?" Johnson enthusiastically accepted. Philip brought enthusiasm and youthful energy, along with his classical education, to invigorate and sustain the project Barr had in mind. Philip's accomplishments at MOMA became the foundation of his career, sustaining his future fame and reputation throughout his lifetime.

When twenty-three-year-old Johnson began his summer journey through Europe in 1929, he personally interviewed many of Europe's leading architects. These emerging masters of European modernism were creating a new style of architecture that would offer an improved way of living: build economically and functionally, standardize where possible, and spend the savings to enhance living standards. Philip wholeheartedly embraced this concept to improve the condition of man. He was witnessing the birth of a new design form that spoke to the needs of the expanding power and numbers of the industrialized Western nation's middle classes: economy over extravagance, functionality rather than high art, standardization rather than expression. Yet, in the ultimate irony, this art form, initially intended to define the emerging middle classes, would ultimately become the iconic symbol of corporate power ruling America's skylines far into the future.

To a young patrician connoisseur like Johnson, it was the opportunity of a lifetime. Philip held the golden keys in his hand: the introduction and translation of a new art form, and the directorship of the new architectural department at MOMA. It must have seemed that the gods of Olympus, with whom he communed during his visit to the Parthenon, had understood and answered his prayers. He would lead the historic introduction of a new style of architecture from the Old World into the New.

M. D. BROSIO

Following Johnson's investigative summer foray in Europe, Barr asked Johnson to tour Europe a second time to gather material for MOMA's first grand exhibition. With Barr's coaching, Johnson began a detailed tour of the continent's new architecture. With his associate, Henry Russell Hitchcock, Philip crisscrossed the continent, touring the new centers of modern architecture, interviewing an impressive group of emerging architectural masters including Van der Rohe, Oud, Gropius, Breuer, and Le Corbusier. In turn, these European architects were pleased to have captured the attention of these young American explorers, speeding around the continent in Johnson's sleek, open-top car, documenting architecture of the future.[11]

When Johnson returned home in the fall of 1930, he had visited France, Belgium, Holland, Germany, Sweden, Denmark, Switzerland, Austria, and Czechoslovakia. He was now officially Director of the Museum of Modern Art, Department of Architecture, and he began the organization of its first exhibition on architecture. It opened in early 1932, featuring Americans Frank Lloyd Wright, Raymond Hood, Howe, Lescaze, Neutra, and the Bowman Brothers. The exhibition, *Modern Architecture—International Exhibition*, stirred New York's architectural scene. It began modestly with a meager amount of lukewarm comment from the media, and some thirty-three thousand people attending its six-week run. Ultimately the exhibition's impact in the United States was profound, and the new style of design was here to stay. International Style modernism's appeal to the American architectural profession, had began with the museum's groundbreaking exhibition, led by its young Director of Architecture. Philip was only 26 years old.

For several years following the exhibition, Johnson was busy with other exhibitions, writing catalogues, and delivering lectures, while maintaining a colorful, fast-paced, social life in Manhattan's elite, Upper East Side salons, amidst the offbeat world of poets, artists, dancers, and musicians. The Rockefellers, Goodyears, and Blisses were museum confidants, and solicitors of his artistic opinions. The gods had surely blessed Philip beyond his wildest expectations, although this young Prometheus was about to embark on the most perilous journey of his lifetime.

Philip Johnson.

Philip Johnson.

THE QUEST TO KNOW HISTORY (AKA) POWER

Art has been defined as the quality, production, expression, or realm, according to aesthetic principles, of what is beautiful, appealing, or of more than ordinary significance. Philip Johnson lived most of his life outside of the boundaries of the ordinary. His body of works are a testament to this. He summed up his body of work in his own words: "It would be impossible to build in as many directions as I have and not hit it once in a while."

He was present at the birth of a great architectural movement and personally knew many of the influential rising architects in America and Europe. The grace of the architectural gods had commissioned him to go forth and spread the gospel of modern architecture, and he had done so. Yet for Philip, there remained a burning question: how would he make his own lasting personal mark within, or perhaps even above, the artistic forces of his time? Would he lead or follow? The more he promoted and advanced the works of others, the more he was sharpening his own sword of Damocles, hovering above him, threatening to render him only a powerful advocate, a celebrated connoisseur, while he himself remained devoid of the powers of creativity.

He desperately needed some primal, liberating event, enabling him to step out of the spotlight of others and claim his own place in history as a creative force. This dilemma, central to Philip's life, would lead him to the doorstep of the most delineative and powerful forces of his time.

He began his own quest for liberation by fulfilling the celebrated remark he so aptly expressed in later years, "We cannot not know history". Philip set out to live history, allowing his classically tuned senses to experience history, not merely as a casual outsider, but in person, as a journalist visiting the brewing pots of the most controversial political figures and arenas of his time. He began with the intentions of highlighting what Philip and his political mentors deemed the failed economic policies of two nations ravaged by depression, America and Germany. He elected to validate his credentials to his audience by reporting history as it happened in real time. Only then could he present and argue for solutions he felt were best for America.

There was an air of excitement to be found across the Atlantic Ocean, in the dynamic forces raising Germany from the ashes of the most severe depression experienced by any Western nation to this time. The Great Depression had left the German nation devastated. Its people were financially, morally, and spiritually depleted as one political solution after another weakened their resolve, and left its people fearing all hope and promise were gone, replaced by endless poverty and degradation. Suicides reached unheard of proportions. It was not uncommon for entire families to commit suicide together, as financial humiliation before their peers shattered and destroyed pride.

Amidst the spiritual exhaustion of the German nation, there arose an insistent hope, carrying with it a terrible gathering storm. It was the defiant and challenging dynamism of the German National Socialist Party, offering if not a clear roadmap to a better world, then at least a thundering denunciation of its failed past. It repeatedly attacked the feebleness of democratic institutions, and the immorality of treaties imposed by shortsighted victorious western nations. It condemned its own democratic spokesmen who devised endless austerity measures, claiming such disciplines were required of a vanquished people to regain the respect of their conquerors.

Philip, with his lifelong cultural appreciation of Germany, was aware from his travels, friends, and international media sources, of the profound effects of the Global Depression in Germany. He was impressed by the way Germany was rebuilding itself, regaining its sense of purpose and dynamic drive, restoring pride in Germanic culture. He was aware that this stunning turnabout was led by one of the most charismatic and controversial leaders in German history, Adolf Hitler. Hitler embodied the persona of the "Great Leader" and seemed to many to be the model for the statesman-politician of tomorrow. By all accounts and accomplishments, Hitler was the physical manifestation of the "Will to power," expressed by the philosopher, Friedrich Nietzsche. The writings and theories of Nietzsche, more than any other philosopher, influenced Philip's concept of man's drive to attain and sustain power.

During his 1932 summer vacation in Europe, Johnson was invited by Helen Appleton Read, a New York art critic for the *Brooklyn Eagle*, to attend a Nazi rally. Hitler spoke to a large crowd in a field in Potsdam, a suburb of Berlin. Johnson was completely magnetized by this new "theater of politics"; the martial songs, the flags, the precise phalanxes of handsome young troops, the bombastic Teutonic orchestration, climaxed by the appearance of Hitler with his explosive harangue, asking his listeners to embrace the unlimited future of Germany, embodied in himself, leader of the new Germanic Reich.

This was a grandly scaled form of visual power that, in the hands of Germany's state architect, Albert Speer, was overwhelming and operatic in effect. Speer was the Reich's master architect, an essential force in fusing art, architecture, and politics in a way the modern world had never witnessed. Far above the emotional effects Johnson had felt at his first view of the Acropolis and the Cathedral of Chartres, these raw displays of power witnessed in the Potsdam and Nuremberg rallies were Philip's first exposure to man's unbridled quest for power in the flesh. Under the guidance of Speer, the great Nuremberg rallies were designed to overwhelm the senses, to hypnotize and subjugate the individual to the will of the great leader, using the powers of light, art, theater, architecture, and emotion to disguise the intellectual and moral vacuity presented under the banner of the Third Reich's brand of German National Socialism.

Driven by his craving to live and know history, Philip undoubtedly understood he was immersed in a unique historical moment that would be remembered either for its glory or infamy, or perhaps both, but nevertheless a turning point in the social and political fabric of the Twentieth Century. Politics, art, and power had been united in one visceral tangible living form in Philip's artistically fertile imagination.

And so on Christmas Day in 1934, Johnson began, what his biographer, Franz Schulze, most appropriately described as the "Inglorious Detour". Leaving behind his unique and privileged position within MOMA, Philip began his quest for solutions to correct America's flawed system of politics and government. Although the premise behind the International Style of

Modern Architecture was to raise the standard of living for the middle classes, the power of political events taking place in Germany promised even more to its people. For the time being, architecture must take a back seat, as the human conditions in America and Germany could no longer be ignored.

He made his fateful decision to resign from MOMA at the moment his efforts in the United States to expand awareness of innovative architecture were bringing public recognition and fame. When viewed through the lens of Johnson's lifelong fascination with power in physical and abstract forms, it may be said that he felt compelled to experience the perhaps, once-in-a-lifetime opportunity to "know" history, and experience man's tangible quest for power first hand.

There was an inherent contradiction that motivated and substantiated the change in direction Philip was ardently pursuing. To understand the contradiction, it is necessary to realize that Johnson had enthusiastically advocated a dehumanizing architectural form, devoid of excess and sensory stimulation, designed only to create a functionally efficient environment for the common man. In a paradoxical twist of fate, he found himself spreading this architectural philosophy precisely at a juncture in time when the Great Depressions in America and Germany were subjecting the common men and women of both nations to the physical reality of dehumanizing living conditions, despair, and social ostracism. Architectural theory and urban street-life had collided in a juxtaposition where either architecture had portended history, or events portended the new style of architecture, in a way none had expected. In either case, promoting de-humanizing architecture seemed to be an unwarranted cruelty in view of the economic and spiritual suffering imposed on the common people of the two nations Philip had hoped to enjoin through architecture.

The contradiction can also be viewed within Philip's mercurial nature attracting him to the brightest lights of a just cause. Just as he been attracted to the power and brilliance of man's greatest architectural structures, and the innovative strength of the International Style of Modern Architecture, he was now attracted to the most powerful and radical spokesmen of the time.

Johnson, the classic parvenu, took on the dual roles of student and leader. As a student of history, he would make a conscious effort to experience power politics by jumping fearlessly into the most controversial political cauldrons of the times. As a leader, he would use this newfound knowledge to guide others toward a better life. It was a momentous decision and would result in interlocking Philip's understanding of art, politics, history, and power for the rest of his life. Where it would all lead, he nor anyone else could be certain, as the degree of social upheaval and displacement was severe by any previous standards, since the beginning of the industrial revolution. That he did not burn his most important human contacts in the world of architecture but was able to maintain them throughout this period in his life, indicates that he visualized, and indeed planned, a return to the highly visible positions in architecture, available to one with his imagination, wealth, and social connections.

While many intellectuals and artists of his time considered the benefits of communism, socialism, and fascism, Johnson became attracted to right-wing writer and fellow Harvard student, Lawrence Dennis. Dennis' most emphatic work, *"Is Capitalism Doomed?"* presented a case for invoking a form of populist fascism. Its goal was to correct the current flaws bringing financial, moral, and emotional hardship to millions of Americans. Dennis predicted that capitalism in the United States was a deeply flawed system and doomed to fail. He stated that only the coming of fascism could save America. Fascist revolt, he explained, would come, not from the masses, but from "The menaced and injured members of the elite who have a will to power, and a will through the capture and use of power, to change conditions they find intolerable."

Dennis argued that all societies were ultimately run by elites. Fascism had the virtue of not being hypocritical, as it "Frankly acknowledges, or rather boasts, that its elite rule." If the economy performed better and the masses were happier under fascism than under communism or capitalism, Dennis concluded, then indeed, it was the right medicine for America.[12]

Johnson was no stranger to Populism, the political philosophy promoting the rights of the common people against the power of the privileged elite. Populism had a long and solid history in the Midwestern United States where Philip grew up. Fascism was not a political system with which he had familiarity, because before World War II, Europe had not yet fallen under German or Italian fascist dominion. However, with Philip's exposure to the concepts of populism and Nitzschean power, it was not an inconceivable leap of faith to believe in the "great men" of history, with their inherent right to rule through whichever political system best served the needs of the common man. The great philosophers, Aristotle, Plato, Socrates, and Nietzsche had guided Johnson's philosophical maturation. However, for Philip, it was to be the outspoken and bold "great leaders" of his time who would demonstrate the physical incarnation of Nietzsche's will to power.

In December 1934, prominent front-page accounts in the *New York Times* and *New York Herald Tribune,* reported that Johnson and Alan Blackburn, a former Harvard classmate and associate at MOMA, had formed their own "Nationalist Party" or "Gray Shirts." Momentarily consumed with a streak of revolutionary fervor, the *Herald Tribune* noted, Johnson's office at the MOMA was filled with catalogs of firearms. Blackburn was in favor of large pistols; Johnson favored the submachine gun.[13] After actively trying to recruit members for their new political party, and holding a few meetings with somewhat desultory results, the pair quit their jobs at MOMA and traveled to Louisiana to offer their services to Senator Huey Long.

The "Kingfish," as Huey Long was popularly called, was in Dennis' words, "The nearest approach to a national fascist leader." Huey Long gave fist-pounding "share the wealth" sermons, taunting the nation's elite to feed the hungry: "What's Morgan and Baruch and Rockefeller going to do with all that grub? We got to call Mr. Rockefeller and say, come back *he-ah!*" Long's staff turned the two eager Ivy Leaguers back after asking how many votes they represented. Johnson never spoke with Long, who was assassinated in Baton Rouge in 1935.

Johnson then turned his considerable energies toward the support of Roman Catholic cleric, Father Charles Coughlin. Coughlin was the other potential candidate for an American fascist party leader in Dennis' eyes. Johnson and Blackburn supported Coughlin in a variety of ways. In what was probably their most notable accomplishment, they successfully organized a rally in Chicago at which eighty-thousand spectators paid fifty cents each to hear Coughlin speak. Johnson himself designed the speaker's podium for Coughlin, modeled after the podium he had seen Hitler use at Potsdam, Germany, in 1932.[14]

Father Coughlin, pastor of a church in suburban Detroit, preached weekly to an audience of fifteen million Americans. Coughlin blamed America's ills primarily on President Roosevelt and his New Deal policies, while also promoting theories of a worldwide Jewish-Communist conspiracy, along with "Godless capitalists," who were all threatening the future of American citizens. At one point, Coughlin was receiving more weekly mail than Roosevelt, and it was no secret within the White House that Roosevelt wanted Coughlin muzzled. FDR's request was ultimately honored in typical back-room political fashion, although the accommodating players were of special eminence.

On October 8, 1936, the Vatican's powerful Secretary of State, Monseigneur Eugenio Pacelli, protegee of Pope Pius XI and destined to become Pope Pius XII, arrived in the United States for a nationwide tour. The primary goal of Pacelli's visit was to gain Vatican support from Roosevelt in the form of a U.S.-Vatican diplomatic relationship. Pacelli and Roosevelt met on November 6, 1936, at Roosevelt's Hyde Park home, a visit arranged by America's Ambassador to Great Britain, Joseph P. Kennedy, father of future American president John F. Kennedy. Roosevelt obliged Pacelli. Following diplomatic maneuvering, designed not to raise the ire of America's Protestant majority, Myron Taylor was appointed as an accredited representative to the Holy See in 1940, thereby establishing formal diplomatic links between the United States and the Vatican.

In return, although Pacelli never indicated his part in the matter, Father Coughlin announced, on November 8, 1936, two days after the Kennedy-arranged Roosevelt-Pacelli meeting, that he was making his final public broadcast. He would never broadcast again. As in the case of Huey

Long, another powerful fascist voice in the United States was silenced, leaving Johnson with no radical political alternative in the form of the "great leader" to support in America.

It is noteworthy that Monseigneur Eugenio Pacelli, as Pope Pius XII, was later to come under severe criticism for accommodating Germany's Nazi fascist regime. In his controversial book, *"Hitler's Pope,"* author John Cornwell documented Pacelli's role, as Vatican Secretary of State, in the formulation and conclusion of the 1938 Reich Concordat with Hitler and the Nazi Government. This concordat effectively muzzled Catholic resistance to Nazi rule and consigned the Catholic Church to a role of noninterference in German politics. In return, Hitler allowed the Catholic Church to retain its religious ministry, property and wealth, and in theory, revoked all coercive measures against the Catholic clergy in Nazi Germany. At this moment, when the fate of governments and religious organizations were at stake, political expedience took precedence. Pacelli likely ended Father Coughlin's reign in American politics, in the interest of strengthening Old and New World relationships before the coming Nazi storm.

The culmination of Johnson's quest for a political solution to poverty in America occurred in 1938, as war enveloped Europe. With Dennis' help, Johnson was invited by the German government to attend a *Somerkurs für Aüslander* in Berlin, an introduction to Nazi politics for foreigners. Without any doubt, the personal highlight of his next Germanic tour was the occasion of Hitler's appearance and speech at the 1938 Nuremberg Party Rally. This rally was the greatest and the last of the Nuremberg rallies. The following year the world would begin its descent into the deadliest war in mankind's history.

"For the benefit of Mr. Kite there will be a show tonight on trampoline.
The Hendersons will all be there late of Pablo Fanque's Fair, what a scene! Over men and horses, hoops and garters, lastly through a hogshead of real fire! In this way Mr. K. will challenge the world!"

— JOHN LENNON, SONGWRITER

"When a hundred men stand together, each of them loses his mind and gets another one."

— FRIEDRICH NIETZSCHE, PHILOSOPHER

THE DESCENT OF MAN

For at least one week every year, from 1932 through 1938, Nuremberg was inundated by Nazi officialdom from all parts of the country. Present were representatives of all branches of the military, paramilitary, militia, fervent German and foreign Nazi adherents, diplomats, correspondents, groups of trade workers, and the curious. Loud, triumphant music was played continuously through public speaker systems throughout the city. The mood of the city nervously approached a tumultuous fever pitch, leading up to the great rally, and the appearance of Adolph Hitler and his entourage.

By 1938, Albert Speer, Hitler's State Architect, had raised the annual Nuremberg celebration to an unprecedented art form. Speer had been given the task of organizing and planning the culmination of the Nuremberg Rally. He designed and developed the Zepplinfeld Stadium, with a capacity of 340,000 people. Speer employed the interplay of architecture and light on a grand scale to serve as a backdrop for the vast blocks of perfectly aligned humanity, the powering stimulus of Wagnerian music, the multi-colored flags and golden standards borne by Nazi legions, and oversized Nazi banners. Above all, there was the hypnotic effect attained by Albert

Speer's innovative and overpowering "Cathedral of Light." When referring to his creation, Speer later stated, "The actual effect far surpassed anything I had imagined!" In a 1987 interview conducted by art critic Robert Hughes, Speer was still unable to hide his unbridled pride in his classic *architectural* feat.

> "I still consider this my best idea I had as an architect. The effect was as I planned, that of a *room*. [italics are the authors] Yes, from the outside it looks like columns, but from the inside it looks like a cathedral."

British Ambassador Sir Neville Henderson, present at the 1938 Nuremberg Rally stated it "Was both solemn and beautiful ... like being in a cathedral of ice." Yet despite its grandiose, artistic effect, Speer's majestic achievement will be remembered for its darker purpose, that of a hypnotic propaganda tool, capturing and enslaving those within its towering walls of light, to a philosophy shaped by one of mankind's most misguided and apocalyptical political and social theories. It forever remains a brilliant distraction, a masterpiece of deception, disguising man's quest for overwhelming power.

Philip Johnson was present at the 1938 Nuremberg Rally and experienced firsthand, the stupendous effect of Albert Speer's creation. Around Philip, the great vertical swords of light from 152 flak searchlights ignited. Placed at precise intervals, one by one, with the onrushing sound of towering light sabers, each pierced the blackness of the night sky, up to a height of 25,000 feet, more than 4 miles upward. Together they created a mighty enclosure of light, surrounding the vast assemblage of humanity. It was a room in which all participants became an entwined mass of nonentities, assuming shape and definition through submission to the sway of the great leader, who would twist and bend their wills to his. Philip's dedicated search had brought him into Herr Speer's room, created by the *luminaria deceptionis,* the lights of deception, erected with the twin purposes of binding its over-stimulated celebrants in a cathedral of the senses to complete their conversion into fervent disciples of the National Socialist gospel; and likewise to surround the great man, as noted American art critic Robert Hughes explains, "With a sort of divine radiance." For Philip it was surely a spiritually and emotionally overwhelming moment, evoking and surpassing memories he had experienced in his first visit to the Parthenon at the age of 22. Nevertheless, it was a tragedy of near calamitous proportion, for Johnson now walked, with so many others, onto the horrific path set forth in Hitler's 1925 book, Mein Kampf.

For the second time in his life, driven by his own fundamental need to "know" history and the nature of power, he found himself at the genesis of a new force. This time he was experiencing an unholy transubstantiation of light into the spoken "word". At Nuremberg he witnessed the creation of the dark Nazi Parthenon, enveloping him and capturing him, within the most ethereal and mysterious of building materials an architect could employ: pure light. Philip absorbed its influence, perhaps more keenly than others, because of his lifelong attraction to power, and a burning desire to portray power through architecture. It would require disillusionment and fear on a grand scale, to make Philip understand that his pursuit of these noble purposes had placed him on a perverse and morally corrupt path. Denial or recognition of the misuse of these powers would threaten his reputation, livelihood, fame, and career with ruin, and perhaps worst of all for Philip, consignment to oblivion as a great "might-have-been." That disillusionment was yet to come.

The official reason for his next visit to Germany in 1939, was to serve as "war correspondent" for Father Coughlin's magazine *Social Justice*. As Johnson has related to his biographer, Franz Schulze, he had become friends with Viola Bodenschatz, wife of Luftwaffe Major General Karl Bodenschatz, then serving as liaison between Reichsmarshal Hermann Goring's Luftwaffe and Adolf Hitler.

A month before the outbreak of war, traveling with Bodenschatz, Philip reported what he had witnessed in an article for Coughlin's magazine, *Social Justice*. He reported conditions that stood in contrast to the tensions and mounting cruelties that existed in Nazi Germany. In this, and other published writings authored by Johnson during this phase, he supported National Socialist policies. At the invitation of the German Propaganda Minister, he was allowed to accompany the German army to witness the invasion of Poland firsthand. It was at this time, amid the ruins of burned out houses and villages, that the sublimated meaning for his own, later renowned structure, the Glass House took shape and remained in his memory. The images of a burned-out home, only retaining the brick and stone chimney or hearth to show where a family had once lived, was a surreal image, capturing the eye of the architect who remained unburdened by the reality of the attendant horrors of war.

Philip's abandonment of his elevated position at MOMA in search of a system of government for the betterment of mankind, had led to a disastrous turn towards the most radical and perverse of all solutions, driven by the age old dictum of survival of the fittest, where the virtues of compassion, brotherhood, and respect for life, are usurped by the will to rule, ascend, and conquer - the very symbols that would arise from his memorial to an American president he would design 30 years later. Philip had once stood in a "room," in an inglorious turn in his life he cared not to discuss and experienced how the horrific release of unrestrained power can transform and destroy men and nations.

Through his later years, Philip Johnson recanted his involvement with Nazi politics to various degrees, perhaps coming as close as possible to admitting he had been seduced by Albert Speer's dark magic. His apology has the ring of a man hypnotized of his own free will. After succumbing to the awesome power of Albert Speer, master hypnotist, he would find to his everlasting horror that his ultimate desire, the fusion of architecture and power had been twisted into a negative image of man's purpose. Philip had been duped on a grandly ceremonious scale, standing shoulder to shoulder with legions of fools, craving the arrival of the great leader, who would lift mankind to the promised land. Johnson would never be adequately able to explain, how he had been in his own words, "carried away" by one of history's most able and darkest magicians.

Perhaps it was much too painful to admit that the art forms he believed could uplift and exalt man, also had nearly destroyed him. In an interview related to his induction into the Academy of Achievement in 1991, Philip stated,

"My worst mistake was going to Germany and liking Hitler too much. I mean, how could you? It's just so unbelievably stupid and asinine and plain wrong, morally and every other way. I just don't know how I could have been carried away. It's like being carried away by a religious revival or something that enables you to cut people's heads off in the next county because they live in the next county. That's not good either. But that I should be psychologically so inept as to be swept along in something so horrible, it really wonders you. How could you? I never found a reason, I never found an excuse, and all I can say is how much I regret it because the racial part of is the worst. I can understand social fascism as done in Italy before Mussolini met Hitler, because that was, If the trains run on time, let's not do it the communist way, let's do it our way. That made some sense and that's what I was doing here in America. But to be caught up in the racial thing was unbelievable, because like everyone else in the intellectual world, nine-tenths of the people I know are Jewish and the outrageousness of that kind of thing that could happen in a world and I didn't know it?! Where the hell was I?! A Harvard graduate! So much for Harvard! I was just stupid. Just unforgivable. That's the worst thing I ever did."[15]

In *Architectural Record,* Johnson biographer Franze Schulze writes:

"Though he shifted from one political objective to another during this period, he remained true to his belief in power, especially if manifest in someone - like Hitler or Long (or Mies van der Rohe, for that matter) - who seemed to Johnson a prophetic figure in the Nietzschean mold. He did not overtly surrender his political orientation until he was identified as a "fascist" . . . By then, Johnson had withdrawn from politics to enroll as an architecture student at

Harvard in the fall of 1940. Even then, the exercise of power, now returned to the aesthetic realm, remained a central motivation."[16]

In the *Architectural Record,* architectural critic, Michael Sorkin writes:

"In a life of nearly a century, Johnson never interested himself in any of the registers through which architecture and its philosophy can help enfranchise; never showed much, if any, concern with housing the poor, with the environment, with the fate of cities. His own philosophy was rooted in a schoolboy Nietzscheanism of supermen and the will to power."[17]

Finally, realizing the misguided direction of Hitler's actions, Johnson, in the fall of 1940, at age thirty-four, applied to Harvard's Graduate School of Design, to study architecture and begin a fresh start. With Houdini-like elasticity at the very last minute of his downward spiraling tragic drama, he was able to throw off the odious stench of Nazi collaboration, and quietly work his way towards the surface of respectability, with the assistance of powerful friends. He narrowly avoided the ensnaring net of the FBI and the disgrace of being labeled a traitor. His own attempts at bringing fascism to America proved to be of no lasting consequence. But, he had fully experienced what Theodore Roosevelt had once written to the poet Edward Arlington Robinson, that a "Devil masters each of us, but that it is not having been in the Dark House, but having left it, that counts."[18]

Johnson may have left the Dark House behind, but he took with him the depths, heights, sights, sounds, and emotions of those times, and an understanding of the physical nature of power, in its most overwhelming and destructive forms. The question he carried, amidst the clutter and remnants of a failed episode, was whether he had the requisite skills to convert man's expressions of power and strength into visible form with glass, metal, and mortar. Harvard was his refuge, where he would allow his experiences, images, and creativity to boil and simmer in the calming halls of academia. Leadership and respect were freely bestowed by students much younger than himself, awed at his former position at the Director's chair at MOMA, by his success in introducing a new style of architecture to America, and by the pre-imminent list of architectural giants Johnson considered associates and friends.

The student within him had been seared and remolded in the hot fires of experience. To dissipate the enormity of that reality he would subsequently don the split theatrical mask of the philosopher/historian, contrasted by the irony, satire, and sarcastic wit of the cynic. As Anne Applebaum wrote in her *Washington Post* article *Remembering Philip Johnson,*

> ". . if you make up a complex, witty persona, use irony and jokes to brush off hard questions, and construct an elaborate philosophy to obfuscate your past, then you're an elder statesman, a trendsetter, a provocateur and -- most tantalizingly -- an enigma."[19]

Johnson had personally witnessed the best and the worst mankind had to offer in the world of architecture. His mission to know history and power had been accomplished, but not without rendering him a classic dupe, and a near-tragic figure. Prometheus had returned home, outwardly intact, but inwardly affected in ways only he would know. Leadership, with a generous sprinkling of cynicism, would now become his enigmatic mantle, his Kevlar vest, his protection against irrelevance and oblivion. Visually, his designs would now be free to reflect new directions and challenge unrealized dimensions. Inspiration would be generated by blending his own vast reservoir of classical and modern art, with the raw images of form, power, and deception he had very nearly sacrificed his career to understand.

Philip Johnson.

"Prometheus shook his head. "I don't know how this box
business got started. It was never a box."

— RICK RIORDAN, AUTHOR

PROMETHEUS RELEASED

In Greek Mythology, Prometheus was both Titan and trickster. He defied
the gods, bringing upon himself the wrath of Olympus. Known for his
intelligence and as a champion of mankind, Prometheus represented human
striving, while running the risk of unintended consequences. These traits
closely parallel the intriguing life and times of Philip Johnson, the eternal
trickster, the intellectual, striving to improve man's condition, yet incurring
tragedy, silenced by his own deeds, reborn, and triumphant.

In choosing architect Philip Johnson to design the JFK Memorial,
Stanley Marcus had made an inspired and politically insightful decision for several critical reasons. Philip was by education, experience, and
travel, a most serious student of history. With his wealth of experiences,
witnessing firsthand the extreme tensions in American and Europe, the
regional struggle between conservative and liberal forces in Texas would
not have been missed by his well-trained political eye. Johnson would have
been highly sensitive to the ebb and flow exhibited by these polarizing
forces. He, perhaps more than any other leading architect of his time,
would recognize the unspoken attitudes and conflicts, present beneath the
public veneer of official statement regarding the construction of the JFK
Memorial. He was an influential member of the elite Eastern United States
artistic community, based in politically liberal New England, yet Johnson
maintained a highly successful architectural practice in the largely right-
wing conservative areas of Houston and Dallas. Stanley Marcus and others
would have been confident that Johnson would recognize the emotional
sensitivities, political land mines, and invisible boundaries encountered
during the project's development. They would be reassured by his well-
developed historical sense, that he would have the political insight and

public relations acumen to successfully navigate the intense and often polarizing world of Dallas and Texas politics, both in his design work, and in his public statements.

Johnson had never designed a memorial. This would be his first. The JFK Memorial presented a fascinating challenge to Johnson. As a student of history, it was an opportunity to symbolically present the place John Kennedy occupied in American and world events. His work would be visited by multitudes of citizens from all over the globe, wishing to honor the memory of a historic and legendary leader. As a successful businessman, he was already deeply involved in many significant and highly visible architectural works in Texas and had a reputation to sustain. As an artist he was presented with a unique opportunity to bring to life a subject central to his own life and career – man's will to power.

Philip described the Memorial as emblematic of the magnetic force of JFK's personality – an interesting choice of words that includes but sublimates the essential "polarizing" characteristics of magnetism. Just as John Kennedy was a polarizing force in America, Philip himself lived and worked in the politically polarized centers of liberal and conservative American politics. Philip's architectural history in Texas began in 1950, when he completed a design for the now famous de Menil House in Houston, Texas, commissioned by John and Dominique de Menil. As word of his architectural activity in Houston spread, along with his fame as an Eastern metropolitan architectural luminary, with excellent social connections, his popularity grew. Philip would have the opportunity to understand the people, and political attitudes of Texas in the 1950s and 1960s. In his own words, "It is Texas that has been responsible for my professional development. As I often say, if I had been a little younger in 1950, when I first worked in Houston, I would have moved to Texas myself."[20]

The absence of financial support for the Dallas JFK Memorial project, both from the state, county, and city, as well as from the upper echelons of Texas elite, would have been significant to Johnson. He was accustomed to the extravagant levels of financial support from the wealthy patrons of the Eastern artists and museums, such as the Rockefellers, Carnegie's, the

DuPonts, and others who routinely and generously supported world class artistic endeavors. Philip himself was often a benefactor of support from wealthy families, business and industry leaders. He was also a major philanthropist in his own right, donating over a hundred significant works to the Museum of Modern Art. Whether Johnson viewed the lack of financial funding for the memorial as a neutral or negative stance, he did not say. He was always sensitive to his client's wishes and once stated, "Architects are pretty much high-class whores. We can turn down projects the way they can turn down some clients, but we've both got to say yes to someone if we want to stay in business." While the remark was made in capricious fashion, Philip believed the client was king and was highly sensitive to his client's positive and negative, spoken and unspoken wishes. The political climate, as well as funding, were significant factors affecting Johnson's approach to the JFK Memorial in determining the materials, size, and features of his design.

Dallas author, Frank Welch, writes that Johnson's original plan for the memorial called for excerpts from Kennedy's speeches to be placed within the memorial. Johnson had been in contact with Kennedy's special counsel, adviser, and speechwriter, Theodore "Ted" Sorensen, regarding selection of John Kennedy's most notable and stirring passages. However, the inclusion of excerpts from Kennedy's speeches proved to be too controversial in the eyes of Dallas civic leadership, and the idea for including these in the memorial was dropped. In a 1998 interview at Philip's iconic glass home in Connecticut, Johnson at first tersely dismissed this aspect of the memorial's development with a simple "Nothing came of it."[21] But wishing perhaps to say more, he added almost casually, "I wish we could have had the quotes included."[22] Johnson never approached any aspect of his works in a casual manner, and there is good reason to believe his comment carried the disappointment of an artist denied the ability to express a fundamental source of power and emotion within his work. This limitation effectively deprived the nation and the world of remembrances of John Kennedy's perceptive, poignant, controversial, and often soaring oratory from the walls of his own monument.

The limitations present in the memorial project surely forced Johnson's thinking into more basic approaches toward the final design. But Johnson's storehouse of history, power, and art, in their myriad forms and presentations, were much too powerful to be defeated by almost any limitations he encountered.

Jacqueline Kennedy had stated to the Memorial Commission her wishes for a memorial that was "Simple, modest, and dignified" perhaps wishing the memorial to be a statesmanlike counterpoint to the violence that occurred in Dallas, and to honor her husband's desire to unite the nation.

The design also had to honor the wishes of Dallas leadership for a memorial devoid of memorialization or political statement, and not a reminder of the tragic events occurring just a few blocks away.

The people of Dallas had paid for this memorial with their hard-earned money, and they were also Philip's clients. They deserved a monument embodying the reality of events, expressing sadness and grief for America's youngest elected leader, who had risked his life to visit them, and had fallen amongst them.

Johnson accepted the memorial commission less than a year after the assassination and was undoubtedly aware of the raw tangible sensitivity still felt in Dallas. The memorial he ultimately erected in Dallas, brilliantly avoided offending sensibilities, inflaming extremists, centrists or liberals, and did not add to the controversy of the assassination.

Part of Philip's design approach to the JFK Memorial may be explained in a speech at Yale University in 1959, four years before he received the memorial commission. He reflected on the important role history plays in his design process: "I have gone back to my own little way of looking at things, which is purely historical, and not revivalist, but eclectic."[24] Ultimately, history existed as an archival source for his inspiration and formed the rationale for his building designs.

But perhaps there was another way to translate his deeper feelings of the consequences of power, in a subtle, even more hidden, almost devious way. A plan might have invaded his mind's eye, an eye acutely tuned to the link between JFK's tragic fate and his own near-calamitous downfall, and his intense desire to portray events in their true historical perspective. A design that would escape the watchful eyes of conservative Dallas guardians.

Perhaps Philip could bring the Memorial forth as a subconscious form and shape that would articulate the horror that awaited man for his savage dedication to the pursuit of power. Yet in some ways, it might also serve as the apology he had never been able to offer clearly enough, to absolve the guilt he carried within himself for the last 40 years. For Phillip, the Memorial might become his best and last chance for redemption.

My second decoding of the Memorial's design occurred in the summer of 2007. I was at home one night at my desk combing through historical images. Being a self-taught student of history, I often searched for articles and video documentaries of history's epic conflicts and crucial turning points, from early Veydic battle accounts, through the Crusades, the Revolutionary and Civil War, and the great clashes of arms in the Twentieth Century. It would not be out of character for me to spend a few hours absorbed in the battle formations of Wellington and Napoleon at Waterloo, or the trails taken by the back-water men of the Carolinas in their decisive defeat of the British at King's Mountain in 1790.

Searching through World War II images, I came upon a black and white photograph of Albert Speer's infamous Cathedral of Light which he perfected at the 1938 Nuremberg Nazi Party Rally. The photo had extremely well-defined resolution for photography of that time, clearly defining the individual rows of searchlight beams, contrasted with the darker environment around them.

However, it was not the resolution that caught my attention, but rather it was the orientation of the searchlights Speer had aligned to create his over-powering luminous structure. As I concentrated on the structure's outline I knew that I recognized that image. It was as if I were looking at the wooden skeletal frame of an ancient vessel that I now perceived in its completed form. Historic structures of the past are mostly unearthed as ruins, or as an outline, and then restored to their original physical form.

I knew this structure in its completed form and its original skeletal shape was not revealed until now. It was the image of a structure I had visited many times. I was transfixed by the luminous columns of light, forming their box-like shape, opened at the center of the right side.

With mounting excitement, I copied the image and used imaging software to produce a negative image of the Cathedral of Light. There, before my eyes was the perfect outline of the John F. Kennedy Memorial in Dallas, Texas, re-created created by master architect Philip Johnson, 40 years later.

I leaned back and gripped the sides of my chair in a combination of joy, surprise, and fear. I was riveted to the images on the screen before me, instinctively knowing that my long search had been additionally answered in a most unexpected way. My journey had in an instant, expanded far beyond the question of who had pulled triggers that day in November 1963. That question was no longer relevant, and not possible to answer, if it ever was.

The Cathedral of Light was a symbol of Fascist rule, capturing and leading millions of German citizens astray, much the way Philip Johnson interpreted the assassination of John Kennedy - the power of the few over

The JFK Memorial, Dallas, Texas.

The JFK Memorial, Dallas, Texas (NEGATIVE IMAGE).

Cathedral of Light, Nuremberg, Germany, 1938.

the many, with all of the resources necessary to deceive and lead the citizens of America astray. The Cathedral of Light was alive again, in Philip Johnson's imaginative, creative mind, to portray as Albert Speer did with light and shadow, man's eternal quest for the privilege of capturing that most elusive of man's goals - the power to guide the history of men and nations.

There was no doubt in my mind that Philip Johnson had re-created a masterpiece in Dallas, Texas, under the watchful eye of Dallas leadership, through all the limitations and restrictions that it was possible to place on an artist. The JFK Memorial is not a monument to any one epoch, era, political force, or ideology, but rather a statement that profoundly reminds the world of the struggles and turmoil necessary to overcome those who are driven to dominate mankind under the guise of any political system. The assassination of John Kennedy was not about the "mechanics" present that day in Dealy Plaza, but rather about the "mechanisms" of power that collide in any system man develops to sustain his rule over other men – be it democratic, communist, fascist, socialist, theocratic, dictatorship, junta, or triumverate. Philip Johnson had experienced first-hand, and well-understood, the awesome forces that can be unleashed in man's primeval hunger for power. He knew man's capability of masking his drive for dominance behind a wall of false illumination, propaganda, and deceptive historical teaching. Albert Speer had shown him how it was done, using the most perfect of all building materials – light.

I believe Philip Johnson's conscious intention was to construct a *sold material* reproduction of the great "room" created by Speer. In 1938, his "room" had entranced and converted Johnson into a blind apostle of the dictates of National Socialist power. It had left him, along with countless millions of others, morally and spiritually bankrupt, his once meteoric career in ruins, rendering him capable of only feeble apologies of his own unfathomable error in being utterly and completely seduced by a master magician, who was himself a slave to man's quest for power.

For Johnson it was a lesson bitterly learned and acknowledged. For others it is a warning of what can happen when individuals and nations surrender their moral compass to the pursuit of power. As National Socialist Germany fell into ruin and moral degradation, the pain of Johnson's fleeting association with fascist power was intentionally buried inside of him, hidden from sight and comment to the greatest extent possible. Except when probed by an occasional interviewer, Philip Johnson entombed his Nazi past deep in his consciousness, until scant apologies were all that remained, along with his silent need for acquittal and redemption. To his credit, he had the courage to remind us that the demon of destructive power had again been released, a quarter of a century later, on November 22, 1963.

To Philip, the images must have been both enthralling and verboten. For here was the ultimate power of architecture, the ability of form and shape to drive men's behaviors, to penetrate man to his core, and drive him to actions he might never have attempted. It was no longer a case of art as an expression of man's feelings and emotions, but art in its most powerful role of driving history - at the wheel of man's future, propelling him into either the heavens or the abyss. It is likely no other architectural structure will ever produce the over-whelming, yet incalculably evil results, as did the Albert Speer's Cathedral of Light.

Philip's most unique feat will likely remain of little or no consequence to many, but of great consequence to perhaps a few. That it was accomplished under the intense public scrutiny of local political stewardship where even the slightest issues of controversy were magnified, is a tribute to the genius of Philip Johnson, and his life-long intent to know and understand the history of man.

Philip's brief description of the JFK Memorial states he wanted to create:

"A 'room' with tall walls open to the sky, would block out the surrounding city."

Albert Speer's brief description of the Cathedral of Light he had created:

"The effect was as I planned, that of a 'room'. Yes from the outside it looks like columns, but from the inside it looks like a cathedral."

Anne Applebaum writes in her February 5, 2005 article, "Remembering Philip Johnson,"

THE JFK MEMORIAL AND POWER IN AMERICA

Asked in 1993 whether he would have built buildings for Adolf Hitler in 1936, he answered, "Who's to say? That would have tempted anyone."

Robert Hughes' 1987 interview with Albert Speer produced this remarkable exchange confirming the architectural link between the two men:

Hughes: "Suppose a new Führer were to appear tomorrow. Perhaps he would need a State architect? You, Herr Speer, are too old for the job. Whom would you pick?"
Speer: "Well," Speer said with a half-smile, "I hope Philip Johnson will not mind if I mention his name. Johnson understands what the small man thinks of as grandeur. The fine materials, the size of the space."
Speer: "Oh, there is one thing," said Speer.
Hughes: "Whatever you like, I said."
Speer: "I wonder if you could take a small present to Philip Johnson."
Hughes: "Why, of course, I would be delighted to."
            Speer reached into the bookshelf behind him
            and fished out a pristine, arctically white copy
            of (his book) "Albert Speer: Arkitectur".
Speer: "Would you very much mind taking that to him?"
Hughes: "Nothing could please me more, I said."

Speer carefully opened the book to the title page, uncapped his heavy gold fountain-pen with the floppy nib, and wrote in blue ink in his peculiarly crabby, vertically squished-up hand: "For Philip Johnson, a fellow architect. With sincere admiration of his most recent designs. Best regards, Albert Speer."

Albert Speer understood.

Speer had transfixed millions with his symbol of power, but none more so than the lifelong student of Neitzschean principles of power, Philip Johnson. When Philip entered the Cathedral of Light, he had entered one of the greatest illusionary inventions of all time. Albert Speer had created nothing more than deception on a grand scale. The candela brilliance of the massed searchlights served their creator well in obscuring the twisted lights of Nazi philosophy. Speer had successfully covered its perverted truths behind pageantry and a blaze of light, and in doing so purchased the minds of many intelligent men and women with the clever hand of a master showman.

In later years, Speer referred to his prolific creation as his greatest work of architecture. Within this admission, the architect of the "luminary deceptionis" confessed the degree to which he himself had been deceived and the depths he had been mesmerized by the National Socialist call to glory, obscuring the deadly message so boldly announced within the pages of Mein Kampf.

Forty years would pass before the master would proclaim the student as his successor and heir. The circle was complete, as both men sought to bring man's fascination with power to life within the architectural creations they left behind; with the critical distinction that Albert Speer's marvel of illumination was created to entrap the minds of the willing and the weak, whereas Johnson's Memorial was a warning.

John Kennedy's tragic demise may speak volumes of the existence of less visible forces behind the throne, who possess power in orders of magnitude beyond the Presidency, that drive men, wittingly or unwittingly to carry out their aims. The Kennedy years represent a unique intersection and polarization of forces fighting for nothing less than the future of the United States of America - its wealth, military might, foreign and domestic policy, and the liberty, potential, and prosperity of its citizens. The victors and pathways leading away from the struggle for power in America would be determined by those willing to wage the most savage battle to capture the keys to the castle. This never-ending warfare throughout human history for the right to rule, was clearly understood by JFK's adversaries, and by Philip Johnson as he began designing his most powerful architectural statement.

The visual, artistic, and esthetic presentation of a structure was foremost in Philip's minds-eye. His John F. Kennedy Memorial in Dallas,

Texas, is his only work serving as a testament to another man's life, work, and historical impact. During the design of the JFK Memorial, Johnson changed the rules of his own architectural substrate, and addressed the historical and political connections between JFK and the world of manifest power in which he lived and died. Johnson was not allowed to emphasize a single unique or compelling characteristic of his subject's life or achievements, as portrayed in other American memorials to its great leaders but could only present the spirit of John Kennedy within the context of his place in history. He would convey this historic perspective using that singular architectural element he respected most - light.

Its properties offered the possibility of a statement and perspective not subject to the directives of man, and created change and effect according to the whims of nature, free from imprisonment in form and shape, at a place and time of its own choosing.

In a commemorative article in the Architectural Record, former Yale professor, Robert A. M. Sterns writes:

"Among the postwar Modernists, Johnson was the compulsive truth-teller . . . Johnson may have proclaimed his dependence on sources a little too much for his own good—he could be self-deprecatory to a fault—but in roaming around history, he always transformed what he saw in the past into something of his own."[25]

Johnson's incomparably creative mind raced through the possibilities. In *Philip Johnson & Texas*, author Frank Welch writes that *Dallas Morning News* architectural critic David Dillon, found strong similarity between the final JFK Memorial design and German architect Mies Van der Rohe's memorial to commemorate German war dead following World War I. There is a possibility that this design served as one of several initial starting points for the memorial's design. Van der Rohes's design featured a marble-like wall to surround a symbolic crypt. Perhaps symbolism without decor, without statement, neutrality in presentation would suit the expectations of some. But how should JFK's symbolic tomb be enclosed? A closed or

open, roofless design? Was it possible to summarize the majesty and tragedy of John Kennedy's meteoric rise and fall, from political wilderness to
the dizzying heights of world leadership, in just a few short years, only to
vanish from the world stage in a tragic Shakespearean ending?

Philip also had to ask himself, what was the appropriate historical
view of JFK's presidency. What was the meaning behind his appearance
on the stage of history, and his untimely departure? Historian, artist,
adventurer, free thinker, student of Nietzsche's philosophy of power -
surely this was the moment to capture the essence of this powerful story -
America's story - one that would reverberate in history forever, more so
than any other project Johnson would complete throughout his life. John
Kennedy was, like Philip, student and leader, dependent on others to
obtain the heights of leadership, but also an independent spirit who would
explore and push the existing limits of power. Philip well understood that
men's lives were traded as easily as coins in a marketplace in the pursuit of
power. America was not exempt from witnessing those seeking or challenging power being struck down like leaves in the fall. JFK was power personified, as were other leaders Philip Johnson had studied and sought out. Yet
all had been silenced or vanquished. This was not simply a repetitive tale
of the pursuit of power dating from ancient history, or a drama based on a
Greek or Shakespearean tragedy. Or was it? As significant and traumatic as
the event was for the global community, might this simply be a part of the
endless tales of power that would continue until man either perished by the
terrible power of his own sword, or passed into the illumination of a new
time, where it was no longer necessary to conquer and divide.

In my visit to the memorial in 2005, when I first encountered the stunning display of Medieval symbology rising on the Memorial wall, I wondered to what extent the architect had consciously taken advantage of the
architecture of the adjoining Old Red Courthouse. Significant deviation
from the Memorial's final design would have prevented the rising tableau
of Medieval symbology from being displayed. As designed, the memorial is
roofless, placed in the best possible location, with walls sufficiently high to
portray the resurrection of all four symbols of ancient and Medieval power.
I believe this could not have happened by accident.

In 2012 I had the unique opportunity to interview noted Dallas architect, author, and photographer, Frank Welch, as part of my research for this book. I had the opportunity to raise this question. Frank Welch is a gentleman of the most kind and gentle nature. Not merely an accomplished architect and author, he is also a careful and sensitive photographer, whose images portray the intricate nature of the more sublime aspects of life with an artist's awareness of light and shadow. We discussed Philip Johnson's extraordinary use of light within his design. As we talked together in Frank's office, he explained that Philip was at the memorial site many times, to evaluate and oversee progress of his work, and to select and inspect the efforts of the project's subcontractors. In *Philip Johnson and Texas,* Welch writes that Johnson used a very personal "hands-on" approach, from initial site inspection through completion. I left Frank Welch's office secure in my mind that master architect, Philip Johnson, was fully aware of the interaction between the fifty-foot high walls of his memorial, and the symbolic shadows cast by the adjoining "Old Red" courthouse.

In the middle of our conversation, Frank's account of the day of the assassination vividly brought to life the emotions felt that day in Dealy Plaza, "I was at a club with friends having lunch and the television set was on in the clubhouse. We all jumped up and ran over to the TV set when the news was aired. I grew up a Democrat and a supporter of JFK. I had followed his nomination and press conferences closely. It was simply terrible! No one could believe what had happened! I did not return to work for three days!"

Welch also indicated that Johnson was not as popular in Dallas at the time as some might have imagined. Johnson was viewed by many as a "dandy," a rich Easterner, with many wealthy East Coast connections, although Philip had many patrons and admirers in Texas.[26] As Frank put it, "Philip had many enemies, but he also had a lot of powerful friends."

I also had the opportunity to discuss my observations of the placement of the JFK Memorial with award-winning architectural photographer, Robin Hill. Robin's extraordinary photo graces the cover of this work.

Hill's written comments describing Philip's sense of urgent sensitivity in developing the JFK Memorial, had warranted a phone call for his additional insights. On his website blog, Robin has constructed a lushly written piece, describing his experience photographing the unique architecture on the grounds of Phillip Johnson's Glass House estate, in New Canaan, Connecticut. In a singularly striking moment when Hill was photographing the Glass House from behind the swimming pool at dawn, he described the effects of Johnson's use of light to elevate architecture. It described my own experience within the memorial. In his piece, Robin writes beautifully of his experience:

"The shutter releases. In this moment I am both observer and participant in the passing light show. There is no distinction between the vast Architecture of Nature and the little Architecture of Man. In such a place there is no distinction. Breathing together in their own crucible, they are one."[27]

This mirrored my feelings at my first exposure to the startling living theatre present within the JFK Memorial. Nature and architecture were fused into one crucible of light, shadow, and stone by the natural motion between sun and earth, creating the vast architecture of Nature and the little architecture of man. Robin Hill had also noticed the striking shadows during a photographic session at the JFK Memorial and shared the cover photo with me capturing this natural creation, precisely and poignantly, on the outer walls of the Memorial. Having witnessed the beautiful interplay of light and shadow several times, I am, each time, astounded by the naturally occurring high degree of contrast between the Memorial palette, and the moving symbolism from above "Old Red." I returned several months later to improve upon my own images but did not account for the seasonal shift moving the shadows slightly off center. The entire tableau is most beautifully framed by the walls of the Memorial in the summer months of July and August.

As Hill and I discussed the memorial's moving tapestry, he also felt that it was highly unlikely that master architect Philip Johnson would have been unaware of this extraordinary, precisely located theater. Almost any design deviation - less height, curved, sloped, or irregular surfaces, non-parallel alignment between the Memorial and Old Red, or another location within the Kennedy Plaza - would have failed to accurately capture this interplay. Johnson himself described how he utilized the effects of the surrounding buildings in one of his works. That structure specifically made use of the surrounding detail to enhance a residential tower constructed on Spring Street, in Manhattan. As written in the Architectural Review, 2001, Johnson stated: "The blocks are Cubist forms, and each will have a different kind of brick to pick up the colors of the neighboring buildings, which are mostly 19th and 20th century warehouses."

The works of Johnson's principle mentor, Mies van der Rohe, liberally made use of the interplay of light and reflection to change and slowly unfold space. Van der Rohe's interior spaces routinely changed with the time of day and the season. Another of Johnson's original mentors, Le Corbusier wrote,

"Architecture is the learned game, correct and magnificent, of forms assembled in the light."

Renowned architect Frank Gehry, a close associate of Philip Johnson, whom Johnson saluted as the greatest architect of our time wrote:

"There are a great many things about architecture that are hidden from the untrained eye."

In bringing the first part of my journey to a close, I had learned much in an unfolding story of historic importance. The City of Dallas had been tested as few American cities have been, and in the end was sustained by the leadership and the will of its citizens, by acknowledge a terrifying event, and responding with honesty and compassion.

I agree with the opinion expressed long ago by Stanley Marcus, that Philip Johnson was the right man for the job. Johnson had sought and gained the understanding and sensitivity to express power through art. He found it at great personal risk to himself, and to his professional standing. He had recognized at an early age that the greatest of man's architectural works contain within themselves, a timeless ability to portray power at its highest levels, leaving mankind in awe of his own natural will.

Despite the arguments of critics, Philip Johnson was not a moral or physical coward. Nothing of the kind could be said of this proud, powerfully intelligent, gay man who chose to live in a glass house in America of the 1950s. Through the force of his own will, he had made his transparent home the most photographed and innovative dwelling in the land. He willingly ventured into the most controversial political and social philosophies of his time, with courage sufficient enough to explore the radical agendas of the most powerful men of his time. He has seemed to his critics to be unable to feel the abject pain of those he witnessed in defeat and subjugation, and perhaps this is true. He was forever drawn to the radiance of light, and could not fathom its cold, enveloping absence. In Dallas, he left behind a memorial that allows others to gain an unconventional perspective of John Kennedy's place in the tapestry of American history. There within the room Philip Johnson created, one may alternately feel the pride, joy, and pain of a past era, standing before the black somber cenotaph where John Kennedy lies in vanquished repose, beneath the castle, the scepter, the obelisk, and the wyvern.

I was aware of the awesome challenge the Memorial presented within my journey. The JFK Memorial suggests a battle of historic importance between men of power, purposefully and consciously waged. Despite his failings, John Kennedy represented the nation, its people, its power, wealth, and its destiny. Perhaps America, more than John Kennedy was the true target in the struggle for power taking place within the years of JFK's presidency.

The questions were daunting. What was the nature of that struggle? On what battlefield was the conflict waged? Who were his adversaries? What was the outcome and the implication for America? These were the questions to be faced if the messages contained within the Memorial were to be validated, understood and placed in their true historic light.

PART TWO: THE STRUGGLE FOR POWER IN AMERICA

". . do you want a name for this world? A solution for all
of its riddles?
A light for you, too, you best-concealed, strongest,
most intrepid, most midnightly
men?— This world is the will to power—and nothing
besides! And you yourselves
are also this will to power—and nothing besides!"

— FRIEDRICH NIETZSCHE, PHILOSOPHER

4

DYNASTIES IN AMERICA

*"I saw no other choice but for Mr. Rockefeller and his son to form
a great series of philanthropies for forwarding civilization in all its
elements in this land and in all lands; philanthropies, if possible,
limitless in time, and amount, broad in scope, and self perpetuating.*

— FREDERICK T. GATES, GUARDIAN AND PLANNER OF
JOHN D. ROCKEFELLER'S WEALTH.

*"It is the essence of the poor that they do not appear in
history."*

— ANONYMOUS

POWER AND THE drive to rule are constant threads running throughout
man's history on every continent, and throughout all ages of recorded
history. From the dynastic kingdoms of Persia and Egypt, through the
medieval ages and to the present, the power to determine the destiny of

nations, has resided with familial dynasties. They have been the prime directors of human history, able to transfer the reins and means of power through the process of next-in-line succession. In a resurgent an enlightened medieval Europe, recovering from the destructive effects of plague and stifling feudalism, the Medici and Rothschild families dominated finance, while the Hapsburg, Plantaget, Hohenzollern, Romanov, and Tudor dynasties provided the blood-lines of European nobility through inter-locking relationships. The Roman Catholic Church, a successful practitioner of line-of-succession rule, solidified its empire throughout Western Europe, maintaining a moral authority that united nations, and crossed oceans, from the old world to the new.

The essential strength of any dynasty is its ability to maintain dominance through successive periods of strife. In today's world, sports dynasties are measured across five to ten seasons, in politics, perhaps one to two generations, and in the life of nations, decades or centuries. The longer it survives, the deeper and stronger its roots become intertwined within the social and cultural strata of its time.

That this level of wealth and power exists, does not in itself create any more hospitable or treacherous conditions for society. It is simply a matter of historical fact that great power exists, beyond the scope and experience of what the common man is accustomed to, or is prepared to manage. The knowledge and ability required for sustaining economic power at the highest levels, is learned from generation to generation, and ensured by trusted guardians and loyal advisors.

A dynasty's power is not measured solely in terms of assets but is properly quantified by its ability to influence human affairs. Its impact may assume the forms of social, cultural, moral, educational, philanthropic and political influence, impacting local, state, and national events, policy, law, social and cultural trends, and developments in the arts and sciences. Wealth for wealths own sake, constitutes an empty venture, with no resulting expression of lasting value to society or history. The ability to influence and direct current events, and more importantly, future events, is where the true essence of power resides. If all the treasure in coin, precious stones, and metal, that has passed through the hands of man, were gathered in one storehouse, it would have little or no value if it remained sealed and unused. Wealth, in its most potent form, creates the means to sustain and expand man's will to power, to steer history itself, and is the prime justification for a dynasty's accumulation of wealth, in a never-ending and expansive cycle.

The greatest dynasties have achieved transcendency beyond national boundaries, overriding the concept of national sovereignty. In reaching beyond national borders, expression of a dynasty's power may exhibit itself through visible or covert forms of control. Their commonality lies in dedication to their self-ordained missions of influencing the lives of men on a vast scale by maintaining a strong regenerative financial base to sustain growth. The Roman Catholic Church creates allegiance through adherence to religious dogma, in return for its bestowal of grace. The Chase Bank achieves growth and dependency through the bestowal of credit. Excommunication and denial of credit are their weapons of ostracism and punishment, although both of these purgatorial states may be redeemed by demonstrating a return to good practices. Both organizations are well-established dynasties in their own right by virtue of maintaining power that transcends generations, geography, and sovereignty. Both have attained true global power.

American dynasties have been exceedingly powerful forces from the inception of the Industrial Age in America. Andrew Carnegie created the Carnegie Steel Company, which he sold to John Pierpont "J.P" Morgan in 1901, for $480 million. Morgan dominated American corporate finance and industrial consolidation prior to 1913. The Du Pont family played a large role in politics during the eighteenth and nineteenth centuries. Cornelius Vanderbilt built an American dynasty through his development of the U.S. railroad industry. The Warburg family was a prominent European financial dynasty, transplanted to America, where Paul Warburg achieved fame as the chief architect of the Federal Reserve System in 1913. William Randolph Hearst built and controlled the nation's largest newspaper chain, whose methods profoundly influenced American journalism, and exercised enormous political influence until the early 1950s. The Getty

family made its fortune in oil in the 20th century, and remains an important sponsor, promoting advancement of the arts in America. The Bush
family has occupied the White House for 12 years from 1989 to 2009.
The Dulles family is unique among those listed, because its contribution
was largely in global politics, and in defining and supporting America's
dynasties, and ensuring the success of their policies through the U.S. State
Department, intelligence gathering, and covert military support.

American dynastic families are powers unto themselves, occasionally
appearing on lists of the wealthiest Americans, accompanied by estimations
of their wealth. Their cumulative fortunes are diversified and re-invested
many times over, with no agency or system capable of determining the
extent of their wealth and influence. Trusts, endowments, philanthropical
activities, mergers, interlocking directorships, and banking practices that
provide impenetrable investor anonymity, serve to render accurate valua-
tion of their true wealth impossible. Family dynasties have played pivotal
roles in defining and directing the financial growth, power, and policies of
the United States. Resource development, banking, education, agriculture,
transportation, science, urban development, support of the arts, medicine
and healthcare, all have been driven by the power and interests of American
family dynasties.

Beyond the normal provisions of a dynasty's philanthropy and profit,
there is the business of war. It is within the context of war between nations,
where the greatest economic potential for industrial corporations resides,
with profits far exceeding peacetime limits. Conversion to wartime production requires an organization with a highly developed degree of engineering skill, and a well-developed understanding of the principles of mass
production. These organizations help ensure a nation's ability to extend its
territory, and political and economic influence, by providing the weapons
of war.

In the 1920's, many major American companies were well-established
and looking beyond America's shores for new markets. Prospering and
evolving in peacetime, many had also helped enable victory in World War

I. Their post-war challenge was one of negotiation with foreign governments to gain access to large untapped markets throughout the world.

An outstanding example of the mechanism by which a dynasty gains access to foreign markets is England's East India Company (EIC), chartered by the queen of England in 1600, but owned by wealthy London aristocrats and merchants. The Company's charter was to arrange international trade agreements with the East Indies. EIC was so successful that, at its height, it accounted for half of the world's trade. It eventually brought about conditions that lead to the creation of the British Empire in India. Its success achieved military and economic control of the Indian sub-continent, with a population of 100 million people.

Following its Revolution of 1917, Russia, was a nation of vast untapped markets with a newly-entrenched communist system of government. By 1930, the opportunity for economic control of the largest country in the world, covering more than one-eighth of the Earth's inhabited land area, with a population of 160 million, was beckoning American dynasties with its vast potential.

The Amtorg Trading Corporation, was the first Soviet trade representation in the United States. Amtorg was stablished in New York, in 1924, by merging Armand Hammer's Allied American Corporation with two other corporate entities. Hammer was a unique American entrepreneur, who had gained access to the Soviet government's top officials through various methods of business operandi. In 1924, at the request of Soviet leader Vladimir Lenin, Hammer was awarded contracts for concessions in Soviet Russia.

Amtorg was the sole purchaser for the Soviet communist government and, prior to the establishment of diplomatic relations between the USA and Soviet Russia, served as a de facto trade delegation, and a quasi-embassy. Amtorg handled almost all imports to the Soviet government. It provided American companies with information about trade opportunities in Russia, and supplied Russian industries with technical goods and blueprints, either through purchase, espionage, or simply the promise of future lucrative business relationships. Amtorg headquarters was located in Manhattan, with branch offices in Chicago, Detroit, Los Angeles, San Francisco, and Seattle.

The November 30, 1930 edition of the *New York Times*, carried an article entitled "44 American Firms Aiding Soviet." The article's headings read:

44 AMERICAN FIRMS ARE AIDING SOVIET

List of Those Working on Contracts for 'Technical Assistance' Is Made Public at Washington.

◆ ◆ ◆

FACTOR IN FIVE YEAR PLAN

◆ ◆ ◆

Commerce Department Holds Its
Success Hinges on This Aid, Which
Is Not Regarded as "Investment."

"Special to the New York Times" (excerpt)

Washington, Nov 29. -While stating that stories of millions of American capital being invested in the industrial enterprises of Soviet Russia are untrue, the Department of Commerce is aware that many American concerns are engaged in "technical assistance" activities in that country.

It has been estimated that about 2,000 American workmen, including engineers and assistants with their families, are now in Russia supervising the building of large manufacturing and electrical plants.

Investments by American citizens in the development of Russian however, are considered impossible because under a ruling of the U.S. State

Department, foreign countries which have not settled their debt to the Unites States, are not allowed to offer securities for sale in this country."

A list of the forty-four companies contracting with Russia for assistance, furnished by the Amtorg Trading Corporation, the Soviet commercial organization in this country is as follows:

Akron Rubber Reclaiming Company - technical assistance to the Soviet Rubber Trust

Allen & Garcia Company - technical assistance to the Donetza Coal Trust

Austin Company - technical assistance to the Nizhni Novgorod automobile plant

Arthur J. Brandt - expansion of the Amo automobile plant for the Avtorest Automobile Trust

Brown-Lipe Gear Company - technical assistance for the Avtorest Automobile Trust

Burrell-Mase Engineering Company - rationalization and expansion of the gasoline industry

Hugh L. Cooper & Company - consulting engineers for the Dneiper River Hydro-Electric Plant

Arthur P. Davis, Lyman Bishop & Associates - consulting engineers on irrigation projects

Frank E. Dickie - technical assistance for construction of Aluminum plants

Du Pont De Nemours & Company - technical assistance in erecting fertilizer plants

Electric Autolite Company - technical assistance, electrical equipment for autos and tractors

Hardy S. Ferguson & Company - technical assistance for construction of a paper mill

Ford Motor Company - technical assistance for operation of the Novgorod automobile factory

Freyn Engineering Company - consulting engineers for the designing of steel mills

Harry D. Gibbs - technical assistance, aniline industry (used for drug, plastic, explosives mfg)

Goodman Manufacturing Company - technical assistance for the coal industry

Hercules Motor Company - assistance for production of truck engines in the Amo Auto Plant

John J. Higgins - technical assistance to the G.E.T (state electro-technical trust)

International General Electric - technical assistance fore the Soviet electrical industry

Irving Air Chute Company - technical assistance for the aviation industry

Albert Kahn, Inc. - designing buildings for the Stalingrad tractor factory

Kopper's Construction Company - building of coke and by-product plant

Lockwood-Greene & Company - reorganization and reconstruction of textile mills

McCormack Company - designing of baking plants

Arthur G. McKee Company - technical assistance, construction of the Magnitogorsk Steel Mill

McDonald Engineering Company - construction of industrial plant

Mechanical Manufacturing Company - technical assistance in the meat packing industry

Newport News Shipbuilding & Drydock Co. - technical assistance in turbine construction

Nitrogen Engineering Company - technical assistance with a large ammonia fertilizing factory

Oglebay Norton Company - technical assistance, design, construction, operation of iron mines

Radio Corporation of America (RCA) - exchange of patents and technical information

Radiore Company - technical assistance in location of ore deposits

C.F.Seabrook Company - technical advisors for road building

Seiberling Rubber Plant - design and assistance in construction of a rubber tire plant

Southwestern Engineering Corporation - assistance in the design of non-ferrous metals industry

Sperry Gyroscope Company - technical assistance in the manufacture of marine instruments

Stuart, James, and Cooke, Inc. - technical assistance in the coal industry

Timken Detroit Axle Company - technical assistance to Avtotrest (automobile trust)

Westvaco Chlorine Products - aid in the production of chlorine

Archer E. Wheeler and Associates - technical assistance to the non-ferrous metals industry

J.G.White Engineering Company - consulting services for a hydroelectric plant

Norman D. Wimmler - technical assistance to the non-ferrous metals industry

W.A.Wood - technical assistance to the non-ferrous metals industry

The technical knowledge provided by these American companies is consistent with the fundamental expertise required to create a strong military capability. Taken together, these manufacturing processes enabled Soviet Russia to create the ground, air, and naval forces needed to survive the Nazi invasion encountered in 1939 and play a role as a major military power in World War II, and the ensuing Cold War.

It should be noted that these early years of Amtorg's trade ventures between American industry and the communist government of Russia, took place during the global Great Depression. It occurred at a time when

American workers were unable to find employment and were reduced to selling apples on city streets to survive. No doubt manufacture of the many items required by the Soviet government, if built in the United States, would have employed an enormous number of American workers. However, this was not the preferred route for American industries headed by Henry Ford, John D. Rockefeller II, the DuPont family, and General Electric and RCA financiers - J.P. Morgan and the Vanderbilt family, who chose to develop the economy of a foreign nation.

Amtorg's main consultant and banker in the United States, was the Chase National Bank. In 1930, the same year that the cited article was published by the *New York Times*, the Chase Bank acquired the Equitable Trust Company of New York, whose major stock holder was John D. Rockefeller Jr. This acquisition made the Chase the largest bank in the world, while strengthening Rockefeller's position as a power broker between Soviet Russia and American high-tech companies. As Amtorg's primary consultant, the Chase Bank was in a unique position to identify those American technologies and industries whose expertise complimented the Soviet government's desire for both a strong industrial manufacturing base, and world-class military capability. A decision to convert the Soviet Union's industrial base to wartime capability, would not be a concern of American financial institutions, but would rest with the Soviet government. American dynasties would not be blamed for such decisions, for their interests lay only in developing their own sphere of financial interests and profits. And as history shows, the Soviet Union was both a critical ally in defeating Hitler in World War II, and our became our primary opponent in the Cold War.

On June 22, 1941, Adolph Hitler unleashed Operation Barbarossa, a stupendous invasion of 153 German divisions against Soviet Russia. Soviet resistance amazed the world, although in retrospect, the world had not taken due note that the Soviet government had been arming itself with American technology as early as 1919 with the purchase of Henry Ford's "Fordson" treaded tractors. The flow of American technology and manufacturing processes increased after the Amtorg contract was initiated in

1924, relying on the guidance of the Chase Bank in 1930 to determine where to mine American technology. Author, Henry Zelchenko, in his book entitled, "Stealing America's Know-How" relates an interesting story. Zelchenko, an American, was paid by both Ford and Amtorg to act as foreman and interpreter for groups of Russian engineers and mechanics, who frequently visited United States manufacturing facilities. He states:

> "One thing always puzzled many Amtorg men engaged in industrial espionage:
>
> How did Moscow know of machines and processes about which we in New York had no inkling? Where did it get the tips which promoted their instructions?

In a complex techno-manufacturing business relationship, such as existed between the Soviet government, Amtorg, and its chief U.S. consultant, the Chase Bank, information is essential. The scope and nature of the involvement of American industry listed in the cited 1930 *New York Times* article, tells a story of industrial espionage and the banker's certain knowledge of where the most cutting-edge American technologies existed, and the more advanced the technology, likely the more the Soviet government would pay for this information. This occurred despite the known idealogical differences that existed between the Soviet government and the democratic government of the United States, and the then-current ban, on foreign investment with debtor nations. Ultimately, American technical expertise, provided to the Soviet Union beginning in 1919, would result in the emergence of an enemy that nearly matched the United States in scientific and military technology from 1947 through 1991.

A little more than ten years after American dynasties had profited enormously by assisting communist Russia in becoming a modern military power, American citizens suffered destruction of their own careers, character, and even imprisonment, at the hands of Senator Joseph McCarthy's hearings, and J. Edgar Hoover's investigations. Those who were called before McCarthy, as alleged communists, or communist sympathizers, were not responsible for the creation of a powerful USSR, not did they profit in any manner near the scale of the profits reaped by American dynastic investment in the rise of the Soviet military. Yet, these individuals were identified as the most odious of American citizens - traitors to their nation, their communities, their friends. Citizens such as composer Leonard Bernstein, entertainers Charley Chaplin, Lucille Ball, Pete Seeger, Lena Horne, Orson Welles, playwright Arthur Miller, scientist Robert Oppenheimer, and Nobel Prize winners Albert Einstein, Thomas Mann, and Linus Pauling were blacklisted, or suffered under McCarthyism. A close friend of mine, recently asked, "What was the point of the McCarthy hearings?" The easiest answer is that war is the most profitable venture known to man, and war requires an enemy. If one is not available, one must be created. Another answer is to recall the symbols of power rising on the walls of the JFK Memorial in Dallas, Texas: the castle, the scepter, the obelisk, and the wyvern. Such is the power of dynasties in America.

THE GENTLEMEN WARRIORS

By the end of World War II, American optimism was at its zenith, having defeated world-class military powers on both sides of its oceans. When John Kennedy stood on the balcony of the Capitol Building to read his inaugural address, American dynasties were poised to carry out America's blueprint for world dominance in the nuclear age. They had developed a clear roadmap to guide America's leaders in her role as the foremost super-power. The next fifty years were to be the American Age, and if the strata-gems planned were fulfilled, America's dynasties would sit atop the world, as preeminent powers for a century or more.

The date often given for the birth of this new age is, March 12, 1947, when President Harry S. Truman delivered a speech enunciating the Truman Doctrine, the first official American proclamation intended to con-tain Soviet communism. This all-encompassing blueprint would be named the Cold War: the most potentially destructive conflict in man's history. The rules of international engagement were re-written, for there was no prece-dent to guide men in the use of weaponry that would obliterate an opponent through the power of science. There was to be no respite in global tension, as the Cold War began almost immediately following the deadliest war in human history, World War Two, where an estimated 60 to 80 million people lost their lives. The ensuing Cold War would cost the American people an estimated eight trillion dollars, and the lives of nearly 100,000 soldiers, lost in the Korean and Vietnam conflicts. It would dominate America's political and military landscape for the second half of the twentieth century. It was a well-planned, enormous undertaking, significantly impacting the quality of life in America, and ultimately bankrupting the Soviet Union. It was fought without a single major military engagement. It was the first time, as one observer stated, "a major opponent was defeated on the battlefield of ideas"

When John Kennedy entered the office of President, there were many Cold War action plans already approved by President Eisenhower's National Security Council. The most important of these plans had been recommended by the NSC's guiding arm, the Central Intelligence Agency.

Covert operations were scheduled in Europe, Central Europe, South America, Southeast Asia, and Africa. These were costly, strategic plans, based on approved doctrines, developed in the 1950's. The existence of these doctrines calls forth a fundamental question that must be answered: who defined these revolutionary doctrines, which formed the basis for America's immense military and economic efforts during the forty-four years of the Cold War? Let us examine the most visible of the men who, while not the actual powers behind the throne, were in the public's mind, the voices and representatives for America's intentions to defeat communism across the globe. The Dulles family maintained a highly visible presence in carrying out America's Cold War plans, as successful lawyers are trained to do, intensely advocating for their less visible clients.

Through the mid-1950s, John Foster Dulles was at the apex of his power as the nation's fiercely anti-communist, deeply religious, Secretary of State, under President Dwight D. Eisenhower. His connections within the Eastern power establishment had been established with his tenure as chairman of the board of the Rockefeller Foundation and the Carnegie Foundation. Dulles' grandfather, John W. Foster, served as Secretary of State in 1892 and 1893, under President Benjamin Harrison. In 1895, Foster authored the Treaty of Shimonoseki, acting as advisor to the Qing Dynasty, the last imperial dynasty of China. The treaty, ending the first Sino-Japanese War, is generally viewed as having the same effect on Japan, as the Versailles Treaty ending World War I, had upon Germany. It engendered a feeling of humiliation, resulting in the rise of a stronger militarist faction, dedicated to the two-fold aims of correcting the perceived weakness of its own government, and the unfair treatment of the nation. Dulles' uncle, Robert Lansing, served as Secretary of State, under Woodrow Wilson, until he resigned at Wilson's request, over their differences of opinion regarding the United Nations.

From the beginning of their public lives, the John Foster, Eleanor, and Allen Dulles had free access to American dynasties of the Twentieth Century, through their social connections, and by virtue of their work as lawyers representing those dynasties. Younger sister, Eleanor Lansing

Dulles, was a significant force in America's economic re-building of Europe, through her work at the State Department's Berlin Desk, a focal point of early Cold War tension.

John Foster Dulles was an intimate of the Rockefeller family from his college days. Their relationship was described by David Rockefeller in his book *Memoirs:* "I had known him (John Foster Dulles) and his family since my college years. Foster had a reputation of being cold, austere, and puritanical, but the man I knew had a sense of humor and could be a wonderful companion. His daughter, Lillias, had been part of a small group of friends during my college years and one of Peggy's (David's future wife, Peggy McGrath) closest friends. In fact, when I was courting Peggy in the 1930s, she always stayed with the Dulles' at their New York town house."[29]

Certified as a representative of entrenched citadels of American power, John Foster Dulles was able to move onto the global stage as Secretary of State from 1953 to 1959, the defining years of the Cold War, where he would be the most visible advocate of America's hard-line response to Soviet communist expansion. He exemplified America's stance against Soviet aggression, and in speech after speech, he unmistakably signaled America's refusal to treat Soviet plans, and their representatives, with nothing more than scorn and contempt. John Foster Dulles wore his mantle of America's foremost sentinel against communism, with the same dedication and zeal as the chain metal armor worn by a Knight Templar.

John Foster's younger brother, Allen Welsh Dulles, had built his impressive reputation as America's master spy in Europe, during World War II. Allen worked for the Office of Strategic Services (OSS), the CIA's predecessor, from his office in Berne, Switzerland, bordering Nazi Germany. He was a virtuoso, orchestrating covert efforts to undermine Hitler's regime. Dulles controlled assets stretching across Europe, from Berlin to the Balkans. He was providing funds for the French Resistance forces, while maintaining close contact with Italian pro-royalist forces. His operatives were infiltrating opposing factions in Yugoslavia, and he was receiving a wealth of classified information from excellent sources within

Nazi Germany. He was simultaneously working with Wehrmacht generals, the head of Germany's intelligence organization, and encouraging Himmler's Gestapo to overthrow Hitler, while financing Communist anti-Nazi groups. He was sending spies into Hungary and Romania, and was watching Soviet, British, and French espionage activities in Switzerland. It was common practice, in the hotbed of Europe's conflicting wartime loyalties, to maintain contact with, and even fund opposing forces, to obtain the secrets of both, in hopes of mining those prized nuggets of information that brought Allied victory a step closer. That these actions might spell imprisonment, torture, or death to the men and women dedicated to their cause, was understood by all engaged in the intricate games of espionage and infiltration, as part of *les risques de guerre*. It was a remarkable tour-de-force, that gained Allen a reputation as one of history's great spymasters, a reputation even failure could not erase.

Following World War II, the Central Intelligence Agency reached its most dominant position of power, pushing its activities far beyond its original mandate of intelligence gathering: to guide the President and U.S. foreign policy. The Cold War required a new methodology for the twin goals of defeating communism and protecting the nation's foreign economic expansion, without inviting escalation toward nuclear exchange. The CIA evolved into the perfect covert instrument for both. Under Allen's guidance and brother John's protection, CIA covert military action resulted in the establishment or overthrow of governments throughout the world, persuading people high in the U.S. government that the CIA could successfully accomplish regime change, without involving United States armed forces. Never before had a covert para-military agency possessed this level of skill and power in replacing governments on a global scale. This was a much-too-irresistible weapon, especially to the economic lords of high finance, searching for means to establish new markets for American goods. The Agency's power and track record would be impossible to resist during the first two years of the Kennedy administration. Only the bitter taste of failure, led John Kennedy to challenge the Agency, and indirectly, the dynasties who relied upon its power.

CHAPULTEPEC TO MOSCOW

During its first three generations of scions, the Rockefeller family in America had a most unique role in shaping American doctrines and policies. John D. Rockefeller I, "Senior," left behind a legacy of economic triumph. He was universally recognized as an unequalled force in neutralizing competitors through his ruthless monopolization tactics, and had clothed the family in a flinty overcoat of distrust. John D. Rockefeller II, "Junior," proved adept at re-casting the family image into a more palatable evening jacket, interwoven with threads of social concern. His five sons, Nelson, David, Laurance, John, and Winthrop, became a blend of "Senior's" and "Junior's" strategies, never fully separating the drive to enhance the family's wealth, from their father's mission for spotlighting the family's dedication to the improvement of society. This proved a difficult task, where altruistic efforts to raise mankind to better heights, collided with an insatiable drive for profitability. This dual approach to philanthropy and profit would be a significant cause of contention in policy and application, that would emerge during the Kennedy White House years, ultimately forcing many in positions of power to choose where their loyalties rested.

For the latter part of his political life, Nelson Rockefeller's obsession would be in gaining the position he envisioned as the capstone of his career, the presidency of the United States. Nelson's campaigns were carried out brilliantly, with the utmost dedication and technical expertise, but could not overcome party challenges and voter distrust. His political aspirations were limited to four, four-year terms, as governor of New York. Not to be denied his ultimate goal and perhaps his perceived birthright, Nelson most likely engaged in covert political maneuvering to have himself appointed by President Gerald Ford to fill the vacant office of Vice President of the United States following the resignation of President Richard M. Nixon in the Watergate debacle. It would be the closest Nelson would come to fulfilling his ultimate ambition. That overriding ambition was a clear departure, perhaps even a violation, of the age-old Medieval dynastic code, which required its most successful adherents to remain the ever-elusive "Powers behind the throne." The family paid a price for Nelson's moment in the sun. Their heretofore hidden wealth and influence became the subject of protracted Senate confirmation hearings, ultimately exposing far more than the tip of the dynasty's economic iceberg, which Nelson was willing to reveal at the beginning of the hearings to satisfy his will to power. Through Nelson's impatient ambition, the nation got it's first look at the inner complexities and interlocking structure of power that the family had carefully and discreetly built since John D. Rockefeller Sr. began the most powerful dynasty the nation will ever likely witness.

Although his latter years in politics brought him the most visibility with the American electorate, Nelson Rockefeller's remarkable achievements began in November 1944, at the conclusion of World War II. President Franklin D. Roosevelt appointed Nelson to the office of Assistant Secretary of State, although he was to hold this post for only nine months. During his tenure, the world experienced three climactic events. First, was the meeting of the "Big Three" - Winston Churchill, Josef Stalin, and Franklin Roosevelt, at the Yalta Conference in the Crimea, in February 1945. It was to be the last of their three wartime conferences. Yalta was convened specifically to discuss Allied post-war cooperation, and to define future spheres of influence for each of the principle victors. The second climactic event was the signing of the United Nations charter in June 1945, in San Francisco, officially creating a body representing 80% of the world's population. The third climactic event was the dropping of the first wartime atomic bombs on Hiroshima and Nagasaki, Japan, on August 6th and 9th, 1945, the beginning of the nuclear age. It was an extraordinary time to hold the position of Assistant Secretary of State. It would have been difficult to find anyone who relished the opportunity to play a leading role in transitioning the world, from global hot war to the new political and military strategies required by the Cold War.

At the conclusion of World War II, American economic powers looked southward, to the vast lands, un-tapped resources, and potential markets in our own hemisphere, Central and South America, and the natural beauty of smaller Caribbean nations. But the conquest of a continent is not for the inexperienced, or those lacking sufficient confidence and power. Mastery of a landmass and diverse collection of peoples requires planning on a military, economic, and social scale at the highest level of human endeavor. In this regard, only the Rockefeller family had the political organization, resources, government and intelligence connections, secure loyalties through their philanthropical networks, and above all, the will to power, for such an undertaking.

The development of South American nations would require a decade or more of dedicated effort to accomplish and would represent the application of dynastic power on a vast scale. The goals were specific: eliminate competition, in this case, America's idealogical opponents, create profitable conditions for the extraction and export of resources, and open a continent to the import of American technology, products, and services. The political and military climate would necessarily require long-term stability in which a flourishing middle class would maintain buying power to purchase American goods. The prime means to accomplish these goals would be military and economic doctrines and policies that sanctioned American involvement, effective intelligence gathering to identify competitors, and their elimination, if necessary, through the application of covert or conspicuous force. With the subsequent creation of stable conditions, American corporate investment would follow.

On March 3, 1945, three months before the founding of the United Nations, Nelson Rockefeller, as Assistant Secretary of State, realized the fruition of his plan to align the military and economic interests of the United States with twenty-one South and Central American nations, through the signing of the Act of Chapultepec.

This Act was Nelson's first foreign policy coup, re-affirming Central and South America as the exclusive domain, or in effect, a virtual protectorate of the United States, binding the nations of the Americas together in a mutual defensive strategy to resist communism. Implicit within this Act, would be the justification and responsibility for a U.S policy to create stable economic and political environments in these nations. In addition to nullifying communist threats, a hemispheric Pax Americana, guaranteed by American military might, would encourage American investment in potentially lucrative Central and South American marketplaces. Financial institutions, such as the Chase Manhattan Bank, soon to be led by younger brother David Rockefeller, would provide funding to U.S. investors, to harvest South America's bountiful supply of oil, gold, silver, copper, tin, and iron ore, as well as stocking market shelves with American goods.

The Act of Chapultepec was to have immediate consequences far beyond a hemispheric or regional defensive treaty. The concept of regional alliances had led the world into two global wars in the previous forty years, resulting in an estimated eighty million deaths world-wide, and potentially greater than two times that amount in total casualties. The twentieth century's system of regional alliances was judged by all the principal victors to have been a largely failed system. The hope for a new guiding principal, to replace the disastrous system of regional dependencies, resided in the global acceptance and authority of the United Nations concept in providing a world forum to eliminate regional warfare.

With the creation of the Act of Chapultepec, Nelson blatantly orchestrated the very type of regional alliance the United Nations was created to replace. As such, he found himself on a collision course with the fundamental principals contained within the United Nations charter. However, it is the prerogative and manifest destiny of dynasties to view the world around them in the most propitious circumstances for the maintenance and development of their own power. Nelson moved among the U.N. political and diplomatic community with the power and authority confirmed on him by virtue of the family's position as America's foremost dynasty. No other American diplomat, holding only an assistant cabinet position, would have had the power and connections to override a new global mandate about to take form in the United Nations.

He drove his position home relentlessly with the American delegation, where his participation was both encouraged and resented. He was supported by U.S. military leaders, hesitant to trade away the traditional system of regional military alliances for a yet-unproven theory of global conflict management. It was also recognized that the Yalta Conference had recognized the concept of global spheres of influence for the victors of

World War II. Nelson's efforts could be viewed as justifiably re-affirming South America as residing within America's sphere of influence, as put forth in the Monroe Doctrine, and as a response to the Soviet Union's encroachment into eastern Europe.

Nelson's efforts were resented by those who stood by President Roosevelt's commitment to our former wartime allies to support a global peace-keeping body. Their argument was admirable and visionary: would not the continuation of regional alliances encourage the Soviet Union, and other nations, to continue expanding their regional alliances, and ulti-mately create the conditions for a third global war?

Nelson gathered enough powerful supporters to establish The Act of Chapultepec, and the age-old practice of establishing regional alliances was upheld. One decade after the conclusion of the deadliest war in human history, with casualty figures never to be fully known, the world was once again divided into opposing military alliances, assuring the continuation of regional conflict. Such was the contributing influence of the Act of Chapultepec, and the will to power of an American dynasty driven to define the future course of a nation, and a continent, in its own terms.

With a U.N. compromise over United States' claims to control South America, the regional concept was formally recognized as a self-defense clause, which became known as Article 51 of the U.N. Charter. Article 51 would later serve as the "legal" basis for post war military alliances. The consequences were played out by the establishment of the Rio Pact of 1947, the North Atlantic Treaty Alliance (NATO) in 1949, the Southeast Asia Treaty Organization (SEATO) on September 8, 1954. The Soviet Union responded with the creation of the Warsaw Pact in May 1955. Regional alli-ances served as the basis for Soviet Union's suppression of the Hungarian Revolution in 1956, the invasion of Czechoslovakia by Warsaw Pact troops in 1968, and United States Armed Forces entering into armed conflict in Viet Nam.

Nelson Rockefeller accomplished this pivotal act, thirteen years before John Kennedy became President. In the process, he had secured a conti-nent for American military and economic domination for the next several decades, with hemispheric protectionism as a cornerstone for establishing a stable environment for American economic investment. Shortly thereafter, Rockefeller himself increased family and business investment in the South American arena. Through his own efforts and family cooperation, Nelson personally provided $3 million in capital, with an additional $21 million provided by Standard Oil to create the International Basic Economy Corporation (IBEC). Standard Oil had a vested interest, as many of IBEC's operations were located in countries where Standard Oil was pumping oil, while nationalist and peasant uprisings were occurring.[30]

IBEC was intended to be an altruistic approach to raise the standard of living in its host countries, as well as a profitable foreign business venture for the family. The effort combined Rockefeller "Senior's" goal of high profitability, with "Junior's" desire to promote social improvement. The most visible structures to evolve from IBEC planning would be a chain of American-style supermarkets stocked with products produced by local agricultural businesses. Venezuela would be IBEC's target market where the expansion of a super-market chain would help solidify a middle class, perpetuating a customer base to purchase IBEC products. It was also thought that the rapid expansion of these food outlets would encourage an influx of American agricultural technology to create a dependable supply system, similar to that found in the American Mid-West. IBEC would emulate the key component of Amtorg's most successful aspect, that of serving as a direct pathway for American technology and investment into the heart of South America. IBEC philosophy was also based on the belief that a capitalist system of food production and supply would be a powerful socio-political deterrent to the revolutionary forces of socialism and communism in South America. It was also a component in the blueprint for economic domination of South America. While the project appeared theoretically possible in planning, it proved difficult to realize under real-world conditions.

IBEC would ultimately experience both success and failure. In their optimistic reliance on American agri-technology, IBEC experts failed to take into account environmental differences in South America weather, soil, flooding, climate conditions, low product output, and inefficient transportation to market. The lag in transporting fresh products to market resulted in the necessity of importing products from American suppliers. But the influx of American goods had the counter-productive result of inflaming anti-American revolutionary's claims of IBEC being an instrument of "Yankee Imperialism," designed to drive local suppliers out of business. IBEC continued, but at a price to America's reputation in South America. When Nelson Rockefeller came to visit in 1969, 14 of the 17 IBEC supermarkets in Buenos Aires were burned to the ground by nationalists.

In *The Rockefellers, An American Dynasty,* authors Collier and Horowitz summarize the eventual impact of IBEC in the twentieth century:

"By its twentieth birthday IBEC sales would increase to more the $200 million a year. It would encompass more than 140 subsidiaries in 33 countries, operating mutual funds, insurance companies, housing construction corporations and a galaxy of other enterprises. It had become a pioneer although perhaps not in the way Nelson Rockefeller had originally projected. In fact, far from being a semi-philanthropy altering the fundamental realities of Latin American dependence, IBEC was an avatar of a new business form - the U.S. multinational with subsidiaries and markets flung far across the globe - which would be a primary fact in the economic life of the underdeveloped world in the second half of the twentieth century."[31]

In 1954, capitalizing on his perceived success in defining South America as America's exclusive economic playground, Nelson Rockefeller was appointed Special Assistant to the President for Foreign Affairs. The position's full title was Special Assistant for Cold War Strategy, covering a much broader spectrum in foreign affairs. He was tasked with providing the President with advice and assistance in developing programs, by which the various departments of the government could counter Soviet challenges. Nelson was, in addition, the President's Coordinator for the

CIA, responsible for overseeing CIA clandestine operations along with the Deputy Secretary of Defense, and the Undersecretary of State. His direct superior was the President of the United States. He now attended meetings of the Cabinet, and the Council on Foreign Economic Policy. He also attended meetings of the National Security Council, the highest policy-making body in the government and functioned as head of a unit called the Operations Coordinating Board, a committee of the National Security Council. The other members of the OCB were the Undersecretary of State, the Deputy Secretary of Defense, the director of the Foreign Operations Administration, and Central Intelligence Agency Director Allen Dulles. The OCB's purpose was to oversee coordinated execution of security policy and plans, *including clandestine operations* [authors italics].[32]

Nelson's second opportunity to use his immense influence to steer Cold War events came on May 10,1955. Soviet negotiators had reversed their nine-year stance on disarmament policy intransigence by accepting the known U.S. plan for military manpower limits, reductions in conventional arms, and the U.S. plan for the elimination of nuclear armaments. Unexpectedly, the U.S.S.R. agreed for the first time to military inspections, including on-site inspections with permanent international control posts, behind the Iron Curtain. It is important to understand that the Soviet concept of control posts, was of "fixed" unmovable monitoring sites.

Rockefeller's opening move, the Quantico I Study, assembled by his hand-picked panel of eleven experts from various disciplines, proposed a new aspect of disarmament monitoring known as "Open Skies," which both startled the Soviets, and regained the "peace initiative" for American negotiators in the important battle for public opinion. Announced by President Eisenhower, "Open Skies" bound the participants to mutual aerial reconnaissance and an exchange of blueprints of military installations to permit each government to verify closely the other's compliance with the terms of arms reduction.

In order to understand the significance of "Open Skies," it is essential to consider the introduction of U.S. U-2 spy-plane technology reaching completion at the same time. Presidential approval for the U-2 project was given on December 1, 1954, six months before the Soviet Union agreed to nuclear arms reduction. This innovative reconnaissance aircraft (the brainchild of Richard Bissell, Jr., later to become Director of CIA "black ops" during John Kennedy's administration) flew at 80,000 feet carrying cameras of unheard-of resolution and accuracy and was technologically far beyond Soviet monitoring capabilities.

The U-2 reconnaissance program gave the United States a tremendous advantage in monitoring Soviet nuclear development. U-2 technology put the Soviet proposal for verifiable disarmament, by ground-based monitoring systems, in its proper light as a method of verification with low reliability. It was now unlikely the Soviets would agree to "Open Skies," with its highly accurate system of mobile airborne monitoring, rather than easily evaded "fixed" monitoring posts, compelling the Soviet Union to trade away its most prized strategic advantage - secrecy.

In the summer of 1955, the first U-2 planes were ready. German chancellor Conrad Adenauer, de-briefed by CIA project leader Richard Bissel, Jr, and CIA Deputy Director, Air Force General Charles Cabell, brother of Dallas mayor, Earl Cabell, embraced the project, and provided German bases for U-2 planes. As expected by the American delegation, Soviet-U.S. negotiations stalled, then broke down, and both sides embarked on the costliest military armament programs the world had ever witnessed.

Nelson's Quantico I Report, which formed the basis for the "Open Skies" policy, was issued by panel chairman, Walt W. Rostow (later advisor to President John Kennedy) on June 10, 1955. These recommendations are extremely important in understanding the far-reaching level of foreign policy control attained by Nelson Rockefeller, years before John Kennedy became responsible for carrying them out. The overall position of American foreign policy, with its desire to curtail negotiation in favor of maintaining military and technological supremacy, would set the stage for the confrontational policies inherited by the Kennedy Administration, and would strengthen the determination of America's foremost Cold War "hawks" in their resolve to never back down in the face of Soviet challenges.

The Quantico panel of experts clearly expected and planned for Soviet rejection of "Open Skies", allowing the U.S. to embark upon and win the nuclear arms race, as stated in Section B.1.b. below. On June 10th, 1955, the panel's report was forwarded to Nelson Rockefeller at the White House:

The Honorable Nelson A. Rockefeller
Special Assistant to the President
The White House

The panel recommended the following positions should be considered by the American government vis-a-vis the Soviet Union in Section B. of the report:

(B.1.) The United States should be prepared to make a series of proposals designed to move towards the control of armaments. These include:

(B.1.a.1) A proposed agreement for mutual inspection of military installations, forces, and armaments, without limitations provisions.

(B.1.a.2) A convention insuring the right of aircraft of any nationality to fly over the territory of any country for peaceful purposes.

(B. 1.b) Proposal of a disarmament plan to the USSR; *after rejection of the plan*, (italics are the Author's) the U.S. to make every effort to win the arms race as the safest way of forcing the Soviet Union to accept a satisfactory arms convention.

In retrospect, the "Open Skies" proposal may have been the best option to monitor future arms reduction between the U.S.S.R. and the U.S.A. prior to the exponentially rising costs of the nuclear arms race. It failed, as planned, to move arms control forward, and contributed to the missed opportunity of signing a treaty of mutual arms control at the very beginning of the nuclear arms race. It would be nearly a decade before John Kennedy's proposals and speeches in pursuit of nuclear arms control and detente, would challenge the doctrines set forth in the Quantico Cold War blueprints. During that time, the world would come to the brink of nuclear war on several occasions.

On the heels of the Quantico I, 1955 report, Nelson, in 1956, persuaded President Eisenhower to allow him to convene a second study, Quantico II. Also known as the "Special Studies Project," its goal was to develop planning to maintain Cold War superiority. Quantico II's mandate was to:

"Define the major problems and opportunities facing the United States, and clarify national purposes and objectives, and to develop principles which could serve as the basis of future national policy".

As clearly stated by its authors, Quantico II was a logically progressive act, commencing where Quantico I's basic directives ended, to create a full-blown blueprint and doctrine for the victorious culmination of the Cold War. The military portion of the report was given an early release in 1957 for the express purpose of earliest possible implementation. It was given maximum exposure on the front page of the New York Times, whose publisher was Arthur Hays Sulzberger, a Rockefeller Fund Trustee from 1937 to 1959. The military component of the report was fully endorsed by President Eisenhower in his January 1958 State of the Union Address. The entire master plan developed by the seven-panel Special Studies planning group, outlined continuation of the Cold War, at a cost of $18 billion dollars over a six-year period, and was finally released in 1961, during John Kennedy's presidency as *Prospect for America, The Rockefeller Panel Reports*. The priorities and directions outlined in the Special Studies Project defined the nuclear military doctrine of the United States of America, as well as military/security strategy, foreign policy, international economic strategy, and defense department and governmental reorganization throughout most of the Cold War period. It gave priority to ever-increasing military and defense industry budgets at the expense of other elements of society such as health, education, and urban and rural infrastructure. The report became the blueprint for what took place over the next thirty-five years, but at a much higher cost, bankrupting the Soviet economy, and impacting the U.S economy far more than originally calculated.[33]

For the Special Studies Project, Nelson had recruited Henry Kissinger, as project director. He also hired Edward Teller, known as the "Father of the hydrogen bomb." Panel member Dean Rusk was later to become JFK's Secretary of State. Also on the panel were John Gardner, president of the Carnegie Corporation, Henry Luce, founder of Time Magazine, and Rockefeller brothers Laurance and John D. III. [34]

The resulting doctrines, already in their action phases, required a vast military and financial commitment. America's military, defense, and banking industries expected John Kennedy to continue theses policies to maintain American Cold War strategic superiority. As his Presidency began, he did not disappoint them. JFK marched in step until events during his Presidency brought him into conflict with Quantico I and II, along with U.S. strategic plans for a complete and final military victory in the nuclear age.

Nelson, while serving as Governor of New York, had also created the New York State Atomic Research and Development Authority, with hopes of New York becoming the capital of the nation's nuclear industry. While serving as President, John Kennedy could not take his focus off Nelson's strategic initiatives, mindful of the fact that so many of his administration's policies were based on plans that Nelson and his advisors had developed. Kennedy, as he was expected to do, upgraded the nation's military posture, increased military spending, stepped-up ICBM construction and counterinsurgency capability - an almost point-by-point implementation of the recommendations of the Rockefeller Brothers Panel Studies. [35]

But throughout this period, Nelson remained more obsessed than ever of carrying out his own policies, and with the image of his own inaugural parade down Pennsylvania Avenue. One week after Kennedy's election, Nelson convened a meeting at the family estate in Pocantico, New York, and began planning for the Presidential Election of 1964. He and his advisors assumed Nelson's most serious challenge would be overcoming

Kennedy's charisma. By 1963, he was sniping at Kennedy's foreign policy for its "soft" attitude toward Communism, and for making "concessions" to the Russians on atomic testing, which Nelson said "Endangered national security."[36] Then, in a calculated move to remind the nation's cold warriors that he was at one with their mindset, he blasted Kennedy for what he considered Kennedy's "failure" in Cuba:

> "It is very hard for me to understand why we are supporting Vietnam freedom fighters and why we are holding them back and preventing them from operating on Cuba . . . I hope it is not to placate or appease the Soviets."[37]

"Appease" was the operative word in Nelson's statement, calculated to ensure that Kennedy patriarch Joseph P. Kennedy's folly in promoting appeasement toward Nazi Germany and Adolph Hitler, would not be forgotten. There were many in America's military, defense, and intelligence establishments who remembered, and understood Nelson's implications.

Nelson successfully ran as the "moderate" Republican candidate for governor for four-year terms, in 1958, 1962 1966, and 1970, while actively seeking the Republican nomination for President in the intervening years of 1960, 1964, and 1968. While citizens of New York obviously benefitted from Nelson's social agenda, they paid a heavy price. During his tenures as Governor of New York, the state budget went from $2.04 billion in 1959–60, to $8.8 billion in his last year, 1973–74. Perhaps most telling, during his administration, the tax burden rose to a higher level than in any other state, and the incidence of taxation shifted, with a greater share being borne by the individual taxpayer."[38]

In their book *Rockefeller of New York: Executive Power in the State House*, Robert Connery and Gerald Benjamin write of Nelson's four terms as Governor of New York:

"Rockefeller was not committed to any ideology. . . . Rockefeller's programs did not consistently follow either liberal or conservative ideology."

It would seem that the core purpose behind Nelson's programs as governor of New York, was the use of that office to establish credentials acceptable to the majority of American voters in a national election. He painted himself as a compassionate Left-of-Center politician, while maintaining his party affiliation with the Right. It was a well-planned resume, available to exploit as a national candidate for President, appealing to both liberal and conservative voters across the nation, had he been able to secure the Republican nomination for President.

Nelson Rockefeller held no elected position within the government during the years he exercised major influence in defining America's Cold War doctrines. The official positions Nelson Rockefeller held were assistant-level department positions. However, the family's dynastic power was utilized in so forceful a manner as to lead the President and his cabinet in directions that he and his hand-picked advisors determined were best suited to the interests of the nation, and to where the Rockefeller dynasty was positioned to reap the benefits of those doctrines and policies. It was another attempt, at the highest level, to merge the spirit of "Senior's" unquenchable drive for profit, and "Junior's" desire to cloak that irrepressible drive in concerns for the benefit of mankind. Theoretically possible, but impossible to achieve, in the glaring light of public awareness.

Nelson's drive to become the Republican Party's standard bearer and Presidential nominee came to a humiliating end, at the 1964, San Francisco, Republican Convention. There, amid the give and take of intense political persuasion, the "soul" of the Republican Party was re-claimed by its most conservative elements. Nelson's intent of moving the party to a more liberal position was firmly and finally rejected.

Some say his finest moment was when he stood courageously, but forlornly, at the convention podium for fifteen minutes, shouted down by his own party. It also illuminated the precise moment where Nelson had irrevocably descended beyond the protective gates of his grandfather's and father's dynastic citadel. His greatest ambition, the Presidency of the United States, was shattered in the raucous banality of the public arena of political combat, meant only for the common man, where dynastic king-makers were never meant to take up the sword.

Nelson Rockefeller would eventually find his way into the office of Vice-President of the United States. Upon the resignation of Vice-President Spiro Agnew, President Richard Nixon appointed Congressman Gerald Ford, to the office of Vice President. Upon Nixon's resignation, Ford became President, and appointed Nelson to the office of Vice President, neither man having been elected to their respective offices. Gerald Ford retains the distinction of being the only person who served as President and Vice-President without being elected to either office.

Despite his almost incredible efforts to lead the nation and attain the highest office in the land, Nelson Rockefeller was never to savor the crowning moment of his own victory parade along Pennsylvania Avenue.

BATTLEGROUND SOUTH AMERICA

During the years of the Kennedy Presidency, a quiet battle for control of a continent took place, not in Southeast Asia, Europe, or Africa, but for America's neighbor, South America. It was not a war of armies, or battlefield tactics, but a slow inexorable entrenchment of American covert, corporate and economic power, over the indigenous peoples of many diverse cultures and historic backgrounds.

Historically, the foreign policy of the United States was a proprietary relationship regarding the nations in South and Central America. In America's earliest efforts to preserve South America as its exclusive economic marketplace, the Monroe Doctrine unequivocally stated that any external attempts at further colonization in the western hemisphere, would be regarded as an act of aggression.

The first significant enforcement of the Monroe Doctrine occurred in the Spanish American War of 1898. As a result, the victorious United States took ownership of nearly all of Spain's colonies in the ensuing treaty, including Puerto Rico and Cuba. Cuba formed its own civil government and gained independence on May 20, 1902. However, the new nation was prohibited from forming its own foreign alliances, and the U.S. reserved the right to intervene, along with maintaining perpetual lease of a military base at Guantanamo Bay, on the island of Cuba. The next major policy event was Nelson Rockefeller's 1945 Act of Chapultepec, discussed earlier, that bound the nations of the America's in a mutual defensive pact to resist communism.

David Rockefeller understood the importance of maintaining a nation's, and even a continent's, social stability, through the power of its leaders, its chosen political system, and the force of its established institutions. David's rise to the position of chairman of the Chase Manhattan Bank, one of the world's most influential financial institutions, followed a carefully orchestrated pathway, always supported by a close circle of trusted family advisors. Working out of family headquarters in Room 5600 in the Rockefeller Center, David and his advisors evaluated changes in the American economic landscape, and understood their implications. His was a unique window to observe social and political change, along with the growing dominance of financial institutions over industry, and of large institutional investors over shareholding individuals, as the legal owners of the country's leading corporations. Banking was the epicenter of these shifts in the ownership of America's wealth. It's driving principles were the age-old economic rules followed by dynasties and institutions, dating back to Medieval times and before. David, and by extension, the Chase Bank was merely carrying on the traditional roles of financiers directing a nation's economy. For David, it was acknowledgement of an historical opportunity and his own willingness to fill that role. He was poised to become one of the most powerful American financiers, at precisely the right time, at precisely the right place, with the perfect instrument in the form of the Chase Bank, in a nation with seemingly unlimited wealth and potential. To David, it might have seemed more than random chance. From everything his grandfather and father had told him, it was proper that he should be seen among the great historic bankers of Western society, bringing another layer of power and glory to a dynasty, already wealthy beyond the wildest imaginations of men.

John Kennedy had offered David the cabinet position of Treasury Secretary within his administration. It may have been a uniquely poignant moment for both men - John Kennedy, president of the most powerful nation on earth, offering a secretarial position to a man who already held the strings of economical control over a vast myriad of American and international industries. David politely turned the offer down. Years later, when he turned down a similar offer from President Richard Nixon, David was chairing a board of directors interlocked with the governing boards of Allied Chemical, Exxon, Standard Oil of Indiana, Shell Oil, AT&T, Honeywell, General Foods and dozens of other major corporations. The Chase Manhattan Bank itself, was a leading stockholder in CBS, Jersey Standard, Atlantic Richfield, United, TWA, Delta, and Braniff Airlines, and a host of other corporations from IBM, to Motorola, and Safeway. The power that this position conferred was immense.[39] Presiding for four years at the Treasury Department, in either the Kennedy or Nixon administrations, would have been four years spent away from the true desk of power guiding American and international economies on a global scale.

John Kennedy initially announced broad support for the Rockefeller Brothers' panel of study on the American economy. But as Kennedy's presidency progressed, his New Frontier ideology had begun to challenge the basic idea that simply putting more goods on supermarket shelves would bring about a better life for Americans, and their counterparts in the southern hemisphere. Kennedy gradually came closer to accepting his advisor John Kenneth Galbraith's theories, much to the growing concern of the business community. Galbraith, in his best-selling book, *The Affluent Society,* wrote that the problem of providing enough consumer goods had already been solved. What remained were "Those problems which lie largely in the realm of public action - bad housing, poverty, recessions, unemployment, discrimination, crowded and obsolete schools, air and water pollution - were in need of attention.[40]

Sensing the direction JFK was moving towards, David Rockefeller made it his sworn duty to influence the young President to enact a tax cut to stimulate the economy with a large tax cut for those most able to stimulate the economy, the wealthy, in opposition to Galbraith's and Kennedy's emerging social agenda. In an address, quoted by the *Wall Street Journal,* Rockefeller seemed to denigrate the value of Kennedy's advocacy of a more compassionate economic approach to America's social problems, stating "Here again sound policy [Rockefeller's] is often at odds with what is made to have popular appeal from the [political] soapbox."[41] In his book, *Battling Wall Street: The Kennedy Presidency,* Professor Donald Gibson wrote:

> "To label a popular president a cultist, a reactionary, a threat to freedom, was to engage in serious conflict with the democratically elected leader of the Republic. It suggested great anger, and it indicated a frustration produced by Kennedy's failure to heed the criticism."[42]

In 1962, The Kennedy Administration accepted the Rockefeller-driven stimulus and accelerated depreciation allowance strategy. Its related tax cut was enacted two years later, during the Johnson Administration. These changes represented a massive redistribution of income in America, from lower income families to the wealthiest. A family earning $200,000 a year received a return of $32,000, while a family earning $3,000 received $60. Corporate taxes were slashed, while their profits soared, in many cases more than 50%. David Rockefeller had clearly won this round.[43]

Like his brother Nelson, David had acquired a sincere interest in directing U.S involvement and investment in South America. David's Chase Manhattan Bank was on the short list of New York banks supplying credit to former Cuban governments and its dictators for half a century. David, himself, was a director of the second largest of the Cuban-based companies, Punta Allegre Sugar Corporation, which produced Cuba's most important export, sugar. Adolph Augustus Berle, Jr., Rockefeller family advisor, who was appointed by Kennedy to chair a task force developing policy guidelines on Latin America, was chairman of the board of SuCrest Corporation, the largest sugar refiner on the East Coast of the United States, and a Chase Manhattan customer. Many of David's close acquaintances were already financial stewards of South and Latin American finance, such as C. Douglas Dillon, John Kennedy's Secretary of the Treasury. Dillon's investment houses underwrote Latin American governments and paved the way for corporate giants such as Standard Oil and ITT to penetrate and overwhelm Latin American markets.[44] David Rockefeller's interests in South American economic involvement were a profitable extension of his older brother Nelson's seminal work in establishing the Act of Chapultepec, which defined America's role in enforcing political stability in the southern hemisphere. David heartily considered this to be an essential pre-condition for Chase endorsements, aimed at stimulating American investment toward South American businesses and society.

By 1959, through investment and acquisitions, the Chase Manhattan Bank, among others, were predicting a most profitable future in Central American investment. All was proceeding as planned, until a young lawyer, turned Marxist-Leninist revolutionary, Fidel Alejandro Castro Ruz and his fiery, second-in command, Ernesto "Che" Guevara captured Havana City, and the island of Cuba. Castro's unexpected victory dealt a severe financial blow to many powerful American banks, investors, and Organized Crime.

"Che" Guevara was among those unique individuals who personify the revolutions they lead. A former doctor turned revolutionary, he was a well-educated, inspiring, and eloquent spokesman, igniting anti-American sentiment in South and Central America, and the Caribbean, at a grass-roots level. He posed a mounting threat to American corporate bankers, who were counting on regime stability to enable the success of their long-term investment strategies.

Ernesto Guevara was increasingly viewed as a deadly adversary of American economic expansion. His brand of anti-capitalist revolution, if it took hold in South America, could become a costly disruption, or even a crippling blow, to dynastic and corporate plans for economic control of a continent. With a revolutionary's fervor, viewed from the southern hemisphere looking northward, he had global and American economic dynasties in mind when he wrote, in December of 1964:

"The laws of capitalism, blind and invisible to the majority, act upon the individual without his thinking about it. He sees only the vastness of a seemingly infinite horizon before him. That is how it is painted by capitalist propagandists, who purport to draw a lesson from the example of Rockefeller whether or not it is true— about the possibilities of success. The amount of poverty and suffering required for the emergence of a Rockefeller and the amount of depravity that the accumulation of a fortune of such magnitude entails, are left out of the picture, and it is not always possible to make the people in general see this."

John Kennedy's long range response to re-define American involvement in Latin America, was the introduction of the Alliance for Progress. Kennedy's plan proposed to re-focus American investment by combining this with real social improvements. Kennedy's Alliance was a rebuke of Nelson Rockefeller's "Stock the shelves" concept attempted through his IBEC venture a decade before. The Alliance for Progress was envisioned by Kennedy along the lines of Galbraith's theories, bearing real substance against the rising influence of Castro and Guevara.

Kennedy understood the economic and strategic importance of a just economic approach to counter anti-American sentiment and hoped to convince South American governments of the long-term viability of his Alliance for Progress. He hoped it would become an antidote to the threats posed by American imperialism, with assurances of an on-going commitment from both the U.S. government and American financial interests, with tangible benefits for South American society. In a Machiavellian act of irony, John Kennedy offered the top position in his Alliance for Progress to David Rockefeller. David politely declined.

President Kennedy announced the Alliance for Progress, with a statement that was not at odds with Che Guevara's vision for South America, a ten-year plan focused on U.S. - Latin American economic cooperation.

". . we propose to complete the revolution of the Americas, to build a hemisphere where all men can hope for a suitable standard of living and all can live out their lives in dignity and in freedom. To achieve this goal, political freedom must accompany material progress . . Let us once again transform the American Continent into a vast crucible of revolutionary ideas and efforts, a tribute to the power of the creative energies of free men and women, an example to all the world, that liberty and progress walk hand in hand. Let us once again awaken our American revolution until it guides the struggles of people everywhere - not with an imperialism of force or fear, but the rule of courage and freedom and hope for the future of man."[45]

The Alliance for Progress was signed at an inter-American conference at Punta del Este, Uruguay, in August 1961. The charter called for:

- an annual increase of 2.5% in per capita income,
- the establishment of democratic governments,
- the elimination of adult illiteracy by 1970
- price stability, to avoid inflation or deflation
- more equitable income distribution, land reform, and
- economic and social planning.[46,47]

First, the plan called for Latin American countries to pledge a capital investment of $80 billion over 10 years, while the United States agreed to supply or guarantee $20 billion within one decade.

Second, Latin American delegates required the participating countries to draw up comprehensive plans for national development. These plans were then to be submitted for approval by an inter-American board of experts.

Third, tax codes had to be changed to demand "More from those who have most," and, land reform was to be implemented.

In retrospect, the Alliance achieved real progress in social conditions, rather than resulting in the burning down of super markets; progress that otherwise may have never came about. Adult illiteracy was reduced. In some countries the number of young people attending universities doubled and even tripled. Secondary educational participation increased. One out of four school-age children were provided with an extra food ration. New schools, textbooks, health clinics, and affordable housing were created. There were some scattered improvements in land use and distribution, slight improvements in tax law, and an increase in the planning of developmental programs. It was a time of emerging hope in Latin America. The Alliance was a positive step in restoring the voices of the South American peoples and enabling them to guide their own destiny.

However, by the end of its first year, the Alliance was beginning to falter. David Rockefeller's Chase Manhattan report, issued on the first year anniversary of the Alliance, suggested that the tendency [charter] of the Alliance to support government [social] projects was likely to discourage private incentive. Although the report's findings were phrased as a prediction, the report itself was a significant warning to Chase clients considering South America investment, weakening the overall level of stimulus provided by the Alliance, and slowing the flow of American capital investment. Along with political de-stabilization, often initiated by CIA covert intervention, the net effect was to render the Alliance for Progress a dying concept. Years later, in 1965, during Lyndon Johnson's presidency, in a complete reversal of the Alliance's original intent, the State Department stressed the primacy of protecting U.S. private investment and disclaimed any responsibility for promoting democratic government in the hemisphere. Two weeks after this announcement by Assistant Secretary of State for Inter-American Affairs, Thomas Mann, a military coup toppled the democratically elected reform government of Brazil. Lyndon Johnson's (formerly Kennedy's) Secretary of State, Dean Rusk, praised this as a "Move to ensure the continuity of Constitutional government". With right wing military coups on the rise in South America, using fear, intimidation, kidnapping, torture, and murder, a numbing sense of forced stability was felt in Latin America. Country after country, returned to political conservatism, advertised as a safeguard against the specter of rising communism, a fear always available to be exploited by America's dynasties. With this enforced return to ultra-conservatism, the Chase could once again, with confidence, advise its clients that South American investments would be a profitable venture, re-opening the flood-gates of American investment into South America. In a 1966 article in *Foreign Affairs,* David Rockefeller stated that the revised version of the Alliance for Progress was better than "The overly ambitious concepts of revolutionary change of the programs early years, because it created a climate more attractive to U.S. business."[48]

John Kennedy's Alliance for Progress, as initially envisioned did not succeed. The major reasons cited for the failure of Kennedy's original concepts were: opposition to meaningful land reform by traditional elites, insufficient financial commitment, and the growing instability of Latin American governments. During the 1960's, thirteen constitutional governments were replaced by military dictatorships.[49,50]

Of all the reasons cited for the Alliance's failure, the latter was the most crippling: John Kennedy's inability to prevent the destabilization and ruin of liberal and progressive South American leaders and their respective governments. Central Intelligence Agency intervention, as most upper echelon American military and policy figures were aware, was a prime factor in South America's political transformation during the early Cold War years.

The U.S. Constitution provides for the Executive and Legislative branches to share in the making of foreign policy. It is the prerogative of the President to issue foreign policy statements, implement that policy, propose legislation to support that policy, negotiate international agreements, and respond to foreign events. Kennedy, as presidents Eisenhower and Truman before him, supported the growth of free market economies, and the defeat of communist influence where ever it was encountered.

For the successful implementation of a President's foreign policy, it requires that U.S. government agencies rightfully understand and interpret the vision and spirit behind that policy. John Kennedy was a newcomer on the stage of global economic and military strategy, arriving without a well-developed power base, and the firmly established loyalties within the government agencies he directed. All American Presidents have been rightfully concerned that the resulting actions of these agencies, upon those societies acted on, are fully consistent with his vision of foreign policy, and consistent with the democratic principles the United States stands for. Whether his policies are carried out in the spirit he intended, or in a manner differing from his vision, would remain a keystone issue throughout the Kennedy presidency. From 1960 through 1963, foreign intelligence gathering and more importantly, its interpretation and recommended actions to support the President's policy, were all under the tactical control of the CIA.

It remains a question still fully unanswered during Kennedy's tenure in the White House: where did CIA loyalties reside? - in the new-found, un-tested theories of a political novice such as John Kennedy, or with the dynastic powers that had guided America's ascendency as a global superpower through the first half of the twentieth century.

It was clear that the Agency was an unswerving champion of U.S. economic opportunism in South America, through supporting, de-stabilizing, installing or overthrowing governments as required, to create the conditions necessary for successful American economic success. A summary of CIA activity before, during, and continuing after John Kennedy's tenure in the White House includes:[51]

Guatemala 1954: A CIA-organized coup overthrew democratically elected Jacobo Arbenz under pressure from American-owned United Fruit Company, whose land was expropriated by Arbenz's progressive land reforms.

British Guiana (Guyana) 1953-64: CIA and British Intelligence funded anti-communist unions to strengthen opposition to democratically elected Dr. Cheddi Jagan.

Cuba 1959-1961: During 1959 and 1960, Marxist Fidel Castro made radical changes in Cuba, nationalizing industry, collectivizing agriculture, seizing American-owned businesses and farms leading to the CIA-orchestrated invasion at the Bay of Pigs.

Ecuador 1960-63: The CIA infiltrated the Ecuadorian government, set up news agencies, radio stations, bombed right-wing agencies and churches and blamed the left, to force democratically elected Velasco Ibarra from office.

Brazil 1961-64: Democratically elected Janio da Silva Quadros resigned citing U.S. pressure. His successor, Joao Goulart, was overthrown by a U.S.-supported military coup. Goulart promoted economic reform, limiting profits of multinational corporations, and nationalized a subsidiary of U.S.-owned ITT, and refused to break relations with Castro's Cuba.

Peru mid-1960's: The CIA set up military training camps and provided arms to the Peruvian government to combat leftist guerrilla forces.

Dominican Republic 1963-65: In 1963, democratically elected Juan Bosch brought forth a new constitution granting citizens expanded freedoms, land reform, affordable housing, modest nationalization of business, and restrictions on foreign investment. Seven months later a right-wing military coup succeeded supported by active U.S. military intervention based on CIA reports of a growing communist insurgency, later proved to be unsustainable.

Chile 1964-1973: The CIA successfully prevented Marxist Salvador Allende from winning the Chilean presidency in 1964. After Allende was elected in 1970, the CIA intervened and dictator General Augusto Pinochet overthrew Allende. Pinochet's rule was remarkable for the staggering degree of brutality inflicted on the citizens of Chile.

Bolivia 1964-75: In 1952, an armed popular revolt defeated the military, displaced the oligarchy, nationalized the mines, instituted land reform, set up a new government, and reduced the military to an impotent force. With financial support from the CIA and Pentagon, the military was re-built and overthrew President Victor Paz in 1964 because of his refusal to support Washington's Cuba policies.

As a counterpoint to the economically opportunistic policies of Nelson and David Rockefeller, brother, Laurance, was an enthusiast of South American development, painting himself as a champion of environmental protection. Laurance created the American Conservation Society in 1958, to champion environmental preservation. In their book *The Rockefellers, an American Dynasty,* authors Collier and Horowitz find sufficient evidence to suggest Laurance was exhibiting a pattern of sponsoring growth, at the expense of the environment. The authors write: "Even as he was giving money to create parks and sanctuaries, he was carving luxury resorts out of the wilderness."

In the Caribbean islands, Laurance had propitiously timed the dedication of his new Caneel Bay Resort, opened in 1957, with the dedication of the Virgin Islands National Park. Flown to Saint John at his expense, were key guests from the press, the Department of the Interior, and Congress. The plan's intent was openly stated as:

> "Purpose - to transfer the title of lands to the government in such a manner as to emphasize the economic and conservation benefits to the islands and the nation. To properly launch a unique resort achievement with maximum impact for promotional carry-over and simultaneously under-scoring Caneel Bay's unique appeal."

By the mid-1960's, Laurance's Caneel Bay Plantation had helped make tourism a $100 million-a-year business in the U.S. Virgin Islands. This meant a dramatic increase in the value of the 4,000 acres Laurance held jointly with his brother David, on the still undeveloped Virgin Island of Saint Croix. Similar opportunity beckoned in Puerto Rico. Laurance was adept at selecting environmentally sound land with potential for the highest return on investment, often collaborating with investment partner and Kennedy Treasury Secretary, C. Douglas Dillon.

Stewart Udall, John Kennedy's Secretary of the Interior, reflected on the polarity of Laurance Rockefeller's propensity for covering his business ventures with environmental advancement:

> "Laurance is a curious study. I've always thought that the hotels are examples of the basic conflict in him. Take the Virgin Islands. In his interests there you see the two elements of his personality - the selfish and the public-spirited - right on the surface. On the one hand, he sees this little island and says, 'Now this is one of the

finest things under the U.S. flag, and it ought to be a park.' But, then he ties it all together with buying up some plush resort right in the middle of all this beauty, but out of the reach of the ordinary person. It makes you wonder where his commitment is."[52]

Charles Stoddard, who worked closely with Laurance says,

"If anybody but a Rockefeller did what Laurance has - donate land for national parks and then develop them and build large hotels nearby and hold a lot of land for development - it would not only be in obvious bad taste, but a conflict of interest too. But as a Rockefeller, he seems to be able to get away with it. . . Let's face it - the environmental problems facing this country aren't a very zealous concern of his."[53]

Again, it was the dual approach of profit and philanthropy at work, requiring Laurance to begin with a project designed to benefit the environment and well-being of the local society, but ultimately providing corporate profits on a scale available only to a select few.

John Kennedy understood who his adversaries were, and as he grew into the office of President, he was learning the true extent of their power. In true Machiavellian style, he offered to bring them within his own Administration in hopes of finding common ground. Yet, Nelson and David Rockefeller always maintained their distance, publicly and privately, from involvement with John and Robert Kennedy.

Nelson and David, and their brothers, were not fated to share the aspirations, pitfalls, and challenges facing those in elected office. Theirs was a strata above politics, where doctrine, policy, and economic plans, both national and global, were conceived and implemented with the power of their own resources, and, when financially feasible or astute, the economic power of the U.S. government. They deemed it acceptable because in the end, society would presumably be elevated by their actions. They moved forward with supreme confidence, viewing leadership as their birthright and their destiny, secure that history would prove them correct.

As the first two years of John Kennedy's presidency passed, the elite leadership of America noticed a change in the young president from whom they expected continued loyalty. As a candidate, and then as President, John Kennedy understood the institution, weapons, and methodology used to destabilize unfavorable political regimes in South America, and to stabilize regimes more favorable to American interests. After failure at the Bay of Pigs, he was determined to take control of America's foreign and economic policies. He, and his brother Robert, felt they stood every chance of success, provided he was victorious in the 1964 presidential election. Gone were the days of blindly following CIA planning and control. He began creating the building blocks necessary to assert the power of the Presidency to direct the nation's foreign policies. Conflict in Viet Nam was looming larger and would be the focus of CIA and military efforts in the next few years. After being misled in Cuba, then check-mated in South America, John Kennedy would enlist military and economic advisors he could count on, to assist in defining a new methodology of directing America's power.

He also had a powerful weapon, far superior to those public men around him - he possessed the charisma of a natural leader, unmatched during his time, allowing him to draw his audience into his vision of the future. His natural ease in public was his greatest strength. Though he may have reached office through the use of Joe Kennedy Sr.'s wealth, Agency information in outflanking Richard Nixon, and alleged cooperation from Organized Crime, he possessed the intellect and abilities to ensure the continuation of his own power, and to begin a Kennedy dynasty. That pathway rested with the American people in the upcoming election. The Republican Party did not seemingly possess a candidate with comparable natural leadership and charisma to defeat him. John Kennedy understood this. So did his adversaries.

But the strengths he possessed would be tested to their limits. For he had gradually come face to face with another form of unspoken, but lethal power, its depth unknown amidst the shadows of hidden loyalties, changing its shape and form as required, undetectable to those outside the inner councils of the citadels of power. Rockefeller biographers, Collier and Horowitz, summarize this unique power of the Rockefeller dynasty:

". . There was another dimension of their power that made them different from even the wealthiest of their peers . . it was the billion dollar investment that (John D. Rockefeller) Senior and (John D. Rockefeller) Junior had made in the superstructure of the social order. Directorships in one or a hundred business corporations had little to do with the ability of the Rockefellers to lift an academic like Henry Kissinger or Dean Rusk into the stratospheres of national power and policy or put together a prestigious body like the Rockefeller panels and establish the framework of national defense strategies over a decade."

When President John Kennedy's National Security Council voted to finalize its decision to invade Cuba at the Bay of Pigs, five of those voting on the Council were David Rockefeller's close friends or associates: Secretary of State Dean Rusk, Secretary of the Treasury C. Douglas Dillon, CIA Director Allen Dulles, and Presidential Advisors Adolph Berle and McGeorge Bundy. All were men who remained mindful of the covert military and economic plans in place for the Cold War, and who was responsible for authoring and initiating those plans. [54]

When John Kennedy refrained from committing regular United States armed forces to rescue the failed CIA-directed Bay of Pigs invasion, he took his first step in opposing the basic tenets of Nelson Rockefeller's government sanctioned Quantico I and II policies, defining U.S. plans for aggressively confronting and defeating communist expansion. At the Bay of Pigs, JFK asserted the power of the Presidency, notifying his formal circle of advisors and their elite sponsors, that henceforth, they would now be the advised. It was a momentous decision, alerting America's defense and military establishment that the continuum of American military doctrine, was no longer a certainty.

Nelson and David Rockefeller's accomplishments were staggering by any stretch of the imagination. Their achievements border on the prodigious in shaping America's Cold War Era. They achieved their goals by first, creating America's Cold War blueprint, and then carrying out the mission for American supremacy in the latter half of the Twentieth Century. Nelson went first and established the doctrines America would follow as the Cold War intensified. He was followed by David, whose accomplishments were more of an economic nature, and his influence was sufficiently strong to guide governmental agencies and their policies. Though neither man held publicly elected positions prior to 1960, they were appointed and assigned to leadership roles, developed panels, study groups, and opportunities virtually at their own request, enabled and emboldened by the immense influence reinforced by 90 years and three generations of accumulated and inestimable family wealth. They created doctrine and policy followed by Presidents, the U.S. military establishment, Departments of State and Defense, the CIA, and numerous other departments and agencies working in concert with national planning. There is no doubt the America we live in today, is a result of their vision for the economic and military plans they defined in the beginning of the second half of the twentieth century.

In 1965, two years after the assassination of his brother John, Senator Robert Kennedy was in Lima, Peru, reviewing the impact of U.S. foreign policy with a group of Peruvian intellectuals. Robert was asked by his hosts about their conflicts with American oil companies. The liberal Senator from Massachusetts responded, "This is your country, and how you handle the dispute is your business." A Peruvian gentleman pointed out "David Rockefeller was down here last week, and he told the government if they didn't give in to the International Petroleum Company, they wouldn't get any aid from the United States." Kennedy leaned forward, the muscles in his face tensing and replied, "Well, we Kennedy's, we eat Rockefeller's for breakfast."[55] The incident was leaked to the press, and on a subsequent leg of the journey in Argentina, a reporter approached Bobby Kennedy and posed a question based on mistranslation of the idiom Robert earlier stated, "Senator, is it true that you have breakfast with Rockefeller every morning?"

As aptly expressed by Rockefeller biographers Collier and Horowitz, the arena in which Robert Kennedy was proposing a contest was far from the touch football fields of Hyannis Port; it was not even the battleground of party politics. David Rockefeller appeared in the national and international arenas as the representative of American and global dynasties, and for the most permanent order of social authority and influence. When he spoke, it was with the voice of power, that Presidents themselves solicited, to receive sanction for their programs.[56]

It remains a fascinating study in contrast between two historic American dynasties: the five dapper, cosmopolitan sons of the House of Rockefeller, none of whom individually possessed the qualities needed to capture a nation's imagination, or its highest elected office, yet all reaching the uppermost heights of American influence and power; and the four dashing, ruggedly charismatic sons of the House of Kennedy, possessing the greatest natural gifts a public man could hope for, capable of securing the common man's loyalty and the nation's highest office, whose lives and public careers ended in violent death, or severely tarnished.

Perhaps it was never possible for two such houses to exist in accord at the summits of American power in the twentieth century. One dynasty's sons remained within the walls of their castle fortress, save one, at their father's request, forever separated from those around them; while the other dynasty eagerly ventured into the fray, also at their father's request, and suffered as severely as Prometheus for bringing the gift of fire to humanity.

5

A Man to Be Reckoned With

*"I don't know what kind of a diplomat I shall be,
probably rotten,
but I promise to get done for you those things that you
want done."*

— Joseph Kennedy, January 1938, in a wire
to President Franklin Roosevelt following
Kennedy's Senate confirmation as U.S. Ambassador
to the United Kingdom

Boston to Palm Beach

In 1930, in the eastern part of the United States, a young man started his career with visions of wealth, power, and dynasty. If he could parlay the fine opening hand he had been dealt, he or his children might someday step onto the great stage of American history. He assumed varying guises and mantles during his rise to fame, and his methods varied from highly visible to superbly well-hidden, but his goal never varied. He wished to sit atop the most coveted position of leadership the country had to offer, the Presidency of the United States. He was possessed of a drive to succeed no matter the cost, and he had great natural charisma. His greatest skill was that of back-room ward boss, as his father before him, the man who cut the secret deals, dispensed the cash, and began a thousand over-lapping intrigues until no one around him knew exactly what he was doing.

Born on September 6, 1888 to Patrick John Kennedy, an east-side Boston pub owner, powerful ward boss, bank president and State Senator, Joseph Kennedy was a natural at managing and manipulating the complexities and opportunities of wealth management in America of the 1920's and 1930's. He had all the requisite gifts for a man destined for the public eye. Noticeably handsome, with a fiercely radiant smile, quick-witted and nimble during public and private conversation, he possessed a unique ruthlessness in maintaining focus on his own career and wealth.

Thomas G. Corcoran, former assistant to President Franklin D. Roosevelt, and later Joe Kennedy's lawyer made the following observations, "Joe was always watching what made power and gentility; he wanted them both. He studied where power came from . . . power came from money, and he was out to get it."

In September 1912, Patrick Joseph Kennedy, "P.J." to his friends, found a job for his son Joe, as a state bank examiner - an ideal start for a young man to learn the mechanics of money management. Joe honed his banking skills, learning to evaluate credit and asset management. He was privy to confidential financial dealings of companies and individuals important to the economical growth of Massachusetts.

In January, 1914, Joseph Kennedy was elected president of Columbia Trust at twenty-five years of age, becoming the "youngest bank president in the country", as he himself explained to the press, a fact not verified at the time. Joe issued his own press releases extolling his takeover of the bank, neglecting to mention the same trust had been owned by his father and his friends.

Joseph Kennedy's successes were extolled by the American press as that of a true American hero. Rising from relatively obscure beginnings, he was a successful business man, who became Chairman of the Securities and Exchange Commission, the Maritime Commission, and United States Ambassador to Great Britain. It was reported Joe had made much of his estimated fortune of $100 million dollars from a few hours of selling short, during the market crash of 1929. Largely undisclosed to the American public throughout Joe's career in public life were his bootlegging partnerships with organized crime during Prohibition, his unscrupulous adventures in Hollywood movie-making, manipulation of the stock market, aggressive management of his liquor distributorship, and his efforts to promote appeasement with Adolph Hitler.

As the country recovered from the calamitous effects of the Great Depression, Joe Kennedy was an emerging name, not possessing the greatest of reputations, but nevertheless, an energetic and impressive rising man. His prowess and successful navigation through the stock market minefields in the aftermath of The Crash, gained the attention of notables in Wall Street and Washington politics. They began to ponder what future role this aggressive, charismatic individual would play in America's return to greatness. Joe was now able to count among his acquaintances, William Randolph Hearst, future treasury secretary Henry Morganthau, and then Governor of New York, Franklin Delano Roosevelt. Joe had become an advisor of sorts, a behind-the-scenes political operative, according to author, Ronald Kessler, in his book, *The Sins of the Father*, aligning his views with Hearst and other newspaper publishers that would be extremely useful in Roosevelt's upcoming campaign. As Kessler states,

"In fact, Joe eventually gave Roosevelt a total of $360,000 for his first two campaigns, according to Joe Kane, Joe's cousin. In today's dollars, this support came to $3.8 million. Moreover, according to Timothy McInerney, who had worked for Joe, Joe not only contributed to the campaign, but was Roosevelt's "money collector" or bag man, collecting cash from those who wanted to hide their identities. [58]

In September 1932, Joe Kennedy was riding high aboard the *Roosevelt Special*, a train carrying the candidate on a 13,000 mile campaign trip, carrying members of what would be called Roosevelt's "brain trust"

- advisers who would play crucial roles in his administration after the election. According to Kessler, Joe was placed in Car D, among Roosevelt's closest friends and advisors, including campaign manager James A. Farley. Roosevelt defeated Herbert Hoover, 472 electoral votes to 59. The nation's and Joe Kennedy's fortunes were about to enter a golden era of prosperity.[59]

But Roosevelt and his closest advisors were cautious and acknowledged their uncertainty of what to do with their talented but suspect associate. Although Joe approached the White House by various means, he felt he was not properly acknowledged nor amply rewarded for his election efforts. In an ingenious end-around, Joe purchased a summer home in Palm Beach Florida, where in another attempt to gain access to White House power, he and wife Rose entertained people close to FDR, including Roosevelt's son James, and Marguerite A. "Missy" Le Hand, Roosevelt's personal secretary. The Boston Kennedy's were now golfing alongside other powerful American moguls including the Woolworth, Dodge, Firestone, and Pulitzer families, and eventually, intelligence community notables, such as Allen Dulles and Richard Bissell, Jr.

How Do You Keep Joe Happy?

Along came greater opportunities. Perhaps the most difficult to understand was President Franklin Roosevelt's selection of Joe Kennedy to sit atop the Securities and Exchange commission, a position author Kessler correctly points out was akin to placing the most cunning of foxes inside the chicken coop. Joe Kennedy, in the eyes and facts many in the know possessed, was the living symbol of all the SEC had been created to eradicate. The five-year appointment as chairman was FDR's way of repaying Joe for helping to finance his 1932 election, as well as FDR's cunning belief "it took a thief to catch a thief," and FDR felt no one could fulfill this mandate as well as Joe Kennedy. It was also, perhaps Roosevelt's way of keeping Joe Kennedy's mind fully occupied, and his attention turned away from politics, specifically at a potential run for the Presidency during the next election.

In the end, FDR's decision proved to be a fairly good choice. Joe Kennedy was adept at recognizing the face and feel of stock manipulations and suspect actions, as Roosevelt knew he would be. In Joe's position as chairman, he was quick and forthright in getting his officers to look in the right places to ensure compliance with the SEC's new regulations and guidelines. Slowly the American public began to trust Wall Street and its investors, in part due to renewed confidence in the oversight Joe Kennedy had restored at the SEC. It was a remarkable performance that enhanced Kennedy's reputation across the nation. Within the Roosevelt White House, he was without doubt, the rising man to keep a watchful eye upon, even though there were those who still contended that Joe had used his SEC position to advance his own portfolio. Perhaps, FDR who was not above political intrigue himself, had presented Kennedy with enough rope to ruin his own career through improper actions, thereby removing a future contender for the office Franklin Roosevelt would hold longer than any other president.

Joe was proving to be a worth adversary, and an even more valuable ally for FDR as Kennedy nimbly stepped through the SEC minefield. Roosevelt then decided to keep Joe busy investigating the political turbulence arising in Europe from the aggressive posturing of National Socialist Germany.

Adolph Hitler was coming to power in Nazi Germany, arm-twisting, rabble-rousing, mugging and thugging his way into the chancellorship of Germany. Hitler's clearly enunciated promises included over-throwing the humiliating dictates of the Treaty of Versailles, imposed upon Germany by the victors of World War I. This promise alone created a growing sense of threat to European peace, and its system of regional alliances.

Joe's European assignment, at FDR's request, would be his first steps onto the stage of international affairs as a political man. He would visit the Old World, representing the highest elected office in the New World. There could be no doubt in anyone's mind that Joe Kennedy was FDR's man. It was, again a deft move on Roosevelt's part, to keep Joe Kennedy fully engaged, but it also gave Joe the opportunity to enhance his international credentials, and gain the experience needed to strengthen his Presidential qualifications.

Dutifully, Joe left America with wife Rose on September 25, 1935, with letters of introduction to the leaders of political parties in Great Britain, France, Italy, Switzerland, and the Netherlands. He met with Winston Churchill, then an outspoken anti-fascist member of Parliament, who had begun to awaken his countrymen to the dangers of a strong National Socialist German government under Adolph Hitler.

In early December 1937, Roosevelt named Joseph Kennedy, the new ambassador to the Court of St. James. Churchill and Roosevelt were already in close harmony about the dangers of Hitlerism to the free world. On September 11, 1939, ten days after German panzers began their over-powering blitzkrieg style of warfare against Poland, FDR penned the first of his many letters to Winston Churchill, the First Sea Lord of the British government. This was an extraordinary act in itself - the head of state of a nation, opening a channel of correspondence with a subordinate minister of another.

It is not clear whether Kennedy ever grasped the unshakeable depth of purpose and intent shared by Roosevelt and Churchill to utterly destroy Hitler and German fascism. Joe did not share these views, and throughout the war years favored appeasement with Hitler, maintaining this stance well past the point of it bringing him any positive political advantage. Joe's often outspoken appeasement tendencies, confirmed Roosevelt's and others perceptions, of Kennedy's penchant for furthering his own fortunes at the expense of others.

Kennedy was certainly not alone in favoring accommodation with Nazi Germany. Appeasement with the new rising Fascist power in Europe, was a view considered in many high circles of power and wealth in Britain and America. There were other wealthy American families involved in trade or finance with Hitler's emerging Third Reich. Averell Harriman, later America's ambassador both to Great Britain and the Soviet Union and Prescott Bush, Wall Street banker, politician, and father of one of America's foremost political families, were not adverse to profiting from business with Nazi Germany. As late as 1942, their businesses were seized under the Trading with the Enemy Act, although Government investigations into both men's business dealings disclosed their interests were purely commercial. Neither man was identified as a Nazi sympathizer, again demonstrating the unique ability of American dynasties to maintain profitable relationships with America's sworn enemies without retribution, or any serious consequences.

However, the clouds of war were fast approaching and appeared unstoppable, and many in high positions were increasingly forced to align their positions before the coming storm. It was becoming clear that Hitler's warlike statements and militant actions, threatened not only world peace, but represented tremendous financial risk, as well as opportunity.

In the turbulent years just prior to World War II, Joe Kennedy became a strong link between Roosevelt and newspaper magnate William Randolph Hearst, and the virulently pro-fascist Catholic priest, Father Charles Coughlin. Hearst had often attacked Roosevelt's foreign and domestic policies, and supported Father Coughlin. Coughlin, for his part, left no doubt in the minds of millions of listeners, tuning into to his regularly scheduled weekly radio broadcasts, that Roosevelt was a soul-less capitalist, leading the country into financial ruin and war, for all the wrong reasons. Coughlin preached that supporting a Roosevelt-led government was the wrong medicine for America. This eloquent Catholic priest from the sub-urbs near Detroit, was also a charismatic leader in the eyes of an up and coming American architect, Philip Johnson, who viewed Father Coughlin's Fascist-leaning stance as a more extreme, but compatible philosophy with Midwest Populism.

Hearst and Coughlin influenced millions of American voters through the powers of the press and radio. Kennedy in his role of Roosevelt ally, offered to talk with Hearst and Coughlin to help temper their anti-admin-istration attacks. It is not known to what extent these meetings affected the content of their media efforts. Coughlin at one point sufficiently admired Joe Kennedy and his sensible approach of appeasement, to name him a "Man of the Week" in his pro-Nazi magazine, *Social Justice*, the same magazine that served as the literary forum for architect and part-time war correspondent, Philip Johnson.

Joe Kennedy, like Johnson, was fascinated with the political power this single Catholic priest had managed to build across the nation, and the use of that power to impact the political thinking of millions. These lessons in media power remained with Joseph Kennedy throughout his life, and he instilled in his sons a strong respect for the power of the media and for radio's successor, television. We witnessed the fruition of the lesson, when Jack Kennedy dramatically changed the course of the 1960 presidential election by his skillful mastery of television, in the historic debates against an unprepared Richard Nixon.

The final silencing of Father Coughlin came about when FDR met with Vatican Secretary of State, and future pontiff, Cardinal Eugenio Pacelli. The meeting took place at FDR's home in Hyde Park, New York, November 5, 1936, arranged by Joe Kennedy.

Cardinal Pacelli, prime mover in the signing of the Vatican-Reich Concordat, needed a strong ally to protect the Vatican from the increas-ingly volatile Nazi efforts to eliminate the Catholic Church's political voice in Germany.

For Roosevelt, a U.S.-Vatican relationship created another brick in the wall of diplomatic encirclement around Hitler, and was therefore in FDR's eyes, a positive step in protecting America's interests. In return, Roosevelt no doubt queried whether the Vatican would assist him in reigning in the powerful opposition voice of Father Coughlin here in America. No record of this conversation exists, but shortly after this meeting, Father Coughlin signed off from the radio airwaves never to return. For Joe Kennedy's part, it was a significant coup in proving his value in sustaining FDR's presidency, and endeared himself to the Cardinal Secretary of State, Eugenio Pacelli, who within three years would be become "Christ's Vicar on Earth" Pope Pius XII.

Joe Kennedy had come a long way from presiding over a small bank in Boston Massachusetts, but he was still searching for pathways to the oval office. Perhaps it was time to take a realistic view of himself. Was he a viable candidate for the office of President? His strengths, if he were honest with himself, were still those of a behind-the-scenes ward boss, dispensing and collecting favors, controlling his minions through contributions, surreptitious loans, and cases of Scotch and Sulka ties at Christmas. Was this the stuff political dynasties were made of, or had Joe missed the bus somewhere between Boston's political wards, and the exercise of power he witnessed in Washington, London, and Rome, personified by the statesmen-like leadership of Roosevelt, Churchill, and Pacelli?

AMBASSADOR OF ACCOMMODATION

Joe Kennedy began to realize there was much more involved in attaining true power, and as usual fate, and FDR, supplied the next step in Joe's ascendency. For FDR, it was the decade long question of "what to do with Joe?" There was significant risk in appointing Joe to highly visible and sensitive positions. It was Joseph Kennedy's window into the mechanisms of power, but a door only opening as wide as Roosevelt desired. That door opened considerably wider as the ambassadorship to Great Britain became available in 1938. There were advantages in naming Joe to the position. He would be out of the country for an indefinite period of time; he would be in an official position as FDR's eyes and ears in England, reporting directly to Roosevelt, although the position was officially controlled by the State Department. Nevertheless, FDR knew Joe was not the type of career diplomat the State Department would prefer, and Kennedy would not likely conform to State Department policy and direction. Roosevelt understood Joe's craving for power and knew he would value his relationship with the office he hoped to gain someday, far above any other political considerations in official Washington. FDR understood this, because he too had been seduced by the quest for the Presidency long ago and remains today the only man to serve four consecutive terms as President.

It was a widely known fact throughout the White House, the State Department, and to Churchill and his advisors, that Joe Kennedy favored appeasement with Hitler's government. Joe held these views while serving as Franklin Roosevelt's, and America's ambassador to England, the western nation most bearing the terrible brunt of defeating Hitlerian fascism. England was risking all in standing up to Germany's brutally efficient military machine. For Joseph Kennedy to personally present views contrary to the President he served, suggests that FDR preferred retaining Kennedy as a troublesome member of his team out of the country, rather than allowing Joe the opportunity to contend for the office FDR would never willingly relinquish.

FDR was often an enigma to his own close associates and advisors. Many of his own supporters, upon speaking intimately with the President, left the Oval Office assured they had swayed Roosevelt to their point of view. All that likely happened, is that Roosevelt had taken the measure of the man, and the dedication to which that individual felt toward his cause. Roosevelt was, by all accounts, an extremely patient political man. He exercised supreme patience in managing Joe Kennedy's career, consistently giving Joe the most highly visible opportunities in the public eye, waiting for Joe to make that one final slip, which would end his aspirations for attaining the Presidency. Basing Kennedy in Great Britain, where Joe found appeasement-minded individuals among Britain's elite who stood to lose most from a Nazi victory, would encourage Joe's appetite for appeasement. It also served to isolate him from the gradually changing opinions of most Americans, who were beginning to realize that Hitler was the universal enemy.

During his tenure as ambassador to Great Britain, Kennedy's written communications with the White House and utterances in London and Washington in favor of appeasement caused him to be viewed as weak-willed and self-serving by Roosevelt and Churchill. Joe's speeches were often edited by the State Department prior to release, to remove Joe's statements either leaning toward appeasement, or re-enforcing American isolationist viewpoints, neither which were indicative of Roosevelt Administration policies.

Joe relished his time and position in England, initially taking the country by storm with his large photogenic family and wining smile. Kennedy met British wartime leaders, the Royal Family, members of Britain's ruling class, and leading American figures such as J.P. Morgan, Bernard Baruch. He also met a rising political advocate for American isolationism and pro-German policy, Charles A. Lindbergh, who became one of Joe's trusted advisors. In return for his pro-German stance, Hitler awarded Lindbergh the Service Cross of the Order of the German Eagle with the Star, the second highest of all German decorations.[60]

Franklin D. Roosevelt remained aware Joseph Kennedy's eyes remained on the viability of his candidacy for the Presidency. In an intriguing Machiavellian intrigue, Roosevelt asked his press secretary, Stephen

Early, to summon *Chicago Tribune* editor, Walter Trohan for a conversation. Following their meeting, an article ran on page one of the June 23, 1938 edition of the *Tribune* entitled, "Kennedy's 1940 Ambitions Open Roosevelt Riff." Joe Kennedy complained vociferously to *Tribune* owner, Colonel McCormick, who had no intention of retracting the story. The next time Kennedy saw Trohan, Kennedy "drew his hand across his throat" in an effort to intimidate Trohan. Trohan was removed from Kennedy's list of favored editors receiving Sulka ties and cases of Haig & Haig scotch. Later, Kennedy mended their relationship. Joe suspected that Roosevelt was behind the article and did not want to confront Roosevelt.[61]

That same month, a *Saturday Evening Post* article exposed FDR's son, James Roosevelt's profiteering. The article also cited James help in getting Joe the ambassadorship to England, and the exclusive rights to the Haig & Haig scotch distributorship in the United Kingdom. The article stated, "Jimmy [Roosevelt] has helped Kennedy to reach the two great positions he now holds - that of ambassador to London, and that of premier Scotch whiskey salesman in America."[62] Kennedy of course, tried to suppress this article before release, knowing it would damage his image with American voters. Earlier in May, a public opinion poll found that Kennedy would finish fifth among potential Democratic candidates, if FDR did not run. No doubt the two articles spotlighting Kennedy's back-room maneuvering to advance his career and profits did not help, as FDR had likely intended.

On September 1938, the Western Powers, Hitler, and Mussolini, met at the historic Munich Conference. The Western powers, headed by British Prime Minister Neville Chamberlain, and French Prime Minister Edouard Daladier, satisfied Hitler's expansionist aims, and ceded a large portion of Czechoslovakia, in return for a vaguely worded promise of future consultation to settle differences. Three weeks later, on October 19, Joe spoke at a Trafalgar Day dinner given by the Navy League in London. His speech caused intense consternation in European and American diplomatic circles when he stated it was "unproductive" for democracies and dictatorships "to widen the division now existing between them, by emphasizing their differences." Kennedy proposed they work toward "solving their common problems." After all he said, we "have to live together in the same world, whether we like it or not."[63] Twenty-five years later, on June 10, 1963, in a commencement speech at American University, his son, President John Kennedy, issued an eerily familiar statement in favor of detente between America and the Soviet Union, when JFK stated:

"And if we cannot end now our differences, at least we can help make the world safe for diversity. For, in the final analysis, our most basic common link is that we all inhabit this small planet. We all breathe the same air. We all cherish our children's future. And we are all mortal."

On March 15, 1939, the futility of appeasement exploded for all to recognize. Nazi tanks rolled into the city of Prague, making Czechoslovakia a puppet state of the new Germania's Third Reich. Joe Kennedy remained one of the few diplomats who continued preaching appeasement, isolating himself from the Roosevelt Administration, and the American and British public.

Harold Ickes, upon returning from a visit to Joe Kennedy in London, dined with FDR at the White House. Roosevelt told Ickes that Joe had "remonstrated with him for criticizing fascism in his (FDR's) speeches. Roosevelt recalled Kennedy wanted him [Roosevelt] to attack Nazism, but not fascism. When the President asked him why, Kennedy responded that he thought we would have to have some form of fascism in America.[64] For Joe Kennedy, to preach advocacy of a fascist government in America, face to face with Franklin Roosevelt, the only man chosen four times by the American electorate for the office of President, was a statement of incomprehensible dimension. To FDR, it was telling conformation of Joe's wish to be among that fascist elite ruling America.

Felix Frankfurter, a Roosevelt appointee to the U.S. Supreme Court complained to FDR, "I wonder if Joe Kennedy understands the implications of public talk by an American ambassador. Such public approval of dictatorships, in part even, plays into their hands." American Press reactions were immediate and violent to Joe's Trafalgar Day speech in London. His comments were denounced by the *New York Post* as tantamount to suggesting "the United States make a friend of the man who boasts he is out to destroy democracy and religion." The paper called the idea shocking to "free Americans." An article in the *Wall Street Journal,* suggested that upon his return to America, Joe should be dropped in Boston Harbor, where a dunking in "alien tea" might restore Joe's Americanism.[64]

The Trafalgar speech spelled the beginning of the end for Joe's bid for political prominence. By now, the State Department was circumventing its own London ambassador, and Roosevelt cabinet members and advisors were discouraged and angry with Kennedy's performance. Many understood FDR's rationale for keeping Kennedy off-shore, but most also felt the charade had gone too far, and so-advised the President. The May 17, 1939 issue of the British newsletter, *The Week,* reported that Joe was making anti-Roosevelt remarks, and that according to Kennedy, "the democratic policy of the United States is a Jewish production," and that 'Roosevelt will fall in 1940."[65] Protests from Jewish organizations in the United States added to the chorus of complaints about America's ambassador to England.

Aside from the advantages the ambassadorship provided to Kennedy's liquor distribution venture, Joe continued to use his position to gain inside information to further his investments, and to manipulate stock markets. From his London sources, Harold Ickes learned "Joe Kennedy was speculating in the stock market very heavily, but under cover, through London agents."[66]

On April 29, 1940, Henry Morgenthau Jr., Roosevelt's Secretary of the Treasury, had a meeting with his top department aides to review Joe Kennedy's latest "typical asinine" letter to FDR. Ten days earlier, Germany invaded Norway, while Joe's eyes were centered on his own pocketbook, urging Roosevelt to propose legislation prohibiting the government from purchasing gold. Morgenthau told FDR there was no need for such action and stated, "The only thinking that has explained Joe Kennedy to me for the last couple of years is that he has been consistently short in the market." Morgenthau subsequently made inquiries and learned that a U.S.

stock market partner of Kennedy's, a notorious market bear, constantly traveled to London to visit Joe. Morgenthau's conclusion was "Every move he [Kennedy] makes is to bear down on our market. It is the only explanation I can get. Every single move he has made is to depress our securities and commodities." As author, Ronald Kessler, writes in his penetrating work on Joseph Kennedy, *The Sins of the Father*, it was a damning commentary on Joe, suggesting his constant predictions of doom were calculated to force down stock market prices, so he could make a killing.[67] An investigation by Roosevelt advisor and right-hand man, Harry Hopkins, concluded with Hopkins confirming to FDR that Joe Kennedy had indeed sold Czechoslovakian securities short, just prior to Germany's invasion of Czechoslovakia, with Joe's profit rumored to be approximately $500,000.[68]

Roosevelt's plan to keep Kennedy out of the country until after the 1942 election was well-founded, from a domestic political perspective. The British had been tapping Joe's communications and learned that he planned, along with Time Magazine owners, Clare and Henry Luce, to endorse Roosevelt's Republican opponent Wendell Willkie, and mount a campaign to encourage America's 2.5 million Catholic voters to throw Roosevelt out of office.

DEMOCRACY IS FINISHED AND SO AM I

Joe left London on October 20, 1940, a month before the presidential election. Immediately upon his return to America, Joe Kennedy attempted to smooth over any differences with FDR, promising to support Roosevelt's election to a third term. On October 29, 1940, Joe gave a radio address over CBS stating, "I believe that Franklin D. Roosevelt should be re-elected President of the United States." Years later Clare Booth Luce, wife of *Time Magazine* owner Henry Luce, asked Joe why he had endorsed FDR. Joe told her "We agreed that if I endorsed him for president in 1940, then he would support my son Joe, for governor of Massachusetts in 1942.[69] Roosevelt invited him to stay at the White House on the evening of October 27. Earlier that day, Roosevelt had lunch with Lyndon Johnson, congressman from Texas. During lunch, Johnson recalls that FDR took a call from Kennedy at the table and said, "Ah Joe, old friend it is so good to hear your voice. Please come over to the White House tonight for a little family dinner. I am dying to talk to you. You have been doing a wonderful job." Johnson said Roosevelt looked at Johnson, and then "drew his forefinger across his throat like a razor."[70]

FDR was elected to his third term on November 5, 1940. In a meeting the next day, Joe resigned, although according to Elliot Roosevelt, FDR's second son, Roosevelt asked for Joe's resignation. Just before Thanksgiving, FDR invited Joe to his home in Hyde Park. Author Kessler writes:

"Now that the election was over, the president could take the gloves off. Just what transpired is a matter of conjecture. But Eleanor recalled that ten minutes after she brought Joe in to see her husband, Roosevelt called her back. He asked Joe to step out of his study while he talked with Eleanor, who had rarely seen him so angry. "I never want to see that son-of-bitch again as long as I live," Roosevelt declared. "Take his resignation and get him out of here."[71]

Joe's parting shot in a November, *Boston Globe* article, was aimed at the heart of democracy and a final attempt to affect the global war the Roosevelt Administration was preparing America to face. It was also an attempt to undermine Winston Churchill's defiant stand against Hitler, and perhaps create panic within the stock market, where Joe would be able to buy stocks at the most favorable prices and position himself in an even stronger position at the conclusion of the war. This was the crowning embarrassment in his blundering career as American ambassador. The *Boston Globe* article elicited the final damning comment from Joe Kennedy, stating "Democracy is all done", bringing down the Press, and the final curtain on Joseph Kennedy's attempts to build a career culminating in the Oval Office.

All throughout Joseph Kennedy's various political and financial maneuvering, he maintained his focus on his political aspirations. Nine months before Joe's final November blunder in the *Boston Globe* article, an issue of the *Boston Post* carried a February 12, 1940 headline on page one, proclaiming "Kennedy May Be a Candidate".[72] Joe had been testing the waters through his network of associates, and found them to be chilly. His reputation had not reached the levels of popularity he had hoped for. He was publicly out of step with the majority of the American people on the issue of appeasement. In addition, the fact that he had never held political office, his religion, and the uncertainty of just how Joseph Kennedy had made his fortune, were issues Joe could not overcome. On February 14, the New York Times quoted Joe as saying he was declining entreaties from "his supporters" that he run for president. Two days later, eldest son, Joseph Kennedy Jr., filed nomination papers as a candidate for delegate to the Democratic National Convention from the ninth congressional district. With this step, Joseph Kennedy Sr. was acknowledging that securing the office of president was beyond his reach. Tragically, Joe Jr. was soon to perish in Europe while piloting a converted B-24 Liberator bomber loaded with high explosives to demolish an enemy fortress. Upon his death, the burden of fulfilling Joe Sr.'s ultimate ambition fell to his second son, Jack Kennedy.

In Palm Beach, Christmas of 1944, Joe Sr. gave Jack his future plans. He was to take his older brother's place and enter politics. Jack later told reporter Bob Considine, "It was like being drafted. My father wanted his eldest son in politics. 'Wanted' isn't the right word. He *demanded* it. You know my father . . ."[73]

After Jack Kennedy had won several primary contests, Kennedy friend Charles Spaulding recalled standing poolside at Joe Kennedy's Palm Beach estate. While the future president was in the pool, Joe Sr. turned to him and said, "Look at him. He's a scrawny kid. He's going to do it. I tried all my life and I couldn't do it. But he's going to do it!"[74]

All evidence points to Joseph Kennedy Sr. using the momentous events he encountered throughout his life to provide a sense of color and shape to an inwardly focused character. He seemingly moved as an exalted con artist in the guise of a statesman; a pretender, operating amidst the epic gathering of the towering political, military, and economic leaders of his time.

According to Henry Luce, Joe never lost sight of his main goal - making money and acquiring power. According to House Speaker Thomas "Tip" O'Neil, "Joe Kennedy was an ongoing factor in Massachusetts politics." Joe spent $300,000 on Jack's first campaign, the equivalent of 2.2 million today. Every time a Democrat ran for governor, he would go down to see Joe, who would send him home with a briefcase full of cash. The word was, if Joe Kennedy liked you, he'd give you $50,000. If he really like you, he'd give you $100,000." On November 5, 1946, Jack Kennedy was elected to Congress. Seven days later he filed a report with the Massachusetts Secretary of State, certifying that no money had been collected for, or spent, on his campaign.[75] True in 1946, and all during Jack Kennedy's rise to power, political gamesmanship and Joe's wealth were unspoken factors, ultimately elevating JFK to the Presidency. Joe's actions were carried out within the law, some outside the law, some unethical, but permissible amongst those who understood the rules of the pursuit of power. Although never able to break into the billionaire's club, Joseph Kennedy's wealth was estimated by the *New York Times* at $500 million at the time of his death in 1969. Joe had amassed a fortune more than sufficient to buy the support he needed to catapult congressman, and then senator, John Kennedy, to national prominence.

Roosevelt and Churchill had given Joseph Kennedy an unparalleled lesson in global politics, and it undoubtedly left a bitter taste. In the final years of the Roosevelt administration, Joe flip-flopped positions, issued countless denials of his former defeatist attitude, anti-semitic statements, predictions of Axis victory, and American and British defeat.

Joe had prospered by observing the dictum that wealth could open any door, and was the key to bending others to his designs. But he fatally underestimated the extensive investments in America's industries and superstructure made by the nation's dynasties, and overestimated the value of his political relationship with Franklin Roosevelt, and by extension, the power of the Presidency. Kennedy believed that this political partnership alone, would be the prime vehicle for creating his own successful dynasty. Blinded by Franklin Roosevelt's grandly symbiotic relationship with the American people, he misunderstood where true power in America resided. Joe Kennedy never realized that America's dynasties never required the sanction of an American president to achieve their rule over the nation's economy and institutions, a fatal error he would pass on to his sons.

In hindsight, it is possible to understand Joe's belief in the power of the presidency. Franklin Roosevelt was an extraordinarily powerful president. A sure-handed leader through America's great financial and military crises. He was revered toward the end of his fourth term, not only by the vast majority of Americans, but had become a beacon and symbol of freedom for countless millions around the world, as his son John would become. Joe himself, owed much of his success to FDR, and was dependent on Roosevelt for the continuation of his political position, and the wealth he accrued through these opportunities.

Having succeeded in most of his endeavors by reducing opportunities and associates to their purchase price, Joseph Kennedy had little reason, and even less requisite experience, to convince his sons that there were dangerous limits that could not, and should not, be exceeded. Fate had placed Joseph Kennedy at a time and place in Europe, when the fate of nations were being decided by the sword. Joe was privileged to hold, perhaps the ultimate observation point, from which he could study the strengths and weaknesses of the statesmen and dynasties that ruled Europe. It was an unsurpassed opportunity to rise to the stature of a true statesman, and an international power-player in his own right. That he chose to ignore the many opportunities to lift himself above the baseness of simple avarice in an epic era, represents a failure of the highest degree for someone with Joe's dynastic ambitions.

As a result, Joe Kennedy would be denied full membership into the true citadels of power. His sons would pay dearly for their father's disbarment, for as they reached the nation's highest offices, they lacked the time-woven trust and confidence of those who were the true directors of economic and military might. Joe never envisioned acquiring the knowledge possessed by economic dynasties, where that knowledge "is" the power needed to secure the control and wealth of nations and continents.

Subsequently, Joseph Kennedy's accrued wealth was sufficient to finance entry to Congress, the Senate, and the White House for his sons. It opened opportunities and connections allowing his sons to enter the high-stakes casino of American politics. But John and Robert Kennedy would always be regarded as students, to be carefully advised and tutored, creating a deep vulnerability for the brothers. They would find that their immediate circle of advisors were often men who owed their political allegiance and survival to others more powerful. John Kennedy would be expected to sanction the established blueprints for America's path to world dominance, as defined by America's centers of power. As a president who believed in his own vision for America, it was a burden John Kennedy would carry from the first day of his Presidency to his last.

Joseph P. Kennedy, Sr. is rightly viewed as the father of a political dynasty that included a president, three senators, an attorney general, three congressmen, and an expanded family, unrivaled in producing so many members elected to public office. "Kennedy charm" was a formidable natural gift, un-matched by any other American political dynasty. His dynasty did not secure a new direction for America through the office of the presidency. The dynastic "next-in-line" rule of succession was fatally broken on a gently slopping grassy plaza in Dallas, and in a kitchen pantry of the Ambassador Hotel in Los Angeles, allegedly by two disaffected loners, one insisting he was innocent, the other unable to recall what he had done.

6

JFK and the Promised Land

Come senators, congressmen, Please heed the call
Don't stand in the doorway Don't block up the hall
For he that gets hurt Will be he who has stalled
There's a battle outside And it is ragin'
It'll soon shake your windows And rattle your walls
For the times they are a-changin'.

— BOB DYLAN, SONGWRITER

"Mankind must put an end to war before war puts an end to mankind."

— JOHN KENNEDY, PRESIDENT

A QUESTION OF BALANCE

THE KENNEDY YEARS in the White House present historians with a dilemma. The short-lived quest to create a Kennedy dynasty began with

John Kennedy's inauguration on January 20, 1961, and ended with the death of Robert Kennedy on June 6, 1968, a period of only seven and a half years. Yet those years retain a significant and highly emotional place in American history. John's and Robert's charismatic personalities, up-lifting oratory, and un-realized promises for peace and the ascent of the rights of man, have defined the Kennedy legacy in American culture. John Kennedy remains to this day, inseparable from the social and cultural rebirth he personified and energized.

In the youngest man elected to the office of President, America found a leader who sensed America's hunger for social and cultural change and was willing to lead. He challenged the youth and energy of America to transform the face of the world, at a time when the Cold War was extending its cloak of numbing fear - fear of a sudden rash act - a miscalculated move - a random provocation escalating too rapidly for logic and reason to diffuse. It was possible mankind had reached the point where Armageddon could not be averted once the threat was presented. America's cold warriors were certain that, if the button was pushed, plans were in place to emerge victorious, although victory in the nuclear age was never to be a quantifiable, nor qualitative condition. Some of America's most virulent military leaders even welcomed the event, as an opportunity to destroy America's idealogical enemies once and for all. Most, however, were horrified at the thought of a nuclear exchange.

Amidst these alarming scenarios, a new call for reason could be heard, and America's youth responded with the first nation-wide, activist movement. College campuses were the logical centers for students to express themselves, believing for the first time, their voices and vision were important in ensuring America's survival and improvement. It was the first of many re-energizing, yet polarizing challenges in American society, encouraged by John Kennedy's speeches and his Presidency. Those in power were not troubled. But there seemed to be a change in the direction of the political winds blowing across the nation.

Humans have an innate need, almost a genetic pre-disposition, to re-invent themselves following periods of arrested-development, digression, or strife. As the Sixties approached, American society was ripe for a cultural rebirth, as an opposite and necessary response to the emotional vacuity of Cold War philosophy. America was experiencing an explosion of art, music, cultural changes, and the glorification of youth, signifying hope in the future. American society was undergoing a process of review, re-design, and re-evaluation, at university forums and family dinner tables across the county. This renewal united those of common cause, yet polarized America into two camps - those defending a comfortable post-war way of life, and those who felt America was failing to deliver its promise of a new imaginative and inclusive culture. Americans of all strata hotly debated these challenges to their national character.

Respected icons and guardians of the past sensed the swelling energy of change, but were not yet certain how to respond. They watched intently from their secure vantage points, as the small-town majesty of Norman Rockwell surrendered to the eye-candy, psychedelia of Andy Warhol; swing dancing swirled into the self-expressive Twist; Elvis began his slow fade in a blaze of glittering nostalgia; Motown began its historic rise, and the Beatles' English invasion was gathering momentum. Robert Frost spoke elegantly at John Kennedy's inauguration, and then quietly passed into the vermillion landscape of Vermont, while Bob Dylan's aggrieved poetry rose with a fiery attack on America's politics of exclusion. The "American way of life" was undergoing a revolution, most devastatingly from its young, who sensed the madness of a world, whose statesmen and respected icons expected them to blindly follow.

Why should they? Their parents had struggled through the most severe depression in the nation's history, two global wars, the Korean conflict, and were now offered the depressing, apocalyptic, Cold War "MAD" doctrine of "mutually assured destruction." At an exalted level, high above the common man's view, nuclear brinkmanship was the ultimate game for dedicated cold warriors and their grim-faced political allies, who spoke of Armageddon as a 50-50 possibility.

Hope for a peaceful world, following the immense individual sacrifices of World War II, was replaced by the construction of underground bunkers, the recommended solution for citizens to raise the probability of their own survival. Power over the continuation of life on Earth, had now become concentrated in the hands of a few integrated councils, under the figurehead of an aging World War II general. This power matrix was to come under severe challenge by America's youth, who refused to embrace a future measured by the odds of survivability.

A re-energized America society was gradually moving toward rejection of the path of destruction. Opposed to nuclear proliferation, and the politics of exclusion, the voices of a new culture driven by students, musicians, poets, artists, and a handful of brave politicians, began speaking out in damning protest. It was becoming a trying time for the forces that had created the key doctrines and policies of the Cold War. Confrontation between men entrenched in their father's castles of power, the directors and guardians of the Pax Americana, and those who envisioned the possibilities of man's ascent in the Age of Aquarius, were destined to collide in a struggle for the soul of America. John Kennedy walked between these worlds.

In the fourth and final debate of the 1960 Presidential election, Kennedy epitomized youth and the future. His Republican opponent, Richard Nixon, appeared as a pale, heavy-jowled spokesman, preaching the sober philosophy of the Eisenhower-Dulles years. John Kennedy spoke to the common man in an uplifting manner, stressing that political re-engagement was the responsibility of all Americans. His message resonated with voters who felt their voices had been forgotten. They responded at the polls, although by a very close margin, reflecting the reality of an almost evenly divided nation split along political, social, and economic lines.

John Kennedy, whose initials "JFK", that seemed to bestow the popularity and leadership reminiscent of "FDR", was changing the public face of the power game. However, beneath the surface of public scrutiny, the role of America's dynasties and key institutions remained unchanged, headed by men dedicated to preserving the nation's plans for global dominance in the twentieth century. Equality, humanitarianism, and peaceful coexistence were not the qualities they required of Americans to sustain a fierce, cold war mentality, and vanquish their sworn enemies at any cost.

Perhaps these cold warriors felt Americans weren't convinced of the importance, or the deadly nature of the struggle. Perhaps Americans did not realize the dangers of fully defeating their proclaimed adversaries, the Soviet Union and Cuba. Thousands of ICBM warheads were installed in their silos, ready to deliver a lethal blow, should the opportunity materialize. And beyond a policy of retaliation, there were those in the highest councils of the U.S. military advocating for a massive pre-emptive nuclear strike to defeat America's philosophical enemies, deciding the issue once and for all.

Yet Americans did understand - even if they were powerless to remove those missiles. They instinctively understood those warheads would never be launched unless America was willing to invite its own destruction. The arms race was continuously justified as necessary to maintain superiority in a never-ending deadly competition. But surely the number of warheads in place, had already guaranteed there would be no winner in a nuclear exchange. Americans did understand the potential cost in human life and health for decades to come, the destruction of the environment, the economy, and the breakdown of the social fabric of everyday life. Nuclear war was simply not a viable military or political response. And so, in their silos, thousands of messengers of death dutifully remained, decade after decade. They remained silent sentinels of both peace and war, while the Cold War quietly absorbed an enormous portion of America's wealth, eventually bankrupting the Soviet economy, and moving the United States towards a staggering national debt. Their existence enriched no one but the architects, warriors, and industries who had created them, out of the self-enriching politics of fear.

John Kennedy was not unmindful of the ebb and flow and realities of political power. He sensed it was within his administration's grasp to capture the sentiments of American voters, after the spirit-dampening Eisenhower years. It was a golden opportunity for a well-reasoned change of vision, to replace the chilling fatalism of the Cold War, with hope and energy. And so, through the first two years of the Kennedy presidency, John and Robert listened and learned, compromised and planned. They were newcomers to the plateau of national and global direction, and there was little time to waste. Events had to be quickly assimilated, evaluated, and utilized to build their own agenda and power base. JFK was both student and teacher, captive, yet cloaked in immense power, dependent on those around him, but instinctively knowing he possessed the vision to embark on his own plans for America. His message was still mixed, for as he moved forward, he must be all things to all powers, and to all people. To the people of America and Western Europe, he offered a message of peace and hope; to the nation's economic powers, he supported their plans to assure profits to come; to America's military leaders he unequivocally stated America would not bend before any foe. It was a time to survive, compromise, and build alliances. Victory in the 1964 presidential election would significantly free him from the restraints threatening to render him powerless beneath the long-established castles and institutions of American power.

Through the records of John Kennedy actions, it is possible to discern his growing willingness to challenge the directors of America's power. Nowhere was the message more clearly conveyed to America's power elite, than through John Kennedy's secret, back-door method of resolving Cold War conflicts, by direct communication with Soviet leadership during the Berlin Crisis and the Cuban Missile Crisis. The Kennedy brothers initiated this clandestine method of crisis management, which was a first concrete step in seizing control of America's Cold War political and military decision-making capability. They were, perhaps, far too self-assured in their positions as Chief Executive, and Attorney General, in believing that excluding the institutions that enforced American policy - the CIA, military leadership, and their elite advisors and directors - would allow this challenge to remain uncontested.

It is not known exactly when Robert Kennedy first met Georgi Bolshakov, a Soviet intelligence officer, posing as a journalist in Washington D. C. Robert Kennedy, utilizing Bolshakov, initiated the back-channel link between the Kennedy White House and the Kremlin. No Soviet documents dealing with this arrangement have been made public, and Robert Kennedy did not disclose when it began in his JFK Library interviews. The

Kennedy brothers allowed other government officials only furtive glimpses of the give-and-take of the Bolshakov back-channel. Not surprisingly, the few officials who knew of it, thought it was a "dangerous game".[76] In a 1964 interview with the Kennedy Library, Bobby Kennedy stated: "Most of the major matters dealing with the Soviet Union and the United States were discussed and arrangements were made between Georgi Bolshakov and myself . . . We used to meet maybe once ever two weeks." Robert Kennedy served as courier to allow his brother plausible deniability, should the back-channel communications become publicly known, or fail.

In the summer of 1961, President Kennedy supported the doctrine of maintaining the over-whelming American military superiority called for in the Quantico I and II studies created under the guidance of Nelson Rockefeller. JFK announced a three billion dollar increase in defense spending and urged Americans to prepare for the worst by constructing nuclear fall-out shelters in basements and backyards. More than two hundred million dollars were added to the defense budget for civil defense. Other moves, not made public, were designed to signal American firmness to Soviet leaders, such as redeployment of the U.S. nuclear submarine fleet, elements of the Strategic Air Command were placed on heightened alert, military leaves were cancelled, and shipments to Europe of military hardware and munitions were stepped up.[77]

Initially, John Kennedy was in step with the very elements of American Cold War planning that Dwight Eisenhower had warned of in his Farewell Address to the nation. However, only two years later, on June 10, 1963, in a major foreign policy speech at American University, Kennedy spoke of his intentions for limiting the arms race, banning nuclear testing, and his long range goal of nuclear disarmament. On that day, five months before the end of his presidency, John Kennedy articulated his vision of the end of the Cold War:

"I have, therefore, chosen this time and this place to discuss a topic on which ignorance too often abounds and the truth is too rarely perceived—yet it is the most important topic on earth: world peace.

What kind of peace do I mean? What kind of peace do we seek? Not a Pax Americana enforced on the world by American weapons of war. Not the peace of the grave, or the security of the slave. I am talking about genuine peace, the kind of peace that makes life on earth worth living, the kind that enables men and nations to grow, and to hope, and to build a better life for their children—not merely peace for Americans, but peace for all men and women— not merely peace in our time, but peace for all time.

I speak of peace because of the new face of war. Total war makes no sense in an age when great powers can maintain large and relatively invulnerable nuclear forces and refuse to surrender without resort to those forces. It makes no sense in an age when a single nuclear weapon contains almost ten times the explosive force delivered by all the allied air forces in the Second World War. It makes no sense in an age when the deadly poisons produced by a nuclear exchange would be carried by wind and water and soil and seed, to the far corners of the globe, and to generations yet unborn.

Today the expenditure of billions of dollars every year on weapons acquired for the purpose of making sure we never need to use them, is essential to keeping the peace. But surely the acquisition of such idle stockpiles--which can only destroy and never create--is not the only, much less the most efficient, means of assuring peace. I speak of peace, therefore, as the necessary rational end of rational men. I realize that the pursuit of peace is not as dramatic as the pursuit of war--and frequently the words of the pursuer fall on deaf ears. But we have no more urgent task.

Kennedy had come to believe that the continued development and production of more destructive power, was an unnecessary solution for men and societies to pursue. Quantico I and II had achieved their goals of Cold War detente, nuclear superiority, and the weapons makers had realized profits

beyond their wildest dreams. John Kennedy clearly articulated the futility of nuclear exchange, and his vision of a change in direction toward a
peacetime economy, offering far more value to its citizens than a cold war
frozen in time, and in the minds of its creators.

Throughout most of JFK's presidency, the aggressive planning of the
Central Intelligence Agency, and the Kremlin, kept his attention focused
on a succession of international crises, preventing Kennedy from advanc-
ing his own initiatives. The value of the President's back-channel circum-
vention of accepted foreign diplomatic channels now became evident - it
afforded his administration the opportunity to find alternative solutions,
closer to his vision of superpower relations - freeing him from the self-
activating, escalating responses called for in Quantico I and II.

President John F. Kennedy meets with the Joint Chiefs of Staff. Photograph includes:
(L-R) United States Marine Corps General David Shoup; United States Army General
Earle Wheeler; United States Air Force General Curtis LeMay, President Kennedy;
Chairman of the Joint Chiefs of Staff General Maxwell Taylor; United States Navy
Admiral George Anderson. West Wing Lawn. White House. Washington, D.C.

*"The first method for estimating the intelligence of a ruler
is to look at the men he has around him".*

— PRINCE NICCOLO MACHIAVELLI - STATESMAN

WHO ADVISES THE ADVISORS?

On a cold clear, frost-bitten Friday winter day, January 20, 1961, John Kennedy's Inaugural Address set the tone for his Presidency:

"Now the trumpet summons us again - not as a call to bear arms, though arms we need; not as a call to battle, though embattled we are - but a call to bear the burden of a long twilight struggle, year in and year out, rejoicing in hope, patient in tribulation - a struggle against the common enemies of man: tyranny, poverty, disease, and war itself."

This revealing portion of Kennedy's address announced his future goal of diminishing the threat of war, and to work toward improvements in the social condition of man. His inaugural call to arms, but not armed struggle, clearly stated his intentions. The address signaled his intent to break with post World War II Cold War mentality and was a signal to the centers of power in America, that existing policies and doctrines would be reviewed. He was no doubt, hopeful, there would be a sufficient degree of synchronicity and support for his agenda.

The record shows that he built his cabinet around men who were neither hawkish nor virulent cold warriors. Kennedy chose men who had distinguished themselves in the worlds of finance and academia; men who might bring new attitudes and vision to push beyond existing boundaries. It is also a matter of record, that despite Kennedy's intentions, many of his cabinet members owed their success to the same dynasties JFK's vision would challenge, as true power in America does not transform or reinvent itself with each presidential election.

Kennedy's Secretary of State, Dean Rusk, was a Rockefeller Foundation Trustee from 1950 to 1961. JFK's Secretary of the Treasury, C. Douglas Dillon, was often a major partner in Rockefeller family investments and their investment strategies in South America. He later served as chairman of the Rockefeller Foundation from 1972 to 1975. Kennedy presidential advisor John J. McCloy, sometimes referred to as the "Chairman of the American Establishment," served as chairman of the Rockefeller-dominated Chase Manhattan Bank from 1953 to 1960 and was a trustee of the Rockefeller Foundation from 1946 to 1949. Presidential advisor, Adolf Berle, Jr., had been instrumental in helping Nelson Rockefeller push through acceptance of the Act of Chapultepec at the 1945 United Nations conference in San Francisco, was a trusted Rockefeller family advisor. Secretary of Defense, Robert McNamara, was a Harvard graduate who had distinguished himself in World War II. As an Air Force captain in the Office of Statistical Control, he was instrumental in the analysis of U.S. bombers' efficiency and effectiveness, especially the B-29 forces commanded by Major General Curtis LeMay in India, China, and the Marianas Islands.[78]

Robert Kennedy was assigned the critical position of Attorney General, where the power of the Justice Department, working in tandem with the Executive Branch of the government, would enforce administration focus and changes to federal law.

The remaining less visible Cabinet positions were offered to men who had distinguished themselves with long careers in public service but were not known for their controversial leadership.

The men who worked directly under this uppermost level of Cabinet appointees and advisors, were men of action, schooled in military and political combat in World War II, Korea, and the formative stages of the Cold War. They believed themselves to be America's first-line of defense, and in their sworn mission to defend her in the most convincing fashion. Defeat was not an option, and if the enemy's will and capacity to wage war was eliminated, the more complete and lasting would be the victory. Total military victory was their objective.

History refers to the period from 1948 as the Cold War, but to the men who carried out this undeclared war, it was a passionate and determined epoch. They were proud of their tradition as warriors of a nation never defeated in war, who's expansionist power was now supported by unparalleled military strength. These were men like Allen Dulles and Richard Bissell of the CIA, and Air Force Generals Curtis LeMay, Edward Landsdale, and Charles Cabell. They had successfully confronted and defeated America's formidable battlefield opponents. Their actions had brought about the rise and fall of foreign governments. They had played critical roles in shaping America's nuclear, conventional, covert, and intelligence forces. They had successfully carried out the military, political, and economic strategies developed by the nation's elite civilian leadership. As John Kennedy would experience, they would be the most formidable opponents of his Presidency, for they were America's pre-eminent warriors whose mission was establishing America's Cold War military and economic dominance during the latter half of the twentieth century.

John Kennedy was also a wartime hero, and his successful attempt to save the lives of his crew had been well-documented. However, to those in America's political and military hierarchy, he seemed increasingly overly-cautious in confronting the nation's ideological adversaries. As his presidency evolved, they began to realize he did not share their win-at-all-cost mentality, and was an unknown, untested entity, carrying the title of Commander-in-Chief, yet not allied with, nor protected by, any American power center or dynasty. Unfairly perhaps, he still carried the distasteful reputation of family patriarch Joseph P. Kennedy, Sr., who only 18 earlier was the appeasement-minded ambassador to Great Britain, and favored accommodation with Adolph Hitler, while England battled Nazi Germany for her right to exist.

As John Kennedy's occupancy in the White House continued, he seemed less an adherent to the accepted plans for expanding America's military and economic dominance, and more a true believer and practitioner of the powers of the Presidency. During the third year of his presidency, John Kennedy, confident of victory in the upcoming presidential election of 1964, set out to gain control the nation's military and foreign policy, and its federal agencies and institutions. The battle for power in America was underway.

Control of M1

As American's are gradually discovering, the Federal Reserve Banking System (FRB) is not a United States Government institution but is instead a closely-harmonized network of privately-owned banks with the authority to print U.S. currency, control interest rates and therefore, inherently control the ebb and flow of the nation's economy. By design, it is not a "Federal" institution, and it has no "Reserve". It is accountable to Congress and the American people through a system of reports, journals, and publications generated by the FRB itself, detailing its actions, and providing justification for those actions.

Publications and meeting minutes are accessible through the FRB's public web site, and do much to support the FRB's claims of transparency and responsibility to the American people. However, upon closer examination, its system of providing information by virtue of its own multi-layered structure and complexity, is not meant to be understood by the average American citizen. The FRB's daily business is based on its own set of procedures and formulations, operating on multiple levels, beginning with input from regional committees and their sub-committees, ultimately resulting in formulation of an economic strategy presented by the FRB's Board of Governors.

Who owns this banking system? This is difficult to answer as the Fed is not a publicly traded corporation, and issues stock to its member banks and others. It is not required by the Securities and Exchange Commission to publish a list of its major shareholders. Who are its original investors? That too is a point of contention, although by virtue of its stockholder policies, it does not seem that any single investor may hold a majority of shares in the FRB. It has been speculated that behind its original banking institutions are familial dynasties long recognized as among the premiere historic banking families of American and Europe. While no doubt, its structure has to a great degree been modeled on European banking principles, it has not been conclusively proven that control of the FRB resides in any foreign entities or established banking dynasties and remains an open issue. Is it a profitable entity? In a 1995 FRB report, its profits were said to be

$23.9 billion, of which it reported paying the U.S. Treasury $23.4 billion, with $231 million paid to its stockholders.

The existence of a central bank in America has a long and troubled history dating back to the earliest days of the republic. The Constitution of the United States empowers Congress and Congress alone, to print the nation's currency. However, the landmark Federal Reserve Act of 1913, transferred control of America's currency to the Federal Reserve System. This legislation was based on the Aldrich-Vreeland Act of 1907, which in turn, established the National Monetary Commission. Senator Nelson W. Aldrich, the powerful senator from Rhode Island, and grandfather on his maternal side to Nelson Aldrich Rockefeller, was largely responsible for the Aldrich-Vreeland Act, and subsequently became the Chairman of the National Monetary Commission. The Commission's study group reviewed the structures of the great central banks of Europe, which were developed and maintained by European familial dynasties. Senator Aldrich felt these were the right models upon which to base a new central banking system for America.

The final push needed for passage of the Federal Reserve Act, was the panic of 1907, in which the New York banking establishment faced the possibility of failure due to heavy runs on the banks by nervous depositors. Panic extended across the nation, as vast numbers of people withdrew deposits from their regional banks. The panic might have deepened if not for the intervention of financier J.P. Morgan, founder of the great Morgan banking and business dynasty. Morgan pledged large sums of his own money and convinced other New York bankers to do the same to shore up the banking system. At that time, the United States did not have a central bank to inject liquidity back into the market.[79]

With the enactment of the Federal Reserve Act, the nation's economy would now be subject to fluctuation based on the monetary policies of the Federal Reserve Bank and its Board of Governors. But it takes no banking experience to understand the basic problem with printing money based on nothing of intrinsic value and charging the government and people of the United States interest on this currency.

Author James Perloff writes in his work, *The Shadows of Power*, "Essential to controlling a government is the establishment of a central bank, with a monopoly on the country's supply of money and credit. Meyer Rothschild, founder of the world's most powerful European banking dynasty is said to have remarked, "Let me issue and control a nation's money and I care not who writes its laws."[80]

Earlier attempts to create a central bank in the United States had been defeated, but attempts never ceased, as the major financial powers of America and Europe, long viewed the United States as the glittering prize of all the modern nations, ripe for monetary control and profits. The First Bank of the United States (1791-1811) was to a large degree successful in paying off the new nation's war debts and repaying Revolutionary soldiers back wages for their wartime service. But problems arose which Thomas Jefferson explained:

"After the expedient of paper money had exhausted itself, certificates of debt were given to the individual creditors with assurance of payment so soon as the United States [government] should be able. When the . . bill would finally pass the base scramble began. Couriers and relay horses by land, and swift sailing pilot boats by sea, were flying in all directions. Active partners and agents were associated and employed in every state, town, and country neighborhood, and this paper [certificates of debt] was bought up . . as low as two shilling in the pound, before the holder knew that Congress had already provided for its redemption at par. Immense sums were thus filched from the poor and ignorant . . "[81]

The Second Bank of the United States (1813-1836) was an attempt to again foist a privately owned, central bank on the citizens of America, but was abolished by President Andrew Jackson who declared:

"The bold effort the present bank had made to control the government, the distress it had wantonly produced . . are but premonitions of the fate that awaits the American people should they be deluded into a perpetuation of this institution or the establishment of another like it."[82]

The current Federal Reserve mission statement falls into four general areas:

1. conducting the nation's monetary policy by influencing the monetary and credit conditions in the economy in pursuit of maximum employment, stable prices, and moderate long-term interest rates
2. supervising and regulating banking institutions to ensure the safety and soundness of the nation's banking and financial system and to protect the credit rights of consumers
3. maintaining the stability of the financial system and containing systemic risk that may arise in financial markets
4. providing financial services to depository institutions, the U.S. government, and foreign official institutions, including playing a major role in operating the nation's payments system

Following the enactment of the Federal Reserve Act of 1913, the nation suffered the greatest depression in its experience, followed by an additional 13 recessions, up to the recession of 2008, all of which were financial disasters the Federal Reserve Banking System was created to prevent. In 2011, the national debt topped $14 trillion, of which $5.5 trillion could be said to be the direct costs of World War I, II, and the Korean and Vietnam Wars, excluding all in-direct costs.[108] While American citizens have enjoyed the highest standards of living the world has known, a strong argument can be made that the Federal Reserve Banking System, introduced by Senator Nelson Aldrich as the solution to American's banking problems, has failed the American people, with often disastrous consequences for American businesses and citizens.

On June 4, 1963, a virtually unknown Presidential decree, Executive Order 11110, was signed by John Kennedy, transferring authority to the Secretary of the Treasury, to issue silver-backed certificates. While the goals of Executive Order 11110 were limited, Kennedy opened a pathway for the United States Government to regain management of its financial well-being. It was a direct challenge to the Federal Reserve Bank who would, if Kennedy's Executive Order continued, might have its mantle of power relegated to that of competitor, and no longer the primary controller of American currency. Executive Order 11110 gave the Treasury Department the explicit authority: "to issue silver certificates against any silver bullion, silver, or standard silver dollars in the Treasury." If the silver-backed United States Notes were widely circulated, they would have increasingly challenged the demand for Federal Reserve Notes, as the United States Note would be backed by silver, and the Federal Reserve Note would not be backed by anything of intrinsic value. Many theories exist, pro and con, for retaining gold or silver standards, with clear benefits for the stability of M1, while creating limitations based on the availability of gold and silver, along with potential for mismanagement for political gains by subsequent White House administrations.

The final act in releasing all restraints on U.S. currency occurred in August 1971, when President Richard Nixon abandoned the gold standard. From that point forward the U.S. moved to fiat currency, or money without any intrinsic value. Taken together with the Federal Reserve Act, the flood gates preventing unlimited swelling of the national debt were opened wide.

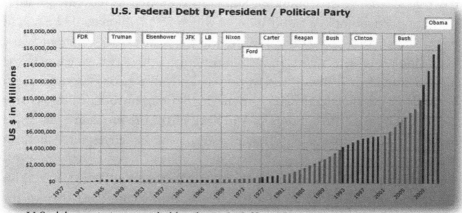

U.S. debt statistics provided by the U.S. Office of Management and Budget.[83]

In 1963, it was reasonable to consider Executive Order 11110 as an opening move for the United States government to regain control of M1. For the Federal Reserve Banking System, it was a slowly ticking time-bomb, ultimately pointed at American and global banking dynasties, who created and profited by the FRB's existence.

Thomas Jefferson once wrote,

"If the America people ever allow private banks to control the issuance of their currencies, first by inflation and then by deflation, the banks and corporations that will grow up around them will deprive the people of all their prosperity until their children will wake up homeless on the continent their fathers conquered."

A century later, another President, statesman, and visionary, Abraham Lincoln wrote in a letter to a friend, about 5 months before his assassination:

"I see in the near future a crisis approaching. It unnerves me and causes me to tremble for the safety of my country. The money powers prey upon the nation in times of peace and conspire against it in times of adversity. It is more despotic than a monarchy, more insolent than autocracy, more selfish than bureaucracy. It denounces, as public enemies, all who question its methods or throw light upon its crimes. I have two great enemies, the Southern Army in front of me & the financial institutions at the rear, the latter is my greatest foe. Corporations have been enthroned, and an era of corruption in high places will follow, and the money power of the country will endeavor to prolong its reign by working upon the prejudices of the people until the wealth is aggregated in the hands of a few, and the Republic is destroyed."

There is no doubt that the Federal Reserve Act of 1913, versus John Kennedy's Executive Order 11110, are opposing strategies for the control of the nation's economic direction. They are mutually exclusive. Both could not exist at the same time. The silver-backed value of the United States Note, created by JFK's Executive Order 1110, would, in time, eventually destroy the confidence and effectiveness of the Federal Reserve Note, and by extension, the Federal Banking System.

All U.S. Presidents residing in the oval office since 1913, have known Federal Reserve Notes issued as legal currency were contrary to the spirit of the mandate written into the Constitution of the United States of America. None have dared to challenge the power of the Federal Reserve Banking System save John Kennedy. Executive Order 11110 was simply too controversial, with its inestimable power to re-direct the economic power and profits of the most prosperous nation the world has ever known.

"We are bigger than General Motors."

— MEIER LANSKY, ACCOUNTANT, ORGANIZED
CRIME SYNDICATE

THE ATTORNEY GENERAL AND THE DONS

The Kennedy's were cognizant of the tentacle-like reach of organized crime into the businesses of America. Clan patriarch Joseph Kennedy himself, had profited from business dealings with Organized Crime during prohibition. No doubt he passed along to his sons and understanding that the Mob was always willing to collude with respectable men of resource who worked in the light of day, while the Mob operated behind the shadows of anonymity.

In 1957, State Senator John D. McClellan headed a Congressional committee known as The United States Senate Select Committee on Improper Activities in Labor and Management. Its chief legal counsel was Robert Kennedy. McClellan stated:

"The existence of such a criminal organization known as Cosa Nostra is frightening. This organization attempts to be a form of government unto itself and outside of the law. This tightly knit association of professional criminals demands and gets complete dedication and unquestioned obedience of its members to orders instructions and commands from the ruling authority or boss . . or bosses thereof. Family, religion and country are all secondary and required to be subservient to the interests of this vicious criminal syndicate."

When John Kennedy won the 1960 Presidential election, the American families of organized crime wondered if, under Attorney General Robert Kennedy, their power in America would soon be under attack by the Department of Justice. La Cosa Nostra's leaders fully understood the intensity shown by Robert Kennedy in the McClellan hearings, and the political advantage to be gained by the Kennedy brothers at the expense of Mob operations. Mob leadership had attempted to buy off the Kennedy's with discreet contributions to John Kennedy's political campaign. In addition, had not the Mob assisted in John Kennedy's presidential campaign by pushing union labor into Kennedy's corner? However, prior to 1960, despite efforts such as the McClellan Committee, the Mafia was as powerful as ever. Its own Cosa Nostra commission was theoretically, its own self-ruling body, with partial jurisdiction over the most important American crime families. By 1960, the Mob controlled large segments of the trucking and construction industries, facilitated money laundering, made use of Teamster funds for bribery, and provided transportation for drugs and guns across state lines.

By the mid 1950s, the Mob understood continual factional warfare was its own worst enemy, since no existing government agency devoted resources to challenge, let alone defeat La Cosa Nostra. Mutual accommodation between competing crime families became necessary to ensure survival and profitability. It was acknowledged there was more than enough opportunity in America, for a group of well-coordinated Organized Crime dynasties, provided regional boundaries were delineated and respected. In many ways, Organized Crime in America taken as a whole, operated much like a true familial dynasty, able to survive and prosper through the changing landscape of war, politics, and the American economy. Mob leadership understood the necessity for maintaining power though familial, next-in-line succession.

The Mob had flourished in America under Edgar J. Hoover's watch as FBI Director, which began in 1924. It is reasonable to believe the highly developed, Federal Bureau of Investigation was aware of the nationwide influence and power of the Mob. During World War II, the FBI had been primarily responsible for identifying foreign spies and their networks and had performed admirably. The FBI had watched the rise of other investigative agencies, such as the Office of Naval Intelligence (ONI), and the CIA, become formidable organizations as part of America's post-war commitment to intelligence gathering. While the CIA and ONI focused on identifying and combating America's foreign and maritime threats, the FBI was, and remains, the nations primary domestic law enforcement agency

Since his appointment as Director J. Edgar Hoover, had been a dynamic and driving force in shaping the FBI into a world renown police agency. By 1957, he was a formidable and admired American icon, but began to appear weak and ineffective against the energy and commitment of Robert Kennedy's highly effective team of Justice Department prosecutors. It was Hoover who stylized the header of own personal memos to contain the letters S.O.G. (Seat of Government). After this significant challenge and subsequent injury to the Director's carefully polished reputation, S.O.G. would no doubt have a much more dampened effect on those who worked with and admired the Director.

Hoover had focused Bureau resources on tracking communist organizers and sympathizers, suspected spies in America, and Hoover's popularly advertised "Ten Most Wanted" list. Prior to 1957, Hoover, consistently refused to acknowledge Organized Crime as a serious threat to American society. In his book, *The Bureau, The Secret History of the FBI*, author Ronald Kessler reports Hoover's comments toward the existence of organized crime as "no single individual or coalition of racketeers dominates organized crime across the country." There was no such thing as "organized crime" or a "Mafia" Hoover said. The claim that there was a national crime syndicate was denounced by Director Hoover as "baloney". [84]

The first public setback for Hoover occurred on November 14, 1957, when New York Police Sargent Edgar L. Croswell, noticed a long, black limousine, followed by dozens more, approaching a secluded estate in the hills outside the village of Appalachin. Croswell obtained the identities of sixty-three Mafia leaders. They came from every part of the country, instantly rendering Hoover's disavowal of organized crime's existence untenable.

The second climactic event, seven years later, were the statements under oath of Mafia soldier Joseph Valachi, who in the 1963 Senate Permanent

Subcommittee on Investigations, revealed the full extent of Mob control over the country. Valachi, a mob lieutenant in the Cosa Nostra family headed by Don Vito Genovese, had turned government informant. With his testimony, the nation had its first look into the Mob's inner workings, and its inter-related, nation-wide structure was laid bare for all to see.

There are popular theories why Hoover took a hands-off approach to the mafia, some have validity, others are of a more sordid nature. Robert Kennedy's relentless pursuit of La Cosa Nostra had raised the unanswerable question of why the FBI ignored the world's largest organized crime syndicate. Author Kessler reports the statements of William G. Hundley, a Justice Department lawyer, who headed the interrogation of Joseph Valachi, as saying, "All of the Attorney Generals were afraid of him [Hoover]. They never knew what he had on them." Robert Kennedy was the only attorney general willing to take on the Director of the Federal Bureau of Investigation. [85]

Robert Kennedy was determined to have the Department of Justice bring indictments and convictions of organized crime members. As a result of those efforts, La Cosa Nostra would experience the highest level of government intrusion in their profitable businesses, since the days of Elliot Ness and his G-Men. Convictions against organized crime families rose 800 percent. The Mob was on the defensive. Previously untouchable Mafia dons, such as Florida's Santos Trafficante, Chicago's Sam Giancana, and Teamster boss Jimmy Hoffa, felt the heat of Justice Department investigations. They would not forgive, nor forget.

But the Kennedy family itself was deeply conflicted about the opportunities Organized Crime presented. In his 1978 biography, *Robert Kennedy and His Times*, Arthur Schlesinger described Joe Kennedy, Sr. as being "deeply, emotionally opposed" to his son Robert's participation on the (McClellan) committee, believing that "an investigation . . . would not produce reform, it would only turn the labor movement against the Kennedy family." Joe Kennedy allegedly went to the extent of asking his good friend, Supreme Court Justice William O. Douglas, to intervene with Bobby. Douglas reported to Joe that Bobby felt the committee represented "too great an opportunity" to give up.

Why did the Kennedy's challenge a powerful, well-entrenched powerful institution such as the Mob, known for their history of violent retribution. The answer is in step with John Kennedy's approach to the re-direction of power in America. Confrontation with Organized Crime was a deadly power struggle between the Judicial and Executive Branches of the United States Government, and a powerful, illegal, nation-wide institution, operating outside of the laws of the government. By the FBI's own estimates, the net worth of the Mafia in America, reached over a trillion dollars at its height, since its first reported appearance toward the close of America's Civil War.

The struggle to break the power of Organized Crime, mirrored the Kennedy's struggle to curtail the independent power of another all-powerful institution, seemingly operating outside the direction of the government, the CIA. Moving against both organizations was a bold gamble, and the message was undoubtedly perceived in different ways. Justice Department action against the Mob carried the implication that even as contract employees of the Central Intelligence Agency, Mob members would not necessarily receive immunity from government prosecution. The second message was a corollary of the first, demonstrating the CIA would no longer have the power to protect its Organized Crime assets from Justice Department investigation. However, both messages would be compromised if John or Robert Kennedy themselves worked in association with Organized Crime. There is compelling evidence that John Kennedy had repeated dealings with Chicago Mob Boss Sam Giancana. Robert Kennedy knew that Mob assets were contracted to assist in the elimination of Fidel Castro within Operation Mongoose, which Robert managed up until November 1963. The Kennedy's were playing an extremely dangerous power game, in attempting to curtail the power of both organizations, each dedicated to rendering their adversaries fully defeated or eliminated.

John and Robert Kennedy challenged historically entrenched powers with the resources and legal power of both the Executive and Judicial Branches of government, working as one closely synchronized force. There is no doubt this was a formidable, and unprecedented challenge to the CIA and the Mob. These challenges were essential components in the struggle for power in America in the final year of the Kennedy Presidency. It was a power exercised by the Kennedy brothers with a growing sense of confidence as the 1964 elections approached, where the extraordinary tandem of JFK and RFK could only be halted by defeat at the polls. The upcoming election was perceived by those competing for power in America as a point of critical mass.

Joe Kennedy Sr. counseled his sons to accommodate themselves to existing powers. They did not heed his advice.

*"And by virtue of the power, and for the purpose aforesaid,
I do order and declare that all persons held as slaves
within said designated States, and parts of States, are,
and henceforward shall be free;*

— ABRAHAM LINCOLN, 16TH PRESIDENT OF THE UNITED
STATES OF AMERICA -

FREEDOM RIDERS

Fast forward ninety-eight years from Abraham Lincoln's driving desire for passage of the 13th Amendment to 1961, and find America still deeply conflicted over the issue of racial equality. From 1863, until John Kennedy's dispatch of federal officers in 1962, to force the entry of James Meredith into the University of Mississippi, there was a continuum moral intent at the Executive level to mend the social fabric of America. Kennedy's record shows a strategy of step-by-step actions to force fundamental change in the social order of the nation. There would be conflict between states preferences and the Federal Government, much as existed in Lincoln's time. Kennedy's efforts were to ultimately bear fruit, in terms of equality before the law, in much the same way as Lincoln's 13th Amendment.

In the latter part of the 1950's, the children of non-white America, were beginning to sense change. It began as a small, growing force, and lasted through the blazing summer heat in larger cities, fanning flames of dis-satisfaction over morally undeniable rights. By 1961, the Civil Rights movement had become a full-fledged firestorm, challenging complacency and fear, bringing America to the realization that states rights alone would no longer remain a sufficient court of law to resolve this issue. African American spokesmen were openly challenging white America to face the issue of equality. Their early attempts at changing social and cultural traditions were dis-organized, spontaneous, and often dangerous.

In Washington D.C., an American President realized only the Executive and Judicial Branches of the government had the resources to begin enforcement of desegregation, who's time had arrived. Although, even Kennedy acknowledged there were limits to what could be accomplished by amending the laws of the land.

Excerpts from John Kennedy's special televised address to the nation on June 11, 1963, on the subject of civil rights in America contains these passages:

"The fires of frustration and discord are burning in every city, North and South, where legal remedies are not at hand. Redress is sought in the streets, in demonstrations, parades, and protests which create tensions and threaten violence and threaten lives.

We face, therefore, a moral crisis as a country and as a people. It cannot be met by repressive police action. It cannot be left to increased demonstrations in the streets. It cannot be quieted by token moves or talk. It is time to act in the Congress, in your State and local legislative body and, above all, in all of our daily lives.

. . . this is a problem which faces us all--in every city of the North as well as the South. . . It seems to me that these are matters which concern us all, not merely Presidents or Congressmen or Governors, but every citizen of the United States."

Kennedy Administration tactics, often consisted of head-on confrontation, and legally challenging local, state, and national authorities and institutions, to re-evaluate their positions towards racial equality in America.

A review of the timeline of John and Robert Kennedy's actions in the area of Civil Rights, shows how the practices of almost two hundred years of racial discord reached a tipping point, and were opposed by the active involvement of the Federal Government.

1961

May 21 – Martin Luther King, Freedom Riders, and a congregation of 1,500 at the First Baptist Church in Montgomery are attacked by segregationists; Attorney General Robert F. Kennedy sends federal marshals to protect them.

May 29 – Attorney General RFK petitions the Interstate Commerce Commission to enforce desegregation in interstate travel.

September 23 – The Interstate Commerce Commission, at RFK's insistence, ends discrimination in interstate travel, effective November 1, 1961.

1962

February 26 – Segregated transportation facilities, both interstate and intrastate, are ruled unconstitutional by U.S. Supreme Court.

April 3 – The Defense Department orders racial integration of military reserve units, except the National Guard.

September 30 – October 1 – Supreme Court Justice Hugo Black orders James Meredith admitted to Ole' Miss' College. Rioting ensues. Robert Kennedy calls in 500 U.S. Marshalls to take control, supported by the 70th Army Engineer Combat Battalion from Ft Campbell, Kentucky. To bolster this force, President Kennedy sends U.S. Army military police from the 503rd Military Police Battalion, and called in troops from the Mississippi Army National Guard.[86]

November 20 – JFK signs Executive Order 11063, banning segregation in federally funded housing.

1963

June 19 – JFK sends to Congress his proposed Civil Rights Act.

November 22 – President Kennedy is assassinated.

1964

July 2 – Civil Rights Act of 1964 signed by Lyndon Johnson.

The Civil Rights Act of 1964, initiated during JFK's administration, and signed into law by President Lyndon Johnson, was the culmination of the emotionally charged events of the previous three years. Taken together, the legislative actions taken by Lincoln, John and Robert Kennedy, and Lyndon Johnson, were necessary advances required of America to fulfill the promise boldly stated in her defining documents. The ultimate rewards were the potential opportunities for a more equitable sharing of power in America. It sought to level the playing field of opportunity through a legislative action. It ended the more blatant and violent aspects of discrimination and provided America's minority citizens a greater share in the nation's educational, employment, and housing opportunities. It forced those who remained undecided, or resistant, to face a new moral standard of equality. And, as with Abraham Lincoln's 13th Amendment, John Kennedy's efforts did not achieve all they were intended to accomplish.

*"The President shall be Commander in Chief of the Army
and Navy of the United States,
and of the Militia of the several States . . ."*

— ARTICLE 2, SECTION 2, CLAUSE 1 OF THE
UNITED STATES CONSTITUTION

JFK AND THE COLDEST WARRIORS

In the areas of military, foreign, and economic policy, America, in 1960, was largely guided by the doctrines put forth in the Quantico I and Quantico II Studies, along with the *Prospect for America, The Rockefeller Panel Reports*, developed by Nelson Rockefeller, and his elite consortium of advisors. The resulting national governmental policies set in motion enormous military and financial commitments, and potential profits for decades to come. There would be tremendous pressure on the incoming president to unequivocally support and champion these undertakings. From a military standpoint, opposition and hesitancy would suggest weakness and lack of resolve, qualities detested by America's highly motivated cold warriors. From an economic perspective, a decrease in commitment to sanctioned Cold War economic strategy, represented a tremendous risk to the immense profits expected by America's major investment and banking institutions.

Kennedy's predecessor in the White House, former General Dwight Eisenhower, departed the stage of American politics with his now famous warning to the incoming president and Congress. His watchword was vigilance against the opportunities that Cold War doctrine had confirmed on America's military and economic powers. Eisenhower's Farewell Address to the nation on January 17, 1961, clearly stated the dangers the Kennedy Administration would face from existing financial powers:

"This conjunction of an immense military establishment and a large arms industry is new in the American experience. The total influence – economic, political, even spiritual – is felt in every city, every Statehouse, every office of the Federal government. We recognize the imperative need for this development. Yet we must not fail to comprehend its grave implications. Our toil, resources and livelihood are all involved; so is the very structure of our society.

In the councils of government, we must guard against the acquisition of unwarranted influence, whether sought or unsought, by the military-industrial complex. The potential for the disastrous rise of misplaced power exists and will persist.

We must never let the weight of this combination endanger our liberties or democratic processes. We should take nothing for granted. Only an alert and knowledgeable citizenry can compel the proper meshing of the huge industrial and military machinery of defense with our peaceful methods and goals, so that security and liberty may prosper together."

Following the conclusion of World War II, and the early days of the Cold War, American military strategy was focused on Southeast Asia, Cuba, Berlin, and South America. The Korean War was an engagement fought with American armed forces providing 88% of United Nations force facing North Korean, Chinese, and Soviet military forces. During the 1961 Berlin Crisis, American military units reported to John Kennedy as Commander-in-Chief, through his personal envoy, Army General Lucius Clay. However, in Saigon, Havana, and South American capitals, the Central Intelligence Agency was leading extensive programs of covert warfare, aimed at the destabilization, or overthrow of nations, leaders, or groups, estimated to be in opposition to U.S. military or economic strategy. CIA action recommendations were then included in National Security Council agendas for presidential review. The question of who was truly determining foreign policy actions, and the application of America's military resources, began to resonate through the White House. Did John

Kennedy, as Commander-in-Chief, truly control the direction and application of American military force, if in fact, CIA-originated operations precipitated military action between regular armed forces of the United States and its adversaries?

John Kennedy's inherited military leaders had risen to prominence in the Roosevelt, Truman, and Eisenhower administrations, and were now major voices within the U.S. military and CIA establishments. These dedicated warriors had been enforcing the doctrines formulated in the Quantico I and II Reports, and within the *Prospect for America, The Rockefeller Panel Reports*. To support these policies, U.S. military leadership now had within their capability, an exponentially increasing capability to deliver crushing payloads of nuclear, or conventional firepower, to any location on the globe, and defeat their ideological enemies per their pre-scripted plans.

It is significant that President Kennedy had extremely mercurial and often adversarial relationships with three of these most dedicated and powerful cold warriors: Air Force Generals Curtis LeMay, Edward Landsdale, and Charles Cabell. Cabell held the position of Deputy Director, CIA. Landsdale had personally lead CIA covert operations in Vietnam and Cuba. LeMay was Air Force Chief of Staff and controlled America's Strategic Air Command. All three generals played significant roles in the most threatening crises defining the Kennedy Administration, the Bay of Pigs, the Cuban Missile Crisis, and Vietnam.

General Cabell was appointed to the position of Deputy Director of the CIA on April 23, 1953, second in command to CIA Director Allen Dulles. Cabell held this position during the formative years of the CIA's development. It was most likely Cabell, who initially briefed Kennedy on the status of CIA Cuban invasion plans during the 1960 Presidential Election campaign. The *San Diego Times* reported that a Kennedy campaign spokesman told the newspaper that General Cabell had come aboard Kennedy's campaign plane to relate "if there is anything important that he needed to know to fulfill his responsibility as a nominee for President." Reportedly, Cabell discussed a CIA study dealing with current global "hot spots" at the request of Robert Kennedy. The study included potential problems with the Soviet Union, the Middle East, Southeast Asia, and "possible action by Cuba against Guantanamo Naval Base," the American naval station located on the eastern tip of Cuba.

In December of 1959, Allen Dulles had approved "thorough consideration be given to the elimination of Fidel Castro, in the form of a typical Latin political upheaval." On March 17, 1960, nine months before JFK reached the White House, President Eisenhower authorized the CIA to organize, train, and equip Cuban refugees as a guerrilla force to overthrown Castro.[87] During August and September, the CIA was pursuing discussions with Organized Crime, seeking their involvement in assassination attempts against Castro. One month after Kennedy's inauguration, the first failed attempts were made to assassinate Fidel Castro using CIA and Mob assets. [88]

The prior knowledge of CIA planning to remove Fidel Castro, allowed Kennedy to seize the initiative and portray himself as an aggressive advocate for eliminating a communist stronghold located 50 miles off-shore. In the November Presidential debates. Kennedy's aggressive position forced Republican candidate, Richard Nixon, to adopt an opposing stance, denouncing Kennedy's position as a violation of international law demonstrating a lack of respect for national sovereignty that would trouble America's Latin American neighbors.

It was an ironic reversal of roles. Nixon, as Vice President in Eisenhower's cabinet, and member of "Ike's" National Security team, was fully aware of, and advocated for CIA intervention in Cuba. Nixon was, as Author Hersh states in *The Dark Side of Camelot*, "trapped", and responded by urging the CIA to remove Castro from power before the election. Hersh states,

"In *RN [Richard Nixon]*, Nixon recalled his assumption that Kennedy had been briefed by Allen Dulles about Cuba and had chosen to take political advantage of that information. Kennedy's statement, he [Nixon] said, jeopardized the project, which could succeed only if it were supported and implemented secretly . . .

I had no choice but to take a completely opposite stand and oppose Kennedy's advocacy of open intervention in Cuba."

Kennedy's tactics required stalling a successful Cuban invasion until after the 1960 election, as a successful pre-election strike against Castro, by the Eisenhower White House, may have tipped the balance decidedly in Nixon's favor. This was a scenario the Kennedy's did not favor. Joe Kennedy, Sr. and Jack, had worked hard, and paid well, during the previous four years, to create the most favorable conditions for JFK's candidacy.

Joseph Kennedy's efforts at elevating the social position of the Kennedy family into the upper reaches of affluent Washington and Palm Beach society, afforded Jack close personal contact with CIA Director, Allen Dulles, and CIA Deputy Director for Plans, Richard Bissell, who controlled CIA black ops. Bissell told a former CIA colleague from the Bay of Pigs, Grayston Lynch, that he and Kennedy were "friends from before" as Lynch recalled in a 1997 interview for *The Dark Side of Camelot*. Bissell made it very clear, Lynch said, that their personal relationship had existed long before Kennedy got to the White House. [89]

CIA Director, Allen Dulles revealed in his oral history for the Kennedy Library in 1964, that he and JFK had "fairly continuous" contact beginning in the early 1950's when he [Dulles] was Deputy Director of the CIA, "because my trips to Palm Beach were quite frequent. He [JFK] was often there, and whenever he was there, we always got together. [90] Jack Kennedy, Dulles added, was always trying to get information. I don't mean secrets or things of that kind particularly, but to get himself informed. He wanted to get my views . . . we had many, many talks together." [91]

By bringing Kennedy into CIA planning, and aware of Richard Nixon's White House participation in Cuban plans, Allen Dulles could be content that he now had both presidential candidates in position to approve CIA plans. Those plans called for the removal of a major embarrassment to America's intelligence community - Fidel Castro's communist Cuba, a strategic forward base for Soviet Russian nuclear capability, located 50 miles off the coast of Florida.

John Kennedy clearly out-maneuvered Richard Nixon in the 1960 presidential election debates. An important part of that strategy, was Kennedy's prior relationship with CIA leadership, enabled by the power of Joseph Kennedy's wealth and social connections. Nothing was being left to chance in Kennedy's quest for the White House, and the classified knowledge secured prior to the election, was essential in trapping and conquering the last remaining hurdle, Richard Nixon

In the games of high-stakes power politics, knowledge is the essential ingredient for survival and success. There was a growing acknowledgement, and perhaps preference, by the men who kept the secrets, in favor of a Kennedy presidency. Allen Dulles was one of two appointments announced by newly-elected President John Kennedy on the day after his election, the other being J. Edgar Hoover at the FBI. Arthur Schlesinger, in his memoir, would recall the reappointment announcements as part of the president-elect's "strategy of reassurance." But who was being reassured? The electorate, or the institutions that were supposed to serve them? The latter would have been more politically expedient, as Kennedy did not have the requisite political muscle to initiate a change of this magnitude. He needed Dulles and Hoover's support and cooperation during the first years of his presidency.

Now the sitting president, and the highest officer of the American government, John Kennedy was looking more closely at the risks posed by the invasion of Cuba. Although Nixon had been outmaneuvered, Kennedy properly understood Nixon's argument during their election debate. It was a legitimate position, based on the doctrine of national sovereignty, and the use of American armed forces in the Southern Hemisphere. He was aware of Dulles's and Bissell's roles in planning the upcoming Cuban invasion. He knew of the involvement of CIA Generals Cabell and Landsdale. If somehow the plan failed, during execution, he was aware of Air Force General Curtis LeMay's outlook and eagerness to push the conflict into a full-blown strategic air attack, using LeMay's Strategic Air Command forces.

In March, 1960, a top-secret policy paper outlining U.S. actions against Cuba was drafted entitled, "A program of Covert Action Against the Castro Regime" (code-named JMARC) to bring about the replacement of the Castro regime with one more acceptable to the United States. The mission was to be carried out in such a manner as to avoid any appearance of U.S. intervention. President-elect John Kennedy was given a copy of the JMARC proposal by Richard Bissell and Allen Dulles, in Palm Beach Florida, on 18 November 1960, ten days after the presidential election. Later, in March 1961, President Kennedy asked the Joint Chiefs of Staff to evaluate the JMARC project. The JCS reported an overall success rating of 30%. Therefore, they could not recommend that Kennedy should approve the JMARC project. Kennedy sent the JMARC plan back to the CIA for modification. After the plan was revised, Kennedy approved it, despite continued objections by his military advisors, and his own misgivings. It was likely a combination of factors resulting in John Kennedy acquiescing to CIA plans:

First, it was the CIA's disclosure of their planning to regain control of Cuba, imparted to JFK before the 1960 election, that presented Kennedy with the opportunity to outmaneuver Richard Nixon. Kennedy would likely have felt a debt of gratitude to the CIA, and in particular, to CIA leadership, or rather a reward he felt must be re-paid.

Second, since those frenetic days of the 1960 Presidential campaign, John Kennedy had consistently portrayed himself as an unwavering opponent of communism. A reversal of his support for the Cuban invasion would have been difficult to explain to the American people, and to the dedicated anti-Castro cold warriors in the CIA, and the U.S. military, along with the fervently anti-Castro community in Florida, now actively involved in CIA invasion plans.

Third, on 18 August 1960, the Eisenhower administration had approved a budget of $13 million for the Cuban operation. Operation planning involved a complex cross-structure of military preparedness, including thousands of invasion and support personnel, fully supplied and armed. In addition, there were supporting American military assets, consisting of aircraft and naval vessels, their supporting crews, and secretly-funded airbases in Central American countries. Dismantling this powerful force would have sent alarming signals that JFK's cold war support was wavering and put the CIA in the embarrassing position of seemingly training this significant force for propaganda purposes only.

Fourth, John Kennedy had never known political defeat. JFK's rise to the Presidency was defined by success. It is likely that Kennedy expected his luck would hold and subsequently raise his popularity to dizzying heights as America's, and the free world's, undisputed leader in the fight against communism. A successful regime change in Cuba would have made Kennedy a resolute leader to be reckoned with by the Soviet Union, a man not hesitating to take risks. Success in Cuba would have given Kennedy a stronger bargaining position in future encounters with Soviet leadership. Most importantly, winning in Cuba, would have guaranteed victory in the 1964 presidential election.

Fifth, the same could be said of the CIA, who's track record up until 1961, was one of success in seizing and directing global power through covert operations. Kennedy was gambling on the continued success of CIA planners to enhance his own political future. Both outgoing and incoming presidents, were presented with CIA information suggesting a CIA sponsored coup would be legitimized by a spontaneous uprising of the Cuban people - although this was a prediction never based on sound information, and ultimately proved incorrect.

Sixth, from an economic viewpoint, South American population in 1960 was around 200 million people, spread over an area of 6.8 million square miles, greater than the United States, in both population and area. With the elimination of a communist threat, the fourth largest continent on Earth was the prize to be secured, with its vast economic and resource potential. With America's global-economic potential unfolding as planned, it would have been heresy and certain political death for an American president to slow the advance of capitalism into the relatively poorer nations of South America.

Conversely, a communist controlled Cuba, could become for American financiers, JFK, and the CIA, the portal from which a genuine anti-capitalist, anti-imperialist, grass-roots revolution of discontent could destroy decades of American economic planning. Cuba had a population of 7 million people, on an island of 42,000 square miles, but the basic problem was that Fidel Castro's revolutionary coup was a successful and popular uprising supported by the majority of the Cuban population. Castro had overthrown a corrupt Cuban government that had executed thousands of its own citizens, and that had richly benefitted from cooperation with American corporate and Organized Crime interests. A Marxist revolution had improbably succeeded on an island 50 miles from the glittering lights of the "capitalist" playgrounds of Norte America, where American military forces maintained a major naval base at Guantanamo Bay. It was inconceivable, but undeniable, that Castro and his iconic lieutenant, Ernesto "Che" Guevara, had succeeded beyond their wildest dreams. The people of South America were astounded by the "Cuban model," viewing it as a stirring modern-day battle, a popular uprising between the people's heroes, over the corporate "Goliath" that America symbolized to the common men of the southern hemisphere. Cuba, unchecked, could become a lasting symbol of American failure to defend its own sphere of influence, and undermine American power implicit in the Monroe Doctrine.

The overthrow of Castro was to be modeled on the CIA operation "PBSUCCESS," which had taken place in Guatemala, in 1954. American business interests had spurred President Eisenhower to approve the overthrow of the democratically elected regime of President Jacobo Arbenz. Arbenz had promoted popular reforms, including expanded voter rights, workers ability to organize, legitimization of political parties, and public debate. But it was primarily Arbenz' agrarian land reforms, enabling seizure of lands for poverty-stricken peasants, that prompted American corporations to act. One such entity, the United Fruit Company, appealed directly, to both Presidents Truman and Eisenhower, to act militarily and politically against Arbenz. Eisenhower's Secretary of State, John Foster Dulles, and his law firm, Sullivan and Cromwell, had negotiated much of the 42 per cent of the fertile land of Guatemala owned by United Fruit. Dulles's younger brother Allen, CIA Director under Eisenhower, sat on United Fruit's board of directors. John and Allen Dulles were on United

Fruit's payroll for thirty-eight years. Both brothers played a leading role in influencing foreign policy and carrying out CIA-sponsored activity to support those policies. "PBSUCCESS" was an astounding example of the CIA's new strategic and tactical covert action plans. To shield corporate involvement, Richard Bissell, CIA Deputy Director of black ops, issued a strong denial of any collusion between American businesses and the U.S. government in this operation, although one would think that to disguise any possible CIA involvement, the denial should have been issued by the U.S. State Department.

At 7 a.m. on April 18, 1961 Deputy Director Richard Bissell, had the most unwelcome task of advising President Kennedy that the CIA-trained invasion force was pinned down on the beaches at the Bay of Pigs, and encircled by Castro's forces. Bissell asked Kennedy to authorize deployment

President John Kennedy and Nelson Rockefeller confer at the White House on April 27, 1961, ten days after American-trained Cuban invasion forces were defeated at the Bay of Pigs.

of regular American armed forces to rescue a rapidly failing CIA operation. Both he and Allen Dulles had fully expected the President to say yes "when the chips were down." Instead, John F. Kennedy, President of the United States, Commander-in-Chief of U.S. Armed Forces, as defined in Article 2, Section 2, Clause 1 of the United States Constitution told his CIA officers, "no."

With this refusal, John Kennedy had taken a major step in regaining control of America's foreign policy. It was his first clear signal that demonstrated he was not bound by the Quantico blueprints for confrontation with the Soviet Union. Kennedy then publicly assumed responsibility for the failed invasion. Bissell and Dulles were removed from their positions of leadership in the CIA. The struggle for control of power in America was intensifying.

John Kennedy was politically adroit and understood that his actions and message were not aimed solely at CIA leadership, but at their sponsors, the dynasties that had created Cold War strategy, for the continuation of global warfare, their own enrichment, and the expansion of the infrastructure President Eisenhower had warned about in his Farewell Address. Defeat at the Bay of Pigs meant many things to domestic and foreign agencies, military staffs, and their foot soldiers, but for John Kennedy, it was a point of no return. He had broken faith with America's most powerful dynasty, choosing to follow his own vision for America

Kennedy and his closest advisors attempted to ensure that CIA leadership would not lead the administration into further unsuccessful adventures. The Kennedy Presidential memorandum to accomplish this change was National Security Action Memorandum (NSAM) No. 55, issued on June 28, 1961. If fully enacted, NSAM No. 55 would exclude the Central Intelligence Agency from providing primary intelligence to the President. Henceforth his principle advisors would be the Joint Chiefs of Staff. This message was understood by CIA hierarchy, as an end to the CIA's reign as the highest planning body for the direction of United States covert military forces. The implications were also understood at the highest levels of American economic leadership. American foreign policy would now be in the hands of its elected leaders, and no longer under the control of the nation's economic powers and their agents.

These action memorandums were never to be enforced. As L. Fletcher Prouty states in *JFK,*

"Kennedy asserted a power of the presidency that he assumed he had, but when his orders were delivered to the men to whom they were addressed, he discovered that his power was all but meaningless. His directives were quietly placed in the bureaucratic files and forgotten. There have been few times in the history of this nation when the limits of the power of the President have been so nakedly exposed."

In a whirling, chaotic, summer of confusing intentions, and over-heated emotions within the White House, Pentagon, and the CIA, signals from John Kennedy indicated he wished to continue the battle against communist Cuba and Fidel Castro. On November 30, 1961, seven months after the Bay of Pigs fiasco, and 5 months after authorizing NSAM No. 55, another abrupt change of administration policy took place. Kennedy authorized a new combined effort of U.S. governmental agencies. It's purpose was to create conditions that would bring about an internal revolt against Castro by October 1962. The "Cuban Project," also known as "Operation Mongoose," involved the CIA, State Department, the Department of Defense, the Joint Chiefs of Staff, the U.S. Army, the departments of the Treasury, Commerce, and Immigration. Kennedy approved the selection of CIA operative, Air Force Major General Edward Landsdale, as mastermind for this project, seemingly in opposition to the chain-of-command responsibilities he had hoped to change in NSAM No. 55.

Edward Landsdale was a unique military officer, who through his personal courage and force of personality, played a significant role in the covert military history of the Cold War. He was a man of action, and was in many ways, a true disciple of Chinese warfare philosopher, Sun Tzu, the real or mythical author of the much-studied work, *The Art of War,* written around 500 B.C. This work advocates clandestine warfare utilizing spies, espionage, and deception to defeat an enemy.[93]

When John Kennedy first asumed office he received two important briefings. One was from outgoing President Dwight D. Eisenhower, who cautioned Kennedy about increased involvement in Vietnam. The other briefing was given by then Colonel Edward G. Landsdale on current conditions in Vietnam. Some of those present at the second briefing, believed Kennedy intended to make Landsdale the next ambassador to Saigon. Indeed, the new President commended Landsdale for his excellent report, and informed Landsdale he could expect to be sent back to Vietnam in a high capacity.[92]

Years before, in 1953, Landsdale's first major cold war assignment, he successfully applied Sun Tzu's techniques to unseat Philippine president Elpido Quirino. With his skill and field credentials established, Landsdale was then assigned to the Vietnam peninsula to develop and employ American counter-insurgency tactics to check the expansion of communist China, and its southern ally, North Vietnam. On January 29, 1954, Allen Dulles, along with CIA Deputy Director Charles Cabell, appointed Colonel Landsdale, as an "unconventional warfare officer" to assist the French military in their fight to retain Vietnam as a French Colony. This marked the beginning of CIA intervention in Indochina.[94] In Landsdale's words:

"Dulles turned to me and said that it had been decided that I was to go to Vietnam to help the Vietnamese, much as I had helped the Filipinos."

Note that Dulles had ordered Landsdale to support the Vietnamese and not the French. France's colonial involvement in Vietnam was subsequently to end in June 1954, following the Battle of Dein Bien Phu, and the signing of the Geneva Accords. Landsdale was then instrumental in establishing the Saigon Military Mission (SMM) in South Vietnam. The SMM became the center for CIA counter-insurgent activity, and the operations center for American military involvement in Vietnam. In his landmark 1992 book, *JFK*, author Fletcher L. Prouty explains "Landsdale would continue to exploit the cover of an air force officer, but he was always an agent of the CIA, and his actual bosses were always CIA."

Within JFK's Operation Mongoose, Landsdale was now coordinating an immense government-wide program of covert military action. Overall control of the project was placed in the hands of Attorney General Robert Kennedy, who represented the President's wishes, and provided the necessary shield of deniability for his brother.

While Operation Mongoose was gathering momentum, the Soviet Union was moving resolutely to secure Cuba, as their beachhead near America's shores. John Kennedy's soft response to the Berlin Crisis, and at the Bay of Pigs, likely convinced Soviet hard-liners that now was the time to move against the young President, who showed he could be outmaneuvered in hard confrontation. The Soviets likely enflamed Castro's fears that another CIA-lead invasion was imminent. Castro was persuaded to accept Russian medium-range missiles, and short-range tactical missiles, equipped with nuclear warheads. It would be an astounding strategic and tactical coup in the Cold War chess game, exposing North American cities to accurate first-strike capability. This would balance the stakes, since the United States had virtually encircled the Soviet Union with missile launch sites, by establishing the North Atlantic Treaty Alliance (NATO). Soviet Cold War planners were both right, and almost deadly wrong, in their assessment of the American response. They underestimated the immense pressure on the young president to unleash the weapons systems that American leadership had been preparing for a decade, to fully defeat the Soviet Union.

Air Force Four-Star General Curtis LeMay was one of America's most influential cold warriors. He had transitioned from innovative strategist during World War II, to a key voice in Cold War air power strategy. During World War II, he was instrumental in the defeat of Japan through the overwhelming application of air power. Napalm fire-bombing of Japan's largest cities, a LeMay tactic, burned the heart out of Japan's war-making industry, and left her urban populations in a near-medieval state of existence with only Japan's rural economy untouched. The New York Times reported at the time of the Pacific campaign against Japan, "Maj. Gen. Curtis E. LeMay, commander of the B-29s of the entire Marianas area, declared "if the war is shortened by a single day, the attack will have served its purpose."[95] He believed it was his duty to carry out bombing attacks in a manner that would end the war in the Pacific theater, as quickly as possible, sparing further loss of American life. He also remarked that had the U.S. lost the war, he fully expected to be tried for war crimes.[96] Both Presidents Roosevelt and Truman supported his tactics, based on estimates that the Allies would suffer a million or more casualties, if the invasion of Japan became a necessity. LeMay was quoted in his 1965 autobiography as saying that his response to North Vietnam would be, "they've got to draw in their horns and stop their aggression, or we're going to bomb them back into the Stone Age," a condition he had reduced Japan to, 20 years earlier.

In 1948, Curtis LeMay was promoted to command of America's Strategic Air Command, responsible for America's air forces and nuclear strike capability, a position he held until 1957. The historical record indicates General LeMay advocated a preemptive attack against the Soviet Union, had it become clear Soviet forces were preparing to attack Strategic Air Command, or the United States. In these documents, which were often transcripts of speeches before groups such as the National War College, or events such as the 1955 Joint Secretaries Conference at the Quantico Marine Corps Base, sponsored by Nelson Rockefeller, LeMay clearly advocated using SAC as a preemptive weapon, if and when such action was necessary. In 1961, LeMay was promoted to Chief of Staff of the United States Air Force. It was widely known in Washington, that he and President John Kennedy shared a barely concealed, mutual contempt for each other. Kennedy had more than once, walked out of a meeting with LeMay, in a fit of pique over LeMay's inflexible attitudes toward Soviet provocations.

President Kennedy was briefed in September 1961, by General Lyman Lemnitzer, Chairman of the Joint Chiefs of Staff, about America's inflexible plan for total, worldwide, nuclear war. The plan was designated SIOP-62, the 'Single Integrated Operational Plan' for Fiscal Year 1962. It was at heart, LeMay's plan, for it reflected LeMay's personal philosophy of massive and continuing retaliation for several days following the outbreak of nuclear war.[97] Kennedy remarked in disgust to Secretary of State Dean Rusk, at the conclusion of the meeting, "And we call ourselves the human race."

The original SIOP-62 target list included one thousand and forty-three, "desired ground zeros" (DGZs), of which 706 were located within the Soviet Union, with an addition 337 DGZs in classified locations in China, and Eastern European communist nations. According to Navy Admiral Roy L. Johnson, Deputy Director of the Joint Strategic Target Planning Staff,

"The SAC people never seemed to be satisfied that to kill once was enough. They want to kill, overkill, overkill, because all of this has built up the prestige of SAC, it created the need for more forces, for a larger budget. …. That's the way their thinking went."[98]

Kennedy also viewed SIOP-62 as a strategy or unnecessary overkill. He was already preoccupied with the danger of accidental nuclear war initiated by mistakes or miscalculation. After this briefing, he ordered SIOP-62 revised to allow for a more flexible response than the obligatory destruction of half of the planet in the event of a minor conflict or miscalculation. The revised plan, called SIOP-63, went into effect just prior to the Cuban Missile Crisis, where LeMay again clashed with Kennedy and Defense Secretary McNamara. LeMay advocated bombing missile sites in Cuba, and opposed the Kennedy Administration's strategy of naval blockade. LeMay strongly supported a Cuban invasion regardless of expected Soviet retaliatory actions.

Shortly after the Cuban Missile Crisis ended, Kennedy met with Secretary of Defense Robert McNamara, Deputy Secretary of Defense Roswell Gilpatric, and the Joint Chiefs of Staff, in the Cabinet Room at the White House. He wished to thank them for their efforts in achieving a negotiated settlement with the Soviet Union. That agreement guaranteed removal of Soviet missiles from Cuba and avoided potential escalation to nuclear war. Kennedy tried to put a good face on what had been a difficult and stressful two weeks with his military leadership, saying he admired them, and had benefited from their advice and counsel. Many in attendance knew, or at least suspected, that Kennedy had made use of his own back-channel communications with Soviet Premier Khrushchev. Suspicions arose that Kennedy resolved the crisis by pledging America would not invade Cuba, along with a lesser known agreement to remove American missiles from areas in Turkey that were within striking distance of the largest Soviet cities.

President Kennedy meets in the Oval Office with General Curtis LeMay
and reconnaissance pilots who flew the Cuban missions.

President Kennedy said, "Gentlemen, we've won. I don't want you to ever say it, but you know we've won, and I know we've won." At this point the Chief of Naval Operations, Admiral George Anderson, naval member of the Joint Chiefs of Staff, exclaimed, "We've been had!" LeMay's own emotional outburst followed immediately thereafter. LeMay, who was enraged that the United States had not bombed and invaded Cuba, pounded the table in the Cabinet room and blurted out, "Won, Hell! We Lost!" We should go in and wipe them out today!" LeMay then proclaimed the resolution to the Cuban Missile Crisis to be "the greatest defeat in our history," and exclaimed, "Mr. President, we should invade today!" - leaving President Kennedy stunned and stammering in amazement.[99]

Unknown to U.S. military leaders, Soviet field commanders in Cuba had been granted authority to launch nuclear weapons on their own, the only time such authority was delegated by the Soviet high command.[100] Among their on-hand arsenal, were surface-to-surface missiles capable of delivering megaton-class warheads to nearly anywhere in the United States; surface-to-air defensive missiles, and Russian fighter planes and light bombers. If President Kennedy had followed LeMay's advice and attacked Cuba, and if Soviet commanders had launched, millions of Americans would have died. The ensuing SAC thermonuclear retaliatory strike would have killed roughly one hundred million Soviet citizens and brought nuclear winter to much of the Northern Hemisphere. The ensuing naval blockade was successful, and the most serious man-made threat to the planet was peacefully concluded.

Author Richard Reeves reported in *President Kennedy: Profile of Power*, JFK had "a kind of a fit" every time someone mentioned LeMay's name. He once stated to an aide, "I don't want that man near me again," after another frustrating exchange with America's foremost hawk.

Operation Mongoose was halted following the Cuban Missile Crisis, but was gradually resumed as U.S. - Soviet tensions faded. Their remained for Kennedy, his pledge to the Soviets of not invading Cuba as part of the Cuban Missile Crisis deal. Kennedy now had to reign in Operation Mongoose, which had acquired immense, unstoppable, momentum, with millions of dollars invested, a highly trained, multilevel structure of dedicated cold warriors, and a collection of inter-department agencies, planning for the dismantling of a foreign government 50 miles from America's shores. Operation Mongoose consisted of a six-phase schedule, aimed at destabilizing Castro's regime, culminating in an open revolt in October 1962. At one point, Mongoose's budget was $50 million per year, employing upwards of 2,500 people, including 500 Americans, and its tenure lasted from 1961 until 1975.

Its program of harassment, sabotage, and propaganda began again in earnest in the summer and fall of 1963. As Mongoose attempts at sabotaging Cuban assets grew bolder and attracted more attention in the world press, they posed an increasing problem for John Kennedy, bound by his pledge to the Soviet government of non-invasion of Cuba. This pledge was considered incredible by many CIA officers and their assets, who understood that Mongoose was a White House-CIA sanctioned operation.

In April,1963, Kennedy began using U.S. Navy and Customs Department ships and planes to intercept Mongoose operatives, who were still conducting harassment raids on Cuban industry and shipping, as well as propaganda activity. As the full details of Kennedy's agreement with Khrushchev emerged there was likely even more determination to continue Mongoose activities at the operational level. Many involved did not believe abandoning the project was Kennedy's true intention. Perhaps it was a politically necessary decoy, to shield the White House and the CIA's true intentions. Others viewed Kennedy in a more disturbing light.

July, 1963, found FBI agents closing down CIA-led training camps in Louisiana in a concerted effort to remove the sting from Operation Mongoose. It was a confusing time for the FBI and CIA agents involved, both of whom believed their missions were approved by the highest officials in the U.S. government. They were both correct. John Kennedy, simultaneously pursing the paths of accommodation, power, peace and war, had become fatally trapped by Cold War doctrine, formulated many years before he reached the Presidency.

There is evidence Kennedy realized he was no longer able to control the mongoose he had unleashed from striking Castro again and again. At a press conference in May of 1963, the he stumbled when responding to a question of whether or not the United States was still aiding Cuban exiles in an attempt to unseat Castro: "We may well be . . . well, none that I am familiar with . . . I don't think as of today that we are." Author Gaeton Fonzi in his book *"The Last Investigation"* properly asks the questions, "Did that mean the President thought his orders to halt aid to the exiles were being obeyed? Didn't he know?"

JFK made a final public jab at LeMay, in his "Peace Speech," cited earlier, at American University in June 1963. Kennedy publicly disavowed those who called for a "Pax Americana enforced on the world by American weapons of war." As author Dino Brugioni states in *Eyeball to Eyeball*, LeMay loved to discuss how Roman strength had produced the Pax Romana; and how the British, through their naval and military strength, had achieved the Pax Britannica; and with unabashed gall, how 'his bombers' had achieved 'Pax Atomica.' Once during a lecture, LeMay resorted to the term 'Pax Americana,' and it was to this phrase, JFK was responding in his commencement address at American University.

BATTLEFIELD CUBA: FINAL ANALYSIS

The consequences of the Cuban Missile Crisis were significant for the Kennedy presidency. America's coldest warriors were aware of options Kennedy could have taken, all attended by risk, as all major military plans contain risks. If Kennedy allowed the invasion of Cuba by introducing American armed forces, the Monroe Doctrine and the Treaty of Rio might have been invoked as legal justification for acting militarily in the Caribbean. Five years later, the Soviet Union justified its brutal invasion of Czechoslovakia under the guise of the Warsaw Pact. Kennedy had chosen to ignore a one hundred and thirty-eight year old established American doctrine, and a new treaty between North and South America, signed by United States government and backed by the most powerful of American dynasties, in favor of his own vision of maintaining detente between superpowers in the nuclear age. His refusal to act militarily, signaled the chiefs of American military and economic dynasties, along with America's adversaries, that he would not commit regular military forces in the Caribbean, Central, or South America, to support America's doctrines and treaties.

Recognizing his deteriorating credibility, it is understandable Kennedy authorized the massive buildup of CIA assets for Operation Mongoose. He wished to reassure U.S. intelligence, defense, and economic powers, of his commitment to oppose Cuban and Soviet influence. Operation Mongoose was as much an attempt to restore his Cold War credentials, as it was to challenge the Kremlin and bring about the removal of Fidel Castro. Kennedy fully understood he was playing *va banque* with the outcome of the Cuban issue.

Just as Abraham Lincoln had discovered, John Kennedy was also fighting a war on two fronts: a militaristic enemy in front, and the advocates of economic warfare behind him. And like Lincoln, Kennedy chose to follow his own beliefs, and use his authority as Commander-in-Chief to direct that battle. By taking the battle into his own hands, he introduced an abrupt change in the process of American global decision-making, and strategic planning. It was a change unacceptable to America's foremost hawks and their benefactors.

There is evidence that Jack Kennedy now realized his extreme vulnerability. He reportedly told Jacqueline Kennedy, after the Cuban Missile

Crisis, "If anyone's going to kill me, it should happen now." In June 1963, five months before Dealy Plaza, he spoke to a group of representatives of national organizations. To the astonishment of everyone present, he ended his speech by pulling a scrap of paper from his pocket, and reading the speech of Blanche of Spain in Shakespeare's *King John*:

> "The sun's o'ercast with blood: Fair day, adieu!
> Which is the side that I must go withal?
> I am with both: each army hath a hand.
> And in their rage, I having hold of both,
> They whirl asunder and dismember me."

It is interesting to speculate about those pleasant social encounters between Allen Dulles and Senator Jack Kennedy, amid the balmy setting of Joe Kennedy's luxurious Palm Beach mansion, enjoying their cool summer drinks amid palm-groved shoreline vistas - whether Jack Kennedy was truly learning global politics from the great 'spymaster" himself, or whether he was being prepped for his future role in rubber-stamping the military and economic plans of America's most powerful dynasties. And did John Kennedy realize they were one and the same?

Allen Dulles.

Ambassador Joseph Kennedy.

Mayor Earle Cabell.

Air Force General Charles Cabell.

Air Force General Curtis LeMay.

Air Force General Edward Landsdale.

Attorney General Robert Kennedy.

Vice President Nelson Rockefeller.

President John Kennedy.

JFK Memorial, Dallas, Texas.

7

JFK in Retrospect

*"Only an America which has fully educated its citizens is
fully capable of tackling the complex problems and perceiving
the hidden dangers of the world in which we live."*

— JFK Un-delivered Remarks Prepared for the
Dallas Trade Mart
November 22, 1963

"All along the watchtower princes kept their view"

— Bob Dylan, songwriter

In retrospect, what was the impact of the Kennedy Presidency on
the contemporary and future history of the United States of America?
Ultimately, historians will take into account the short duration that John
Kennedy served in the Oval Office, the turbulence of the era in which
he was an integral figure, and his unfulfilled vision for America. He

accomplished much in the short time available. There were advances in Civil Rights, the re-engagement of American citizens, especially young Americans, in their nation's political process at home, and through the Peace Corp abroad. His tenure included the first effective government attack against Organized Crime. Ultimately he should be remembered for the avoidance of nuclear war, during its most threatening and precarious moments, when the continued existence of life on this planet hung in the balance, as never before in human history. Many in the highest councils of finance, government, and the military, did not approve of John Kennedy's methods of global conflict resolution. He chose to follow his own vision, much as Lincoln did. We should never forget the inner strength and compassion he possessed, enabling him to resolve issues threatening the continuation of life on this planet.

Likely left un-addressed by historians, will be the interpretation that John Kennedy's presidency was rapidly evolving during his 1,036 days in power - from its early days of unquestioned support for established Cold War plans, to the moment, as Commander-in-Chief, he refused to rescue a failed CIA plan to overthrow a foreign government.

The CIA, and U.S. military planners were accustomed to the premise that Agency actions on foreign soil, would lead to the introduction of formal U.S. military forces. It was an accepted protocol, with men serving in the councils that proposed the original action, and who would then be called upon to sanction the required escalation of force to achieve mission fulfillment. With Kennedy's refusal to support this principle, a critical link in the chain of the nation's military-economic protocol had been ruptured. From that moment, John Kennedy began re-defining the decision-making process dictated by America's dynasties. As a result, he became fully isolated from the citadels of American power and mistrusted by America's coldest warriors. In some unwritten and unspoken ways, he was now left unguarded by the institutions designed to protect him. His only hope for political survival rested in the over-whelming sanctioning of his vision for America, in the presidential election of November 1964, an election he and most everyone in power sensed he would win. If the trip to Dallas in

November, 1963, posed risks, they would have to be taken, if John Kennedy was going to be President in fact, and not just in name.

The Presidency of the United States is a dangerous occupation. Of the 45 men to hold the office of President, 20 have experienced assassination attempts; 6 have been injured in assassination attempts; 4 have been killed in office. With a 9% mortality rate, and a 46% chance of attempted assassination, the President easily holds the most dangerous job in America. The second most dangerous occupation in America, that of fisherman, has a 0.2% mortality rate.

If these statistics, represented a third world, or undeveloped nation's record, they would be brushed off as understandable in an unstable country, lacking an established history of strong institutions and leadership. Yet, these statistics are America's, a democratic nation with a long history of respected institutions and leadership. *This is our record.* Nearly half of our elected leaders have experienced attempts to violently remove them from office.

In addition to the relatively short tenure of the office, too brief to allow any one individual to fully consolidate a power base, there are inherent risks for Presidents who challenge existing powers and institutions. Our history holds countless tales of political isolation, inability to advance legislation, impeachment, resignation, and assassination as effective means to render leaders ineffective, remove them, or influence the policies of the nation.

Ironically, JFK, in his remaining months in office, was labelled an appeaser, as his father before him. But this case, rather he failed to appease the warlords of his own kingdom, by refusing to lead them through the gates of Armageddon.

He was fully aware of the goals defined in the Quantico Studies that took place before his presidency began. He once remarked, "Things do not happen; things are made to happen!" In a nation's life, abrupt change can introduce a state of instability, certainly not a condition in which investment, banking, and economic institutions flourish. Stable economic growth requires a stable political environment.

Kennedy addressed this issue stating that "Efforts and courage are not enough without purpose and direction," perhaps mindful that his rapidly evolving decision-making process was perceived as random, lacking vision, and potentially destroying the well-developed plans for the American century. Those residing in the halls of American power were no longer being consulted. The opinions of those more experienced in global management, were no longer taken into account. None who had authored the great plans for America's position as preeminent global power, seemed to be have John Kennedy's direct attention. His back-channel negotiations with the Soviet Union were strong indications of his lack of commitment to the decision-making structure of the past. The well-funded, carefully developed, and surely profitable plans for the next several decades of American prosperity seemed to be threatened. The directors of American power had every reason to suspect that a Kennedy victory in the 1964 presidential election would usher in more uncertainty and change. The struggle for the control of America, had become the age old historical clash of power, between an ambitious and rebellious young king, and the most powerful nobles of the realm.

Therein lies the central issue with which the Kennedy years must be evaluated, and is at the crux of the question posed in this work: what was the nature of the struggle for power that John Kennedy faced, as president of the United States? This question must be viewed in the light of John Kennedy's attempts to enforce the executive powers of the presidency, as embodied in the Constitution of the United States. This epic document, written by men dedicated to ensuring that the principles and laws of the new nation they were defining, would ensure that America's true source of power would rest with the people, and their elected representatives. America's founding statesmen authored a system of government, specifically designed to prevent the will of the people from being unsurped by the nation's wealthiest dynasties and institutions. John Kennedy's actions supported those Constitutional principles to ensure that United States government policies and military actions would serve only the interests of the

American people, and not exist to enrich the plans of America's economic dynasties or organized crime.

This work has presented numerous facts that portray the intentions of America's elite financial powers, to establish military and economic supremacy over the continent of South and Central America. This work documents the actions of the nation's most powerful intelligence gathering institution, the Central Intelligence Agency, and its role of sustaining the economic interests of the nation's financial elite. By enforcing the guidelines established in the Act of Chapultepec, the Treaty of Rio, and the Quantico Studies, formulated primarily by Nelson Rockefeller and the Rockefeller Dynasty, the Central Intelligence Agency acted as agents for America's financial elite. The numerous studies and panels, convened by this dynasty, contained the blueprints for their political and economic strategy, to be won at the expense of the common people of the Southern hemisphere, under the often cynical guise of combating communism. John Foster Dulles and Allen Dulles, Wall Street lawyers - first and always - behaved until the end, as lawyers are trained to do, as unrelenting advocates for their client's interests. John Kennedy encountered this powerful tandem of client and advocate, and recognized it for what it was, an illegal form of government, not representative of the will of the people, as called forth in the Constitution. It amounted to a form of elite facism in America, the rule of the few over the many, not the government foreseen by Washington, Jefferson, Adams, Madison, and Monroe.

In the third year of John Kennedy's presidency, he put in motion the legal, financial, and military processes and procedures to limit, reduce, and eliminate this illegal form of government. His concerted attack consisted of authorizing the creation of silver-backed currency, curbing the power of the CIA, the Mafia, and the Federal Reserve, promoting social change in South America, establishing detente with the Soviet Union, and scaling back military plans for nuclear confrontation, and war. It was a bold counter to the existing plans of America's elite for economic domination throughout the latter half of the Twentieth Century, ensured by America's unmatched military power. JFK was, as world events progressed, clearly not the kind of aggressive hawk, desired by America's dynasties, to lead them forward through the upcoming battlefields in Southeast Asia, and beyond.

With the premature departure of the Kennedy's, the grim-faced coterie of cold warriors, and their supporting politicians, returned to preside over a largely discouraged and cynical American electorate, who would never again view politics and government in the same hopeful light. As the Vietnam War expanded, citizen support for government actions diminished in the same proportion. Nuclear weaponry continued to stockpile, enriching its manufacturers. The Cold War finally extinguished itself with the removal of the Berlin Wall in 1989. The following year, the existing principles of Cold War military and economic strategy, including the concept of regional alliances, were incorporated into its less lethal, but similarly expensive, concept of Low Intensity Conflict. According to the December 5, 1990, United States Department of the Army Field Manual:

"Low-intensity conflict ranges from subversion to the use of armed forces. It is waged by a combination of means, employing political, economic, informational, and military instruments. Low-intensity conflicts are often localized, generally in the Third World but contain regional and global security implications."[102]

The same manual also states:

"... successful LIC operations, consistent with US interests and laws can advance US international goals such as the growth of freedom, democratic institutions, and free market economies."[103]

It is worthwhile to note that the Army Manual's definition for LIC clearly included the "advance of US international goals such as . . . free market economies." Clearly, John Kennedy failed to disconnect the strategy of military-supported economic warfare envisioned in 1961, by Nelson and David Rockefeller, in their *Prospect for America, The Rockefeller Panel*

Reports - a strategy designed to benefit the global interests of America's foremost dynasties.

By 1963, an ailing Joseph P. Kennedy Sr. was attended by round-the-clock nurses at the Kennedy family home in Hyannis Port. The morning after the assassination, Ted and Eunice Kennedy came into his room and informed him of Jack's death. When nurse Rita Dallas later entered the room, she noticed the front page of the morning newspaper lying face up on the floor. She looked at Joe, who was sitting up in bed gripping the bed sheet in a tight knot. His eyes were closed, and tears were running down his cheeks.[104] The struggle for control of power in America had ended. Joe Kennedy no doubt reflected on the events that had transpired, and perhaps, for the first time in his life, considered that he may never have fully realized the force and nature of true power.

John Fitzgerald Kennedy was far from a perfect man, and perhaps much further from the idealized portrait many American's remember. But he was a brilliant man, a quick learner, compassionate, and carried the idealism of youth. He favored providing Americans, and those far from our shores, with the tools to construct a better life for themselves and their future generations. He preferred not to exalt the pursuit of nuclear war, and the policies that supported foreign economic domination, without an equitable measure of benefit to those nation's economies and standards of living. It became increasingly clear from his speeches that he wished to offer common men the opportunity to guide their own destiny, rather than permitting others to define that future, the ultimate goal of dynastic power. Toward the later stages of his abbreviated presidency, he began a courageous effort to re-route the American ship of state onto a different course.

The story of man is invariably defined by most historians, by the conquests of the warrior and the conqueror. It is their stories that mark the beginning and the end of the epochs of nations and empires. The history of the peacemaker is considered an exception in human affairs, a detour, a temporary distraction in the building of epic historic tales of power.

A short distance from the JFK Memorial in Dallas, Texas, there is a small white "X" on a gently curving street, running through a quiet, grief-laden plaza. Together with the Memorial to America's youngest elected president, they serve as reminders of another pathway to the future that America might have taken.

EPILOGUE

"The most effective way to destroy people is to deny and obliterate their own understanding of their history"

— GEORGE ORWELL, AUTHOR

Since 1963, political, military, and technological landscapes have changed profoundly. We are digitally connected to each other and to events around the world instantaneously. Eyewitnesses to major events can share their perspectives with a global community in a few minutes. The printed word has surrendered to the digital word. If we tune into the traditional nightly news at all, it is only to add a human face and voice to the digital information we have already processed. As cognitive receptors of rapid-fire information, the task of determining the truth is even more difficult, as we navigate through spin, opinion, obfuscation, and hidden agendas, that challenge clarity and perception. Digital streams encourage passivity, instead of effective action. Compassion is subordinated to success, formulated by corporate mission statements. Finding employment is an electronic exercise, providing the ultimate firewall from personal interaction. Trending events are viewed in high definition, but the lines of reason have become blurred. Those seeking media impact understand the value of image over truth. The inherent danger for all, then becomes the passive acceptance of the world as explained to us, not as our senses, mind, and heart know it should be.

Out of World War II came the Cold War, which morphed into the concept of Low Intensity Conflict, which lasted 21 years, until the War on Terror began on 9/11. This war will, as the others before it, absorb millions of dollars of the world's economies, and may prove to be the longest war of all, in our time. It follows the Cold War formula of maintaining casualties at an acceptable level, while ensuring profits for military-related industries, and their financial backers. With fiat currency in place, there is no limit to the profits to be made by the existence of war. World War II was fought to preserve liberty and vanquish extreme dictatorships and totalitarianism. The Cold War was cynically fought over competing political philosophies. The War on Terror springs from differences between theocracies and democracies. The justifications are ever changing while the results remain the same

True perception may still be found through research and exploration, to understand and tame the uncontrollable beast that Frederick Nietzsche proclaims lies at the heart of all human endeavor, the will to power - a pursuit that has hypnotized men of all eras into blind avarice or equally blind servitude, with the regularity of the setting sun.

Standing within the walls of the JFK Memorial, as I did in the spring of 2005, one may witness the symbols of man's desire to rule, arise in their nightly ritual of ascendency. The metaphor is clear and allows us to put historical power in its true perspective.

Thomas Jefferson well understood, having watched his friends and neighbors fall to remove the yoke of servitude, that the cost of freedom lies buried in the ground. He was clear in identifying the danger that powerful, self-serving dynasties can present to the well being of the citizen:

> "I hope we shall crush in its birth the aristocracy of our monied corporations which dare already to challenge our government to a trial by strength and bid defiance to the laws of our country."

The JFK Memorial supports his declaration by showing us the true encompassing nature of historic power. Power that attempts to define the course of nations and the history of man, rendering the elected representatives of the people mere transitory figures, treading lightly through the halls and castles of wealth and power.

It is also advisable to remember Jefferson's warning if we break faith with our responsibilities,

> "The condition upon which God hath given liberty to man is eternal vigilance; which condition if he breaks, servitude is at once the consequence of his crime, and the punishment of his guilt."

Within this work, I have written of the plans developed by leaders of the Cold War era, that have defined America's course in the second half of the twentieth century. My research led me to the inescapable conclusion that the policies John Kennedy attempted to enact as his presidency matured, moved him into fatal opposition against the military and economic planning of the nation's Cold War leadership. Those plans were defined by America's elite financial powers, not by America's elected leaders. Those plans were not consistent with the ideals clearly outlined by America's founding fathers, nor were they ever sanctioned by the American people.

With the arrival of John Kennedy in the White House, a new force was asserting its determination to lead with the growing power of a people's support. Were these challenges appropriately feared or greatly exaggerated by America's elite? There is historical precedence to answer that question, precedence that speaks of a time when well-entrenched powers were eliminated by forces of fundamental change. It occurred as a result of William the Conqueror's successful invasion of England, following the Battle of Hastings in 1066. The battle heralded the last days of the "thegns," the nobility ruling England at that time. Author Michael Woods, in his book *"In Search of the Dark Ages"* writes:

> "The record of the *Domesday Book* completed only twenty years after Hastings, shows that although some Englishmen [thegns] still held considerable estates, very few held any position of influence. . . that society was effectively shattered. The lower reaches of society, the peasants and free farmers were less hard hit - they continued on paying their rents to a new master . . But for the top men, their world had been upturned . . and they had no place in a new order . . Of those who survived the grim period of the late sixties and early seventies, many saw no reason to stay in England, once the Conqueror's grip was assured."[105]

At some point during the third year of John Kennedy's presidency his policies had reached a tipping point and assassination was, as John Kennedy himself foresaw, highly probable, and perhaps even inevitable. No specific order from America's highest military, intelligence, or economic leadership was likely given to end John Kennedy's presidency. If it occurred, and if it was a domestic affair, America's institutions would know what to do. They served a greater purpose and answered to a higher force than the office of the President of the United States. They would surround and contain the event with all the power at their command, as the JFK Memorial portrays.

Memorial architect, Philip Johnson, well-understood the awesome forces unleashed in man's will to power, and his design for the JFK Memorial faithfully adhered to these philosophical teachings of Friedrich Nietzsche's *The Will to Power*. Life in Johnson's view was based on perception, and he took every opportunity to stretch and reshape the geometric prisons of form and dimension to release their force and convey through architecture, what Nietzsche tried so valiantly to express in words - that power is man, and man is power. Johnson kept faith with Jacqueline Kennedy's request for a simple, dignified memorial, and presented the leadership and citizens of Dallas with a design that offers serenity and quiet reflection yet speaks eloquently of a gifted man's efforts and courage, surrounded by forces that over-whelmed his presidency.

Along the base of the JFK Memorial's symbolic crypt there are twenty-one letters of a man's name, whose fate has irrevocably become part of America's fate. It would be entirely appropriate to add an additional 21 letters, beneath those of John Kennedy's:

J O H N F I T Z G E R A L D K E N N E D Y
U N I T E D S T A T E S O F A M E R I C A

Within his Memorial, when we are willing, we may observe the castle, the scepter, the obelisk, and the dragon, continuing their battle for the soul of a nation. And within this silent, ever-changing room, each of us in our own way, may fleetingly glimpse the majesty and tragedy of man's eternal quest for power.

Such is the tale elegantly portrayed by the JFK Memorial.

ACKNOWLEDGMENTS

There have been many who graciously and patiently assisted me during the research phase of this book. Their guidance has been absolutely essential for the realization of this story. Support for the first part of this story, the Creation of a Memorial, began with Krishna Shenoy, Librarian/Archivist at the Sixth Floor Museum in Dallas, Texas, who made The Sixth Floor Museum's archives available and helped me locate essential reference documents. Mark Davies, at The Sixth Floor Museum, also helped me secure vital images and documents critical to the success of this project.

I was most fortunate to have the kind assistance of Pamalla Anderson, Public Services and Reference Specialist, at the DeGolyer Library at Southern Methodist University. With her help, I was able to develop my understanding of the challenges facing the citizens and leadership of Dallas in completing the Memorial, Therein, the Private Collection Papers of Stanley Marcus, and Mayor Earle Cabell, eloquently portrayed the intense emotions beneath the tumultuous political environment that existed in Dallas prior to, and during, the construction of the JFK Memorial.

While completing research in Dallas, it was an exceptional pleasure to visit photographer, author, and architect Frank Welch, who graciously spoke with my research assistant and I in his offices. Mr. Welch offered his sincere first-hand account of those difficult Dallas days, along with his valuable insights of Philip Johnson's involvement during the construction of the JFK Memorial. Mr. Welch's parting words to me were, "Don't be afraid to write something that's controversial." Those words were far more prophetic than I could have imagined at the time and helped sustain me throughout the days ahead.

Further into the journey, I made the acquaintance of award-winning architectural photographer, Robin Hill, of Miami, Florida. Robin provided the unparalleled cover-photo that captures the essence of my story and offered his keen insights into Philip Johnson's use of light and shadow within his architectural works.

Franz Schulze, Professor Emeritus at Lake Forest College, provide important initial insights into the personality of Philip Johnson, and encouragement to a first-time author.

I would also like to thank my good friend of many years, Mr. Charles Lenatti, journalist and publishing industry veteran, who provided necessary guidance, enabling me to properly focus on what was essential to my story, and what was not.

The support given by my wife Denise, and my daughter Cassy, who was also my research assistant, were invaluable. Together we weathered the highs and lows of a seemingly interminable journey. I am eternally grateful for their love and support.

M. D. Brosio

ENDNOTES

PART 1. Creation of a Memorial

1. The American Presidency Project. http://www.presidency.ucsb.edu/ws/index.php?pid=25770]

2. Warren Commission Exhibit 710

3. http://www.jfk.org/go/exhibits/dealey-plaza/change-of-focus]

4. Blumenthal, Ralph, article in New York Times, published November 20, 2003, "Dallas Comes to Terms With the Day That Defined It".

5. http://www.youtube.com/watch?v=4xr4YqYmntA"10Garmonbozia01"-Mayor of Dallas, Earle Cabell, standard YouTube license

6. Frank Welch, Philip Johnson and Texas, University of Texas Press, Austin, Tx, 2000.pg. 125

7. http://en.wikipedia.org/wiki/Stanley_Marcus. Source: Tom Stuckey, Associated Press. "Musicians barred from class – Longhairs promise school rule battle," Indiana Evening Gazette, September 10, 1966, page 14.

8. Frank Welch, Philip Johnson and Texas, University of Texas Press, Austin, Tx, 2000.pg. 123

9. Welch, Frank D., interviewed by M. D. Brosio, Dallas, Tx, August __, 2012

10. Welch, Frank D.. Philip Johnson and Texas, University of Texas Press, Austin, Tx, 2000.pg. 124

11. Welch, Frank D.. Philip Johnson and Texas, University of Texas Press, Austin, Tx, 2000. pg. 12

12. Varnelis, Kazys. Philip Johnson's Politics and Cynical Survival, Journal of Architectural Education, November 1994. http://varnelis. net/articles/we_cannot_not_know_history

13. Schulze, Franz. Philip Johnson, Life and Work. University of Chicago Press, Chicago, 1994, pg. 114.

14. Varnelis, Kazys. Philip Johnson's Politics and Cynical Survival, Journal of Architectural Education, November 1994. http://varnelis. net/articles/we_cannot_not_know_history

15. Academy of Achievement, Interview with Philip Johnson, New York, N.Y. Febraury 28, 1992. http://www.achievement.org/autodoc/ printmember/joh0int-1

16. Shulze, Franz, Philip Johnson: An Essay by Franze Shulze, Architectural Record. http://archrecord.construction.com/people/ profiles/archives/0505johnsonProfile_shulze.asp

17. Sorkin, Michael, Philip Johnson: An Essay by Michael Sorkin, Architectural Record.

18. Welch, Frank D. Philip Johnson and Texas, University of Texas Press, Austin, Tx, 2000.pg. 18

19. Applebaum, Anne, 'Remembering' Philip Johnson. The Washington Post February 2, 2005, Page A23. http://www.washingtonpost.com/ wp-dyn/articles/A55664-2005Feb1.html

20. Welch, Frank D.. Philip Johnson and Texas, University of Texas Press, Austin, Tx, 2000. Forward.

21, 22. Philip Johnson oral history, Interview by Dr. Rick Brettell, curator for the Dallas Museum of Art, filmed by Jeff West, the Executive Director of the Sixth Floor Museum at Dealey Plaza, August 11, 1998.

23. Welch, Frank D.. Philip Johnson and Texas, University of Texas Press, Austin, Tx, 2000.pg. 129

24. Johnson, Philip, Speech at Yale University, 1959

25. Sterns, Robert A.M., , Philip Johnson: An Essay by Robert Sterns, Architectural Record.

26. Welch, Frank D., interviewed by M. D. Brosio, Dallas, Tx, August __, 2012

27. Hill, Robin, Through These Photographers Eyes: The Glass House, Part One. Feb 6, 2012. http://robinhillphotography.blogspot.com.

28. Hughes, Robert. Interview with Albert Speer, Of Gods and Monsters, The Guardian, January 31, 2003. http://www.theguardian.com/artanddesign/2003/feb/01/architecture.artsfeatures

PART 2: The Struggle for Power in America

29. Rockefeller, David Memoirs, New York: Random House, 2002 (pp.28-9,323)].

30. Institute for Agriculture and Trade Policy. Posted March 26, 2013 by Dale Wiehoff. http://www.iatp.org/blog/201303/how-the-chicken-of-tomorrow-became-the-chicken-of-the-world.

31. Collier, Peter, and Horowitz, David. The Rockefellers, an American Dynasty. Holt, Rinehart, and Winston. New York, N.Y. pg. 265

32. Reich, Cary (1996). The Life of Nelson A. Rockefeller: Worlds to Conquer, 1908-1958. Doubleday, New York, N.Y.

33, 34. http://en.wikipedia.org/wiki/Nelson_Rockefeller

35. Collier, Peter, and Horowitz, David. The Rockefellers, an American Dynasty. Holt, Rinehart, and Winston. New York, N.Y. pg. 344

36-37. Collier, Peter, and Horowitz, David. The Rockefellers, an American Dynasty. Holt, Rinehart, and Winston. New York, N.Y. pg. 344-345.

38. http://en.wikipedia.org/wiki/Nelson_Rockefeller. Connery, Robert H.; Benjamin, Gerald (1979). Rockefeller of New York; Executive Power in the Statehouse. Ithaca, New York

39. Collier, Peter, and Horowitz, David. The Rockefellers, an American Dynasty. Holt, Rinehart, and Winston. New York, N.Y. pg. 407-408

40. Collier, Peter, and Horowitz, David. The Rockefellers, an American Dynasty. Holt, Rinehart, and Winston. New York, N.Y. pg. 411.

41. Collier, Peter, and Horowitz, David. The Rockefellers, an American Dynasty. Holt, Rinehart, and Winston. New York, N.Y. pg. 412

42. Gibson, Donald "Battling Wall Street: The Kennedy Presidency, 1994, Sheridan Square Press. pgs. 532-76

43. Collier, Peter, and Horowitz, David. The Rockefellers, an American Dynasty. Holt, Rinehart, and Winston. New York, N.Y. pg. 413

44. Collier, Peter, and Horowitz, David. The Rockefellers, an American Dynasty. Holt, Rinehart, and Winston. New York, N.Y. pg. 414

45. President John F. Kennedy: On the Alliance for Progress, 1961"Modern History Sourcebook. Archived from the original on 3 September 2006. Retrieved 2006-07-30.

46. Smith, Peter H (1999). Talons of the Eagle: Dynamics of U.S.-Latin American Relations. Oxford University Press. pgs. 150-152

47. "Alliance for Progress", The Columbia Encyclopedia (6 ed.). 2001.

48. http://www.geopoliticalmonitor.com/about/ - Info on CIA Activity in S. America.

49. Wright, Thomas C. Latin America in the Era of the Cuban Revolution. http://en.wikipedia.org/wiki/Alliance_for_Progress.

50. Schmitz, David F. The United States and Right-wing Dictatorships, 1965-1989. http://en.wikipedia.org/wiki/Alliance_for_Progress.

51. Blum, William. Rogue State: A Guide to the Worlds Only Superpower. Common Courage Press, 2005.
Blum, William. Killing Hope: US and CIA Interventions Since World War II. Common Courage Press2003

52. Collier, Peter, and Horowitz, David. The Rockefellers, an American Dynasty. Holt, Rinehart, and Winston. New York, N.Y. pg. 400

53. Collier, Peter, and Horowitz, David. The Rockefellers, an American Dynasty. Holt, Rinehart, and Winston. New York, N.Y. pg. 400

54. Collier, Peter, and Horowitz, David. The Rockefellers, an American Dynasty. Holt, Rinehart, and Winston. New York, N.Y. pg. 414

55. Collier, Peter, and Horowitz, David. The Rockefellers, an American Dynasty. Holt, Rinehart, and Winston. New York, N.Y. pg. 417

56. Collier, Peter, and Horowitz, David. The Rockefellers, an American Dynasty. Holt, Rinehart, and Winston. New York, N.Y. pg. 417

57. "National Register Information System". National Register of Historic Places. National Park Service. 2007-01-23.

58. Kessler, Ronald. The Sins of the Father. Warner Books, New York, N.Y. pg. 94

59. Kessler, Ronald. The Sins of the Father. Warner Books, New York, N.Y. pg. 97

60. Kessler, Ronald. The Sins of the Father. Warner Books, New York, N.Y. pg. 160

61. Kessler, Ronald. The Sins of the Father. Warner Books, New York, N.Y. pg. 165

62. Kessler, Ronald. The Sins of the Father. Warner Books, New York, N.Y. pg. 168

63. Kessler, Ronald. The Sins of the Father. Warner Books, New York, N.Y. pg. 175

64. Kessler, Ronald. The Sins of the Father. Warner Books, New York, N.Y. pg. 176

65. Kessler, Ronald. The Sins of the Father. Warner Books, New York, N.Y. pg. 191

66. Kessler, Ronald. The Sins of the Father. Warner Books, New York, N.Y. pg. 195

67. Kessler, Ronald. The Sins of the Father. Warner Books, New York, N.Y. pg. 212-213

68. Kessler, Ronald. The Sins of the Father. Warner Books, New York, N.Y. pg. 237

69. Kessler, Ronald. The Sins of the Father. Warner Books, New York, N.Y. pg. 225

70. Kessler, Ronald. The Sins of the Father. Warner Books, New York, N.Y. pg. 224

71. Kessler, Ronald. The Sins of the Father. Warner Books, New York, N.Y. pg. 230

72. Kessler, Ronald. The Sins of the Father. Warner Books, New York, N.Y. pg. 206

73. Kessler, Ronald. The Sins of the Father. Warner Books, New York, N.Y. pg. 287

74. Kessler, Ronald. The Sins of the Father. Warner Books, New York, N.Y. pg. 380-381

75. Kessler, Ronald. The Sins of the Father. Warner Books, New York, N.Y. pg. 297-298

76. Hersch, Seymour. The Dark Side of Camelot, Little, Brown, and Company, New York, N.Y. pg 254

77. Hersch, Seymour. The Dark Side of Camelot, Little, Brown, and Company, New York, N.Y. pg 257

78. Rich Frank: Downfall, Random House, 1999. http://en.wikipedia.org/wiki/Robert_McNamara

79. http://en.wikipedia.org/wiki/Panic_of_1907

80. Perloff, James. The Shadows of Power, Western Islands, Appleton, Wisconsin, 1988, pg. 19

81. Jefferson, Thomas. The Life and Selected Writings of Thomas Jefferson, The Modern Library, New York, N.Y. 1944. pg. 122

82. Adelmann, Bob "The Federal Reserve System," The New American, October 27, 1986

83. http://www.truthfulpolitics.com/http:/truthfulpolitics.com/comments/u-s-federal-debt-by-president-political-party/

84. Kessler, Ronald. The Bureau: The Secret History of the FBI. St. Martin's Paperbacks. 2003.

85. Kessler, Ronald. The Bureau: The Secret History of the FBI. St. Martin's Paperbacks. 2003. pg. 116

86. Schlesinger, Jr., Arthur (2002) [1978]. Robert Kennedy and His Times. New York: First Mariner Books.

87. Fonzi, Gaeton, The Last Investigation, Thunder's Mouth Press, New York, N.Y. 1993, pg. 415

88. Fonzi, Gaeton, The Last Investigation, Thunder's Mouth Press, New York, N.Y. 1993, pg. 415

89. Hersch, Seymour. The Dark Side of Camelot, Little, Brown, and Company, New York, N.Y. pg 172

90. Hersch, Seymour. The Dark Side of Camelot, Little, Brown, and Company, New York, N.Y. pg 173

91. Hersch, Seymour. The Dark Side of Camelot, Little, Brown, and Company, New York, N.Y. pg 180

92. Prouty, l. Fletcher, JFK, the CIA, Vietnam and the Plot to Assassinate John F. Kennedy. Birch Lane Press Book, New York, N.Y. 1992, pg. 165

93. Sawyer, Ralph D. The Seven Military Classics of Ancient China. New York: Basic Books. 2007. p. 423.

94. Prouty, l. Fletcher, JFK, the CIA, Vietnam and the Plot to Assassinate John F. Kennedy. Birch Lane Press Book, New York, N.Y. 1992, pg. 39

95. http://en.wikipedia.org/wiki/Curtis_LeMayCoffey, [6] Iron Eagle and [7] Tillman, LeMay

96. PBS. American Experience. Race for the Superbomb. General Curtis E. Lemay, (1906-1990). 2009. http://www.pbs.org/wgbh/amex/bomb/peopleevents/pandeAMEX61.html

97. Horne, Douglas. Chief Analyst for Military Records (ARRB). Deep Background: The Rift between President Kennedy and General LeMay,

98. Johnson, Admiral Roy L., USN (ret'd), Deputy Director of Joint Strategic Target Planning Staff (1961-1963) 6 December 1980. [fn: Reminiscences of Admiral Roy L. Johnson, USN (Ret.), US. Naval Institute, Annapolis MD.

99. Deep Background: The Rift between President Kennedy and General LeMay, Douglas Horne, Chief Analyst for Military Records (ARRB).

100. http://en.wikipedia.org/wiki/Curtis_LeMay, citing [36] Rhodes, 1995, pp. 574–76

101. http://jfkcountercoup.blogspot.com/2012/02/deep-background-lemay-jfk.html

102, 103. Wiki, United States Department of the Army (5 December 1990), Field Manual 100-20: Military Operations in Low Intensity Conflict, GlobalSecurity.org. http://en.wikipedia.org/wiki/Irregular_Warfare

104. Kessler, Ronald. The Bureau: The Secret History of the FBI. St. Martin's Paperbacks. 2003. pg. 413

EPILOGUE
105. Wood, Michael. In Search of the Dark Ages; pgs. 232-233

BIBLIOGRAPHY - WORKS CITED

Ballinger, Lacie and Rugg, Ruth Ann. JFK Memorial Rededication Booklet, The Sixth Floor Museum, Dallas, Tx. 2004

Collier, Peter and Horowitz, David. The Rockefellers. New York, N.Y. Holt, Reinhart and Winston. 1976

Welch, Frank D. Philip Johnson & Texas, Austin Tx. University of Texas Press, 2000

Kessler, Ronald, The Sins of the Father. New York, N.Y. Warner Books, Inc. 1996

Koch, Adrienne and Peden, William (editors) The Life and Selected Writings of Thomas Jefferson, New York, N.Y. The Modern Library by Random House, 1944

Fonzi, Gaeton. The Last Investigation, New York, N.Y. Thunder's Mouth Press, 1993

Schulze, Franz. Philip Johnson Life and Work, Chicago, Il. The University of Chicago Press, 1994

Prouty, L. Fletcher. JFK: The CIA, Vietnam, and the Plot to Assassinate John F. Kennedy. New York, N.Y. Birch Lane Press, 1992

Hersh, Seymour M. The Dark Side of Camelot. Boston, MA. Little, Brown, and Company, 1997

Lash, Joseph P. Roosevelt and Churchill 1939-1941. New York, N.Y. W.W. Norton and Company, Inc. 1976

Mosely, Leonard. Dulles: A Biography of Eleanor, Allen, and John Foster Dulles and Their Family Network. New York, N.Y. The Dial Press/ James Wade, 1978

Allen, Gary. The Rockefeller File. Seal Beach, CA. '76 Press, 1976

Kessler, Ronald. The Bureau, The Secret History of the FBI. New York, N.Y. St. Martin's Press, 2002

Cornwell, John. Hitler's Pope. New York, N.Y. Viking/Penguin Group, 1999.

Perloff, James. The Shadows of Power, Appleton, WI, Western Islands Publishers, 1988

Wood, Michael. In Search of the Middle Ages. New York. Facts on File Publications, 1987.

Rockefeller, David. Memoirs. New York, Randon House, 2002

Horne, Douglas, Chief Analyst for Military Records (ARRB). Deep Background: The Rift between President Kennedy and General LeMay

Sawyer, Ralph D. The Seven Military Classics of Ancient China. New York: Basic Books. 2007

Schlesinger, Jr., Arthur (2002) [1978]. Robert Kennedy and His Times. New York: First Mariner Books.

Gibson, Donald "Battling Wall Street: The Kennedy Presidency, 1994, Sheridan Square Press.

Smith, Peter H (1999). Talons of the Eagle: Dynamics of U.S.-Latin American Relations. Oxford University Press.

Columbia Encyclopedia, "Alliance for Progress", (6 ed.). 2001.

Web Resources Cited

Varnelis, Kazys. We Cannot Not Know History, Phillip Johnson's Politics and Cynical Survival. Abstract, Journal of Architectural Education. November 1994, http://varnelis.net/articles/we_cannot_not_know_history

The American Presidency Project. http://www.presidency.ucsb.edu/ws/index.php?pid=25770]

http://www.jfk.org/go/exhibits/dealey-plaza/change-of-focus]

Blumenthal, Ralph, article in New York Times, published November 20, 2003, "Dallas Comes to Terms With the Day That Defined It".

http://www.youtube.com/watch?v=4xr4YqYmntA   "10Garmonbozia01"-Mayor of Dallas, Earle Cabell, standard YouTube license

http://en.wikipedia.org/wiki/Stanley_Marcus. Source: Tom Stuckey, Associated Press. "Musicians barred from class – Longhairs promise school rule battle," Indiana Evening Gazette, September 10, 1966, page 14.

Academy of Achievement, Interview with Philip Johnson, New York, N.Y. Febraury 28, 1992. http://www.achievement.org/autodoc/printmember/joh0int-1

Sorkin, Michael, Philip Johnson: An Essay by Michael Sorkin, Architectural Record.

Applebaum, Anne, 'Remembering' Philip Johnson. The Washington Post February 2, 2005, Page A23. http://www.washingtonpost.com/wp-dyn/articles/A55664-2005Feb1.html

Philip Johnson oral history, Interview by Dr. Rick Brettell, curator for the Dallas Museum of Art, filmed by Jeff West, the Executive Director of the Sixth Floor Museum at Dealey Plaza, August 11, 1998.

Sterns, Robert A.M., , Philip Johnson: An Essay by Robert Sterns, Architectural Record.

Hughes, Robert. Interview with Albert Speer, Of Gods and Monsters, The Guardian, January 31, 2003. http://www.theguardian.com/artand-design/2003/feb/01/architecture.artsfeatures

Institute for Agriculture and Trade Policy. Posted March 26, 2013 by Dale Wiehoff. http://www.iatp.org/blog/201303/how-the-chicken-of-tomorrow-became-the-chicken-of-the-world

http://www.geopoliticalmonitor.com/about/ - Info on CIA Activity in S. America.

Wright, Thomas C. Latin America in the Era of the Cuban Revolution. http://en.wikipedia.org/wiki/Alliance_for_Progress.

Schmitz, David F. The United States and Right-wing Dictatorships, 1965-1989. http://en.wikipedia.org/wiki/Alliance_for_Progress

Blum, William. Rogue State: A Guide to the Worlds Only Superpower and Killing Hope: US and CIA Interventions Since World War II. Common Courage Press, 2005.

"National Register Information System". National Register of Historic Places. National Park Service. 2007-01-23.

Rich Frank: Downfall, Random House, 1999. http://en.wikipedia.org/wiki/Robert_McNamara

http://en.wikipedia.org/wiki/Panic_of_1907

Adelmann, Bob "The Federal Reserve System," The New American, October 27, 1986

http://www.truthfulpolitics.com/http:/truthfulpolitics.com/comments/u-s-federal-debt-by-president-political-party/

Schlesinger, Jr., Arthur (2002) [1978]. Robert Kennedy and His Times. New York: First Mariner Books.

http://en.wikipedia.org/wiki/Curtis_LeMay.

PBS. American Experience. Race for the Superbomb. General Curtis E. Lemay, (1906-1990). 2009. http://www.pbs.org/wgbh/amex/bomb/peopleevents/pandeAMEX61.html

Johnson, Admiral Roy L., USN (ret'd), Deputy Director of Joint Strategic Target Planning Staff (1961-1963) 6 December 1980. [fn: Reminiscences of Admiral Roy L. Johnson, USN (Ret.), US. Naval Institute, Annapolis MD.

http://en.wikipedia.org/wiki/Curtis_LeMay, citing [36] Rhodes, 1995

http://jfkcountercoup.blogspot.com/2012/02/deep-background-lemay-jfk.html

1. JFK Memorial, Dallas Texas. Authors Collection

2. JFK Memorial, Dallas Texas, Cenotaph, Authors Collection

3. JFK Memorial, Dalas, Texas, Shadows. Authors Collection

4. "Old Red Courthouse, Dallas, Texas. Authors Collection

5. Wyvern, "Old Red Courthouse, Dallas, Texas. Authors Collection

6. Wyvern, entrance, City of London, Wiki Commons

7. Wyvern, entrance, City of London, Wiki Commons

8. Dallas citizens memorial in Dealy Plaza, Dallas Texas, by Permission of the Sixth Floor Museum, George Reid Collection, Dallas Texas

9. Philip Johnson. Library of Congress, Prints and Photographs Division, Van Vechten Collection, reproduction number LC-USZ62-127285 DLC 9b&w film copy neg.)

10. Philip Johnson. Library of Congress, Prints and Photographs Division, Van Vechten Collection, reproduction number LC-USZ62-103665 DLC 9b&w film copy neg.)

11. Philip Johnson. 2002.FILARDO.jpg. Licensed under Creative Commons Attribution-ShareAlike 3.0 Unported License

12. JFK and JCS. Credit: Robert Knudsen. White House Photographs. John F. Kennedy Presidential Library and Museum, Boston from the

article: http://govbooktalk.gpo.gov/2012/10/18/hawks-vs-doves-the-joint-chiefs-and-the-cuban-missile-crisis/

13. U.S. National Debt Clock. http//www.brillig.com/debt_clock/[83]

14. JFK and Nelson Rockefeller, White House. Source Criticalpast.com.; order#1372192064, 25 June 2013

15. JFK and General Curtis LeMay, White House. Courtesy of CIA. Attribute: W:en:User:Signaler: File:LeMay Cuban Missile Crisis. jpg;{{PD-USGov-CIA}}

16. Allen Dulles. From en:Wikipedia en:Image:Allen w dulles.jpg 05:51, 17 Oct 2004

17. Joseph Kennedy http://coommons.wikimedia.org/wiki/File:Joseph P. Kennedy, Sr. 1940.jpg

18. Earle Cabell. Congressional Pictorial Directory, 91st Congress, p. 137

19. Charles Cabell. http://en.wikipedia.org/wiki/Charles_P._Cabell PD-USGOV-MILITARY-AIR FORCE

20. Curtis LeMay. Source: http://www.af.mil/bios/bio.asp?bioID=6178 {{PD-USGov-AirForce}}

21. Edward Landsdale. http://en.wikipedia.org/wiki/File:Major-general-lansdale.jpg. Major General Edward Lansdale, 1963 (US Air Force Photograph).

22. Robert Kennedy. http://en.wikipedia.org/wiki File:Robert_F_Kennedy_crop.jpg. Image:Robert F. Kennedy appearing before Platform Committee, August 19, 1964.jpg: Warren K. Leffler

23. Nelson   Rockefellerhttp://commons.wikimedia.org/wiki/File:Nelson_
    Rockefeller_talking_to_LBJ,_color-cropped.jpg

24. John   Kennedy   http://en.wikipedia.org/wiki/File:John_F._Kennedy,_
    White_House_color_photo_portrait.jpg
    http://www.jfklibrary.org/Asset+Tree/Asset+Viewers/Image+Asset+
    Viewer.htm?guid={B9C835C6-2EF1-4C3F-A600-B4BE064F1A20}
    &type=Image

25. JFK Memorial, Dallas, Texas. Courtesy of Robin Hill Photography

Made in USA - Kendallville, IN
1089705_9781492861874
04 23 2020 1048